Critical Cultural Studies of Childhood

Series Editors
Marianne Bloch
Department of Curriculum and Instruction
University of Wisconsin-Madison
Madison, WI, USA

Elizabeth Blue Swadener
School of Social Transformation
Arizona State University
Tempe, AZ, USA

This series focuses on reframings of theory, research, policy, and pedagogies in childhood. A critical cultural study of childhood is one that offers a 'prism' of possibilities for writing about power and its relationship to the cultural constructions of childhood, family, and education in broad societal, local, and global contexts. Books in the series open up new spaces for dialogue and reconceptualization based on critical theoretical and methodological framings, including critical pedagogy; advocacy and social justice perspectives; cultural, historical, and comparative studies of childhood; and post-structural, postcolonial, and/or feminist studies of childhood, family, and education. The intent of the series is to examine the relations between power, language, and what is taken as normal/abnormal, good, and natural, to understand the construction of the 'other,' difference and inclusions/exclusions that are embedded in current notions of childhood, family, educational reforms, policies, and the practices of schooling. Critical Cultural Studies of Childhood will open up dialogue about new possibilities for action and research. Single-authored as well as edited volumes focusing on critical studies of childhood from a variety of disciplinary and theoretical perspectives are included in the series. A particular focus is in a reimagining and critical reflection on policy and practice in early childhood, primary, and elementary education. The series intends to open up new spaces for reconceptualizing theories and traditions of research, policies, cultural reasonings, and practices at all of these levels, in the United States, as well as comparatively.

More information about this series at
http://www.palgrave.com/gp/series/14933

Ashley L. Sullivan · Laurie L. Urraro

Voices of Transgender Children in Early Childhood Education

Reflections on Resistance and Resiliency

palgrave
macmillan

Ashley L. Sullivan
Penn State Behrend
Erie, PA, USA

Laurie L. Urraro
Penn State Behrend
Erie, PA, USA

Critical Cultural Studies of Childhood
ISBN 978-3-030-13482-2   ISBN 978-3-030-13483-9 (eBook)
https://doi.org/10.1007/978-3-030-13483-9

© The Editor(s) (if applicable) and The Author(s), under exclusive license to Springer Nature Switzerland AG, part of Springer Nature 2019
This work is subject to copyright. All rights are solely and exclusively licensed by the Publisher, whether the whole or part of the material is concerned, specifically the rights of translation, reprinting, reuse of illustrations, recitation, broadcasting, reproduction on microfilms or in any other physical way, and transmission or information storage and retrieval, electronic adaptation, computer software, or by similar or dissimilar methodology now known or hereafter developed.
The use of general descriptive names, registered names, trademarks, service marks, etc. in this publication does not imply, even in the absence of a specific statement, that such names are exempt from the relevant protective laws and regulations and therefore free for general use.
The publisher, the authors and the editors are safe to assume that the advice and information in this book are believed to be true and accurate at the date of publication. Neither the publisher nor the authors or the editors give a warranty, expressed or implied, with respect to the material contained herein or for any errors or omissions that may have been made. The publisher remains neutral with regard to jurisdictional claims in published maps and institutional affiliations.

Cover illustration: © Alexmia/iStock/Getty Images Plus

This Palgrave Macmillan imprint is published by the registered company Springer Nature Switzerland AG
The registered company address is: Gewerbestrasse 11, 6330 Cham, Switzerland

Series Editors' Preface

We enthusiastically welcome this volume to our series, *Critical Cultural Studies of Childhood*, as it reflects timely and critical issues nested in US early childhood contexts and adult memories. Foregrounding the voices and life experiences of children growing up transgender, with emphasis on their experiences in early education contexts, this book will contribute much to the growing literature on transgender issues in early childhood. While there is more public recognition, affirmation of rights and general support for transgender individuals in the United States, the adults who share their narratives in this book grew up in a with an array of barriers, struggles, othering and a desire for belonging. These experiences have not changed substantially in present, persistently transphobic educational contexts. The focal narratives also reflect persistence, hope, and examples of confronting mandatory gender binaries and offer strategies for creating more inclusive educational communities and practices. The authors draw on these narratives to engage questions including, "Who are 'trans' children? What does it mean to be 'trans' and a child in US schools? What kinds of experiences do they grapple with and what are adult reflections?"

Voices of Transgender Children in Early Childhood Education: Reflections on Resistance and Resiliency draws on post-structural, queer theory and feminist approaches to connect theory with praxis in early childhood—a context in which fixed gender categories and internalized body normalization persist. Working with ten transgender research partners, the original study for the book focused on their reflections on schooling from ages three to eight. Written in an engaging and accessible style, the book unpacks themes across the narratives including ways children navigated transphobic social interactions, formed friendship with those of the same gender identity or inhabited liminal classroom spaces. Barriers to friendship increased with age and all reported being teased and assaulted, and each found different ways to cope with being bullied (including self-induced isolation, retaliation, building relationships with allies, and providing beneficial services to peers). When reflecting on interactions with teachers, the interviewees recalled far more negative interactions than positive ones. Included in these narratives were discussions of maximum control over the physical body, restrictive curriculum methods, and public humiliation.

The research partners also recalled the effects of gender normative physical spaces and typically regarded the music classroom, art room, auditorium and library as safe and empowering spaces and the gymnasium, cafeteria, bathrooms, and principal's office as unsafe and disempowering locations. Foucault's normalization of the body theory was explored in relationship to the studied population. The findings suggest that gender performativity, gender segregation, gender normalization/gender role conformity are of concern for transgender children in early childhood education. The book concludes with suggestions for creating more inclusive classrooms for diverse students including allowing children to be themselves, abandoning assumptions, eliminating gender segregation, involving parents, creating a safe environment, and supporting/protecting transgender children. Ultimately, the book aims to illuminate the realities and experiences of transgender individuals, in their own words, and provide them with an arena in which their voices may be heard. May readers listen and learn and work to create spaces of belonging in early childhood and beyond and be energized in this important struggle!

Tempe, USA   Elizabeth Blue Swadener
Madison, USA   Marianne Bloch

We wish to dedicate this research project to our partners Aidan, Beth, Chris, Erin, Lady Gazelle, Lana, Lluvy Rae, Maria, Margo, and Mary. We are lucky and honored to be the vehicle through which your stories of courage and fortitude have been transmitted. We also dedicate this text to every transgender individual who reads it. May these stories remind you that you are not alone in the world, and through the telling of these tales, may society develop an understanding of and compassion for you and other members of the transgender community.

To the teachers who have found this text, we hope that you are inspired to act as strong advocates, activists, and allies for the gender creative, genderqueer, nonbinary, transgender etc. students who are entrusted to your care. Your passion, dedication, and willingness to learn and grow can help shape a generation.

Acknowledgements

We wish to thank, first and foremost, the research partners: Aidan, Beth, Chris, Erin, Lady Gazelle, Lana, Lluvy Rae, Maria, Margo, Mary. We would also like to thank Jackson Millarker, the 10-year-old boy who contributed a prologue for the book. We would like to acknowledge Linda Braus, Milana Vernikova, and the entire Palgrave Macmillan team for their support and assistance in the actualization of this project. A special thank you to the book reviewers for providing valuable feedback for drafts of our work. In addition, we wish to thank Arizona State University and Dr. Beth Blue Swadener (faculty adviser and mentor of Ashley Sullivan) and Dr. Mimi Bloch for their input, support, and encouragement. We also are deeply indebted to Penn State Erie, the Behrend College, specifically the School of Humanities and Social Sciences, for supporting us in our research endeavors which allowed this project to come to fruition. Lastly, we want to thank our dear friend and community activist, educator, and mentor Caitlyn Strohmeyer for her support and guidance throughout this process.

We wish to dedicate this book in loving memory to our friend, Dr. Jeanine Ruhsam, transgender advocate, educator, and scholar. Your warmth, generosity, kindness, and consideration for those around you will never be forgotten. Thank you for serving as an extraordinary example of the sublime power of perseverance, hard work, and standing up for what you believe in. The life you lived and the legacy you leave behind will never be forgotten.

About This Book

Who are transgender children? What does it mean to be a transgender child in schools today? What kinds of realities do trans children grapple with while growing up? Though there has been a recent shift toward increased understanding and support for trans youth, their experiences in the education system can often be fraught with challenges and barriers. Nonetheless, there have been and will continue to be arenas of hope that permit and foster a gradual erosion of the often firmly demarcated line between 'cisgender' and 'transgender.'

This book is a qualitative study of transgender children and internalized body normalization in early childhood education settings, steeped in critical methodologies including post-structuralism, queer theory, and feminist approaches. As the struggles and triumphs of trans individuals have reached a watershed moment in the social fabric of the United States, this text aims to proffer a snapshot into the lives of ten transgender people as they reflect on their earliest memories in the American educational system. The book marries theory and praxis, submitting to current and future teachers a text that not only presents authentic narratives about trans children in early childhood education, but also analyzes the forces at work behind gender policing, gender segregation, and transphobic education policies.

The trans people who participated in our study (our "research partners") reflect on their schooling from the ages of three through eight years old. From their narratives, multiple themes arose regarding navigating transphobic social interactions. Most interviewees befriended peers who held the same gender identity and/or were considered "outcasts." There were barriers to friendship that stemmed from perceived gender non-conforming behavior, and these seemed to increase with age. All were teased and assaulted, and each found different ways to cope with being bullied (including self-induced isolation, retaliation, building relationships with allies, and providing beneficial services to peers). When reflecting on interactions with teachers, the research partners recalled double the amount of negative interactions than positive ones. Included in these narratives were discussions of maximum control over the physical body, restrictive curriculum methods, and public humiliation.

The research partners also recalled the effects of gender normative physical spaces and typically regarded the music classroom, art room, auditorium, and library as safe and empowering spaces and the gymnasium, cafeteria, bathrooms, and principal's office as unsafe and disempowering locations. Foucault's normalization of the body theory was explored in relationship to the studied population. The findings suggest that gender performativity, gender segregation, gender normalization/gender role conformity are of particular concern for transgender children in early childhood education. The book concludes with suggestions for creating more inclusive classrooms for diverse students including allowing children to be themselves, abandoning assumptions, eliminating gender segregation, involving parents, creating a safe environment, and supporting/protecting transgender children. Ultimately, the book aims to illuminate the realities and experiences of transgender individuals, in their own words, and to inspire early childhood teachers to fortify the rights, address the needs, and encourage the authentic individuality of the young transgender children in their care.

Note

This book is based, in large part, on the dissertation of Ashley Lauren Sullivan (with excerpts from a more recent GEMS article) (Sullivan 2009, 2014). Though the interviews were conducted a decade ago, this work has never been more relevant or timely. The recent political attacks specifically directed at transgender children have provoked the publication of this book at this time. The stories told on these pages illuminate the struggles faced by young trans children over four decades in the United States. Please dear reader, do not take comfort in the fact that these are not the most recent of tales. They mirror, with precision, the same difficulties children face in 2019. The bullying has only morphed in its method of delivery (modern students endure cyber harassment as well). The deplorable insults remain the same. Gender segregation is still rampant. The very week that the final edits of this book were submitted to the publisher, we witnessed a kindergarten teacher mindlessly lining children up by sex. We have come a long way indeed, though we still have far to go. Thus, we strongly believe that this book can easily be read in a modern context, and that we were called to publish it at the exact time when it was most needed.

REFERENCES

Sullivan, A. L. (2009). *Hiding in the open: Navigating education at the gender poles: A study of transgender children in early childhood* (Order No. 3361853). Available from ProQuest Dissertations and Theses A&I. (304843384). Retrieved from http://ezaccess.libraries.psu.edu/login?url=https://search-proquest-com.ezaccess.libraries.psu.edu/docview/304843384?accountid=13158.

Sullivan, A. (2014). Seeking solace in the music room: Normalized physical spaces in the early childhood environment and the resulting impact on transgender children. *Gender, Education, Music, and Society, 7*(2), 12–24. Retrieved from https://ojs.library.queensu.ca/index.php/gems/article/view/5168.

Prologue

January 14, 2019

Dear Teachers,

I entered kindergarten as a pretty average kindergartener girl. As the year went on, I felt like I was more than just that. I was a boy inside, but even I still couldn't understand that. The summer after kindergarten, I was still feeling that way. Some days I would wear clothing that was not very typical to see on a five-year-old girl. It was either a superhero shirt and a bright pink skirt or an Elsa shirt and khaki shorts. I knew I was not like other girls.

In first grade, I had some more struggles with what gender I was. One day, toward the middle of the first grade, it was picture day and we were put into two lines—the boy's line and the girl's line. I stayed in the middle.

I truly did not know what to do. That was the first time that I really felt supported by my teacher. My teacher pulled me to the side and told me that I needed to choose a line and I explained that I couldn't. We stood there for a moment and I could tell that she was confused. After a little while, she told me to go to the boy's line and that made me feel happy. I explained this to my parents, hoping that they would be supportive of me. This is when they explained to me what it meant to be transgender. I now knew who and what I was. I was a boy, a transgender boy.

I chose to enter second grade, as my true self, a boy. Over the summer, I had decided on a new name—Jackson, which was the most "boyish" name I knew. Imagine the surprise of my classmates when I said that my name was "Jackson." It was a confusing day, but I knew that my teacher was supporting me. This was the year that I would begin using the boy's bathroom, stand in the boy's line, and truly live as a boy. Without the support of my teachers, I would not have had the confidence to go about my day as my true self.

As the years went on, my classmates began to understand more about me and accepted me for who I was. While my classmates and friends have been supportive, we still have to explain to my teachers every year that I am transgender. I am amazed every year to have a teacher that is so nice and supportive. I know that I am lucky because many transgender students do not have that opportunity. I am now in 5th grade and am the happiest that I have been. My hope is that you are able to provide the same support to your students, all of your students—especially those that are transgender or gender non-conforming. The most important advice that I can give is to truly get to know your students, respect their choice of pronouns, and treat them equally.

Sincerely,
Jackson Millarker, age 10

Contents

1 **Trans Who?! Understanding Transgender Children**   1
The "Bathroom Bill": Legislated Hate in the Twenty-First Century   1
Explain This to Me: Who Are Trans People?!   3
Some Facts and Figures About Trans Individuals   4
So, Here's an Idea: Purpose of Our Project   5
Peering Behind the Curtain: Research Design   7
References   12

2 **Being Young and Trans in School**   17
Pink or Blue? Pick a Side Already! Gender Identity Development in Young Children   17
Cracks in the Foundation: Cisnormative Educational Settings   18
Punctured Pedagogies: Teacher Educator Training   21
Trapped in the Box: Absence of Trans Youth in Early Childhood Education Curricula   24
A Game of Dodgeball: Social Interactions of Trans Youth   28
The Charade: Gender Performativity and Survival   33
References   36

3 Theory, History, and Realities of Transgender Individuals 41
   Queerly Speaking 41
   Let's Talk About Sex, Baby!: Sex v. Gender v. Sexual Orientation 43
   Assigned, Designed, Refined: Psychological Treatment of Trans Children and Youth 46
   Some Stark Realities of Trans Children: Struggles and Barriers 50
   Stories for Sale: Mass Media and the Telling of Transgender Tales 52
   References 55

4 Hiding in the Open: Portraits of Trans Partners
   (Birth-Age Eight) 59
   Aidan 60
   Beth 63
   Chris 66
   Erin 70
   Lady Gazelle 73
   Lana 76
   Lluvy Rae 80
   Maria 83
   Margo 86
   Mary 89
   Reference 92

5 Spaces, Places, Faces- Erases and Embraces: Actions
   and Experiences of the Trans Child Within Normative
   Frameworks 93
   Navigating the Social Circle: Trans Children and Their Relationships with Others 93
   Friendships 94
   Bullying and Violence 103
   Teacher Relationships: Positive 112
   Teacher Relationships: Negative 119
   Spaces of Resistance: Disciplinary Issues 131
   Academic Performance 136
   Parent Interactions at School 138
   Diagnosis, Treatment, and Special Education 141
   Chapter Summary 146
   References 147

6	**Art Studios Versus Locker Rooms: Safe and Unsafe Places for Trans Children**	**149**
	Research Partners' Drawings	150
	Comfort and Safety	160
	Empowerment	166
	Playground	169
	Specials Classrooms: Music, Art, Gym	170
	Larger School Environment: Cafeteria, Auditorium, Library, Bathrooms, Principal's Office	173
	Chapter Summary	178
	References	179
7	**Focusing the Lens: Theoretical Perspectives of Body Normalization**	**181**
	An Analysis of U.S. Societal Discourses: Purpose and Process of Body Normalization	181
	Transgender Children and the Body Normalization Process: A Theoretical Model	184
	Let's Play Dress Up! Gender Performativity	185
	Tea Parties and Trucks: Gender Segregation	187
	'No Place for Me as I Am': Gender Role Conformity and Internalized Self-Regulation	191
	Preschool Outlaws, Rebels with a Cause: Gender Rebellion	195
	Chapter Summary	197
	References	197
8	**Where Do We Go from Here? Dos and Don'ts When Working with Trans Children**	**199**
	Advice for Teachers	200
	Advice for Students	212
	Advice for Administrators	217
	Conclusions	221
	References	224

Epilogue   **227**

Appendix A 231

Appendix B 233

Index 235

About the Authors

Dr. Ashley L. Sullivan is an Assistant Professor of Early Childhood Education at Penn State Erie, the Behrend College. Her research focuses on young transgender children in early education settings, children's literature containing transgender characters, children in poverty, reconceptualist methodologies, and kindergarten "readiness." She teaches Early Childhood Education courses at Penn State Behrend. Ashley is currently working on a co-authored book (with Gaile Cannella) titled *Introducing Critical Childhood Perspectives: Reconceptualist Thought, Diversity, and Social Justice Expectations*, with an anticipated release date in fall, 2019.

Dr. Laurie L. Urraro holds a position as Assistant Teaching Professor of Spanish at Penn State Erie, the Behrend College (since 2011). Her area of expertise is contemporary peninsular literature and culture, and she specializes in Spanish drama. Areas of interest include sex and sexuality in contemporary female-authored Spanish drama, gender and sexuality studies, and women's studies, to name a few. She teaches Spanish language and culture courses at Penn State Erie, and has co-authored a Medical Spanish textbook (*Medical Spanish for Nurses: A Self-Teaching Guide*, Springer Publishing Co.) that came out in 2016.

Both Ashley and Laurie are currently collaborating on an ongoing project that analyzes transgender characters in bilingual (Spanish–English) children's picture books.

List of Figures

Fig. 3.1	Sex, gender, and sexual orientation continuum (Sullivan, 2009, pp. 14–15)	44
Fig. 6.1	Aidan's classroom drawing	151
Fig. 6.2	Mary's classroom drawing	152
Fig. 6.3	Beth's classroom drawing	153
Fig. 6.4	Chris's classroom drawing	154
Fig. 6.5	Erin's classroom drawing	155
Fig. 6.6	Margo's classroom drawing	156
Fig. 6.7	Maria's classroom drawing	157
Fig. 6.8	Lady Gazelle's classroom drawing	158
Fig. 6.9	Lana's classroom drawing	159
Fig. 6.10	Lluvy Rae's classroom drawing	160
Fig. 7.1	Theoretical model of body normalization	183

CHAPTER 1

Trans Who?! Understanding Transgender Children

THE "BATHROOM BILL": LEGISLATED HATE IN THE TWENTY-FIRST CENTURY

On March 23, 2016, North Carolina governor Pat McCrory signed into law a piece of legislation, the effects of which would cause ripples of shock, discord, and contention throughout the social fabric of the United States. The law, House Bill 2 (HB 2), often referred to as the "bathroom bill," prohibited the use of public restrooms in all public spaces, including government buildings and schools, for those individuals whose gender identity differed from the sex that appeared on their birth certificates (Gordon, Price, & Peralta, 2016). The law was aimed at transgender individuals. The term transgender is often defined as "An umbrella term for people whose gender identity and/or gender expression differs from the sex they were assigned at birth" (GLAAD Media Reference Guide, n.d.), although the term signifies different things for different people (Sullivan, 2009, p. 71).

Governor McCrory justified this horrific bill as an effort to buffer children and women from purported 'sexual predators' in public restrooms (despite there being no facts to support this assertion). In addition to legalizing discrimination against transgender individuals, HB 2 also made it impossible for workers to sue on the grounds of discrimination in state court, as well as prevented cities from actualizing social policies, such as an increase in minimum wage (Blest, 2017). McCroy, along with

Lieutenant Governor Dan Forest and Speaker Tim Moore, also blocked a Charlotte, NC ordinance that sought to augment nondiscrimination practices for LGBTQ individuals (Blest, 2017).

Although the "bathroom bill" was repealed in 2017 after overwhelming pressure from citizens and businesses, many cite that a "compromise bill" (sometimes called HB 2.0) cropped up in its place, "leaving state legislators in charge of policy over multi-stall bathrooms, and [putting] a temporary halt on local governments passing nondiscrimination ordinances until 2020" (Silva, 2017). Since the bill's initial emergence in the NC house, repercussions have reverberated throughout the nation. Copycat bills were proposed, seeking to dismantle the rights of LGBTQ individuals. Likewise, droves of supporters fought to protect LGBTQ persons. There has been an increased amount of violence against transgender individuals since 2016, with GLAAD (Gay and Lesbian Alliance Against Defamation) reporting that 2016 was the deadliest year on record for transgender people (Schmider, 2016). Twenty-seven people were murdered (including a 16-year old). This is a rate of over two killings per month. Most of the murder victims were transgender women of color (Schmider, 2016). It is important to note that many murders of transgender people are delayed for inclusion or not included in the yearly tallies of these homicides. This is due to a variety of factors, including lack of knowledge, acknowledgment, or reporting of the gender identity of the victim (Human Rights Campaign, n.d.). There have also been accounts of individuals barging into bathrooms to verify the physical sex of the people using the restroom (Blest, 2017).

Nonetheless, some of the reaction to the bill has been overwhelmingly supportive of trans individuals: the NBA All-Star game refused to hold its event in North Carolina, the NCAA and ACC changed venues for their championship and tournament games so as not to play in North Carolina. Artists such as Bruce Springsteen refused to perform in the state, DeutscheBank and PayPal cancelled plans to expand in North Carolina, and Google Ventures decided not to invest further in the state (Blest, 2017). Unfortunately, other states have followed North Carolina's lead. Texas' Senate Bill 6 (SB 6) was sent for a vote by the full Texas Senate in March 2017 and passed (Ura, 2017). Though eventually defeated, SB 6 would have punished trans individuals with fines of up to $10,500 (for a second offense) when apprehended using bathrooms that do not align with the sex listed on their birth certificates. In addition to the aforementioned legislation aimed at reducing rights of trans individuals, over 100 anti-LGBTQ bills throughout twenty-nine states were introduced in 2017, with dangerous repercussions for trans individuals (Miller, 2017). Such legislation, for example, would allow universities and high schools to discriminate against LGBTQ individuals (SB 17 in Kentucky), or forbid changes to an individual's gender marker on their birth certificates (HB 1894 in Arkansas).

Even more recently, President Trump has stated that he is seriously considering defining gender as "as a biological, immutable condition determined by genitalia at birth" (Green, Benner, & Pear, 2018), with the sex listed on one's birth certificate serving as the defining criteria for one's identity. Such a move would undoubtedly restrict the rights of transgender individuals even further. In July 2017, Trump announced via Twitter that he was rescinding an Obama-era policy allowing transgender individuals to serve in the military and receive funding for gender confirmation surgery. This "transgender military ban" has been blocked by several lower courts, and as of December 2018 is being considered by the 9th Circuit US Court of Appeals (Barnes, 2018). It is likely that this policy change will make its way to the Supreme Court, where it will be addressed by newly reconfigured conservative court (with the recent addition of Justice Brett Kavanaugh) (Barnes, 2018). Thus, as fear and misunderstanding of trans people have heightened to a fever pitch of legislated hatred, a more in-depth discussion of transgender individuals is urgently needed.

EXPLAIN THIS TO ME: WHO ARE TRANS PEOPLE?!

Transgender people, also referred to as "trans" individuals, are persons whose gender identity does not align to the sex assigned to them by medical professionals at birth. However, the term transgender can signify a plethora of different things for different people. Some who fall under the transgender umbrella include people who are 'agender' or 'genderless,' identifying as neither male nor female (Weber, 2014), 'androgynous,' having both male and female characteristics (Weber, 2014), 'bigender,' identifying as male or female at different times and switching between the two (Weber, 2014), 'demigender,' having a partial connection to a particular gender (Gender Wiki, 2016), 'gender creative,' in which individuals (typically children) do not conform to particular gender norms (Sirois, 2016), 'gender expansive,' one who expresses their gender in ways that broaden the culturally defined behavior expectations

(Welcoming Schools, 2019), 'genderfluid,' one who expresses both male and female characteristics at different times (Weber, 2014), 'gender non-conforming/variant,' one who does not act according to societal expectations for their sex (Weber, 2014), 'gender questioning,' one who questions their own gender identity (Weber, 2014), 'gender non-binary,' who disregard the idea of male/female dichotomy or continuum with androgyny in the middle and view gender as more of a web or three-dimensional model (Weber, 2014), 'two spirit,' indigenous Americans who possess attributes of both genders with distinct social/tribal roles (GLAAD, n.d.), 'intersex,' those individuals born with indeterminate genitalia/reproductive organs, and/or different chromosomal constitution (GLAAD, n.d.), and 'pangender,' those who identify as a third gender with both male and female aspects (Weber, 2014), to name just a few.

SOME FACTS AND FIGURES ABOUT TRANS INDIVIDUALS

In order to understand transgender persons, it is imperative to examine the psychosocial forces at work while they were children. Kohlberg's theory of gender development (1966) is a useful lens by which to study the trajectory of trans individuals, as it suggests that a child's own understanding of gender proceeds in stages. Progressive development through these stages solidifies and becomes more complex. The first stage, *gender identity*, is usually reached around age two, at which point, the child is able to identify their own gender. The child is also able to understand that others have a gender label. The stage of *gender stability* follows and occurs around age four, where a child realizes that gender (typically) remains the same across time; nonetheless, that same child's understanding of gender is influenced by external societal factors such as clothing, hair style, toy choices, etc. Here, a child who was assigned male at birth may say that wearing a dress would make him a girl. At the third stage, *gender constancy*, achieved between the ages of five and seven, the child begins to understand that gender is unrelated to external features, and thus begins internalizing his/her/their own concept of gender (Sammons, n.d.).

Despite the fact that children as young as two are able to arrive at conclusions about their own biological sex, and, by age seven have developed the ability to begin to process the disconnect between external factors and gender, there are varied estimates regarding the number of trans children (Hoffman, 2016). There are no national surveys whereby physicians are able to report on the number of transgender patients they have. The Centers for Disease Control and Prevention (which provides analysis for behavioral health data) has not finalized an appropriate health survey that would include a question about one's gender identity (Hoffman, 2016). In addition, the U.S. Census Bureau does not ask who is transgender, and, even when people answer the question, the reliability of their answers poses a problem, as many might be frightened to answer, or disagree on the meaning of the word transgender (Chalabi, 2014).

Flores, Herman, Gates, and Brown (2016) estimate that approximately 0.6% of the population, or 1.4 million individuals in the US, identifies as transgender. Other estimates put the number of transgender people at 1.3% of the population, or 4.2 million individuals (Berli et al., 2017). In the 2018–2019 school year, there were 56.6 million US school children (National Center for Education Statistics, n.d.), and at 1.3%, as many as 735,000 of them are transgender (Berli et al., 2017). However, the exact cipher of transgender children continues to remain a mystery. Reasons for this paucity of data include factors such as parents' lack of knowledge about their child's gender identity until that child is an adolescent or older, lack of parental support regarding their child's gender identity when it is disclosed a young age, the transgender child's own fear of disclosure, or the fact that, despite Kohlberg's theory, some children take much longer, even decades, to come to terms with or identify their own gender (Hoffman, 2016). Also, for some individuals, their gender identity is not fixed and can shift over time (Wiseman & Davidson, 2012). While society has historically pressured children to arrive at conclusions about their gender, "young children are still actively in the process of constructing these concepts" (Casper & Schultz, 1999). With as many as ¾ of a million transgender US school children, and the likelihood that teachers will educate at least one trans child over the course of their careers, understanding and advocating for this vulnerable population is a critical role of early childhood educators.

So, Here's an Idea: Purpose of Our Project

In reflecting on the legislation aimed at restricting or removing rights for transgender individuals, concomitant with the facts and figures about this population, one may pose the obvious question: why are transgender persons (as young as two years old) in public spaces a contemporary target for legalized discrimination? Public bathrooms are not the only communal location of focus. There is another public space that our study focuses on more closely: the school. In order to conceptualize how we arrived at the passage of a discriminatory "bathroom bill," it is imperative to examine the experiences of trans individuals in the United States to examine both the causes and implications of institutionalized transphobia. As a means to achieve this goal, we led an investigation into the lived experiences of ten transgender adults to address the research question: what are the lived experiences of young transgender children in early childhood education? This overarching question was developed in response to the presenting problem of transphobic school settings. The methods employed enabled those interviewed in our study to recall specific elements from their first educational experiences. The interview process sought to illuminate our understanding of the propagation and preservation of normalized social and physical early childhood spaces. This narrative, reflective approach served to explore the effects of internalized body normalization on the social, emotional, and educational experiences of transgender children (Hale, Snow-Gerono, & Morales, 2008). Through a critical lens, these recollections were evaluated to explore the process of body and gender role normalization from a historical perspective (as those who participated in the study represented a variety of differing ages). The analysis of narratives, though recalled and unpacked by adults reflecting on their childhoods, explored the experiences of three to eight year old transgender children (Hale et al., 2008). Jointly, a qualitative methodological approach allowed for a post-structural content analysis of literature as a means to investigate ways in which gender has been dichotomized (Capper, 1992; Sullivan, 2009, pp. 69–70; 2014, p. 15).

Persons interviewed for this study were viewed fully as "partners" in the research and not "participants" or "subjects" (Pillow, 2002; Pole, Mizen, & Bolton, 1999). Although eligibility requirements for transgender research partners included an eighteen year age minimum, the "true" unit of study was transgender children in early childhood academic settings. We sought to study body normalization in the classroom as a means to gain greater insight into the lived experiences of this underprivileged, underrepresented group (Foucault, 1995 [1975]), examining the concept of normalization from micro, mezzo, and macro levels of social interaction, influence, and decision-making (Foucault, 1995 [1975]; Sullivan, 2009, p. 70; 2014, p. 15).

Anyone who identified as transgender, genderqueer, two spirit, bigender (or the other non-cisgender categories mentioned in this chapter) were eligible for inclusion in this study. Those who are cisgender (possessing a gender identity that corresponds to their sex assigned at birth) were ineligible for inclusion in this study. Though none participated, intersex individuals would have been included (Sullivan, 2009, pp. 70–71).

PEERING BEHIND THE CURTAIN: RESEARCH DESIGN

Methodology and Data Collection

This study followed a qualitative process steeped in grounded theory (Creswell, 1998). This methodological approach proved to be the best means to explore the extent of gender normalization within the early childhood education system and the effect that such messages have on transgender students (Jaggar & Bordo, 1989). As a result of a series of conversations with members of the transgender community, paired with extensive research on the subject, several themes arose that begged for further investigation (Creswell, 1998). These included social interactions, experienced curriculum, and physical environment (including layout of the classroom, available books, and aesthetics). Four interview questions emerged from these themes (Creswell, 1998). They were broad and open ended and once utilized, allowed for the facilitation of hours of narratives propelled forward with occasional requests to elaborate. These questions appear in the appendix of this text (Creswell & Miller, 2000; Sullivan, 2009, pp. 72–73; 2014, p. 16).

Through in-person interviews with ten transgender adults in 2008, research questions were addressed regarding external methods of body normalization and the internalizing effects of this process. The interviews focused around pre-established questions with the opportunity for follow up questions (Creswell & Miller, 2000). As the IRB determined this study to be exempt, each partner received a letter of information specifically detailing all of their rights and protections as an interviewee. All who participated in the study were asked to complete a demographic information sheet prior to interview commencement. The interviews took place over one or more occasions, depending on the availability of the partners (Gubrium & Holstein, 2001). In some cases, the interview questions created in-depth discussions and time did not permit responses to each of them in a single session. All of the interviews were audio recorded. The sessions were held in a quiet location of the partners' choosing (Gubrium & Holstein, 2001; Sullivan, 2009, pp. 74–74; 2014, p. 16).

One of the interview questions asked the partners to draw the first classroom/child-care room that they can remember. The purpose of this activity was to stimulate old memories that might have been forgotten otherwise. To draw something from such a distant time requires that a person mentally place themselves back in that location. How was the room decorated? What did it smell like? Where did I sit? Who was in the room with me and how did I feel about them? The purpose of this activity was the process and not the product (Sullivan, 2009, p. 94; 2014, p. 16).

As grounded theory was utilized as the primary method of data analysis, patterns of response from the interviews were categorized through a system of layering (Creswell, 1998). An initial coding process was conducted, at which time major themes were identified. A second round of analysis uncovered sub-themes in the data (Pole et al., 1999). Critical methodologies (particularly queer theory and poststructural theory) guided the entire research process, particularly during the data analysis stage. None who were asked to participate chose to decline. The partners were located through snowball sampling (Noy, 2008). Throughout the analysis process, ongoing communication was held with the partners. They made suggestions for inclusion or exclusion of certain elements, added new stories they had forgotten during the initial interviews, and offered opinions regarding interpretation (Johnson, 2007; Sullivan, 2009, p. 77; 2014, p. 16).

All research partners were asked to select pseudonyms to protect their anonymity. Although several of the research partners are quite visible and active in the community, and would not have opposed the use of their real names, a decision was made to utilize pseudonyms as this population faces a disproportionately high risk of violence (Schmider, 2016). The protection of this disenfranchised group was crucial (Sullivan, 2009, pp. 89–90; 2014, p. 16).

Relationship Building with Research Partners

A point was made to try and meet every partner prior to interviewing them. It was important to build relationships with each person so that the audio taping process did not seem as intimidating (Brayboy & Deyhle, 2000; Nguyen, Tanjasiri, Kagawa-Singer, Tran, & Foo, 2008).

During these meetings, the interview questions were provided so that they would be prepared for the kinds of things that would be asked. Aside from these pre-interview meetings, food was utilized as a tool to build relationships. The research partners were sharing a great deal of their personal lives, and so at minimum it felt important that something was shared with them as well. A lot of pizza was ordered during this time period (Sullivan, 2009, p. 85).

It was easier to build relationships and trust with some of the partners than with others. For example, friendships had been established with Erin and Aidan (two research partners) for years prior to collecting their interview data. Although they answered the questions and provided numerous helpful resources, the interview with them felt more like spending time with old friends than a formal, structured interview. Mary was introduced to the project by Lady Gazelle (Noy, 2008). Lady Gazelle regards Mary as one of her mentors. Once the research goals were explained to Mary, she was so grateful for the project; she took every opportunity to express her gratitude for the study. She opened up quite easily. Lluvy Rae is a shy person, reserved, thoughtful, and helpful. She had so much to share that we ran out of tape, and the interview continued on another day. Chris was known to the researcher from a variety of campus and community activities. He was very busy and managed to squeeze in an interview. Less contact was had with Chris than any of the other partners, and we are grateful for the time he was able to provide (Sullivan, 2009, pp. 84–85).

Margo and Beth facilitate an annual community event. The researcher met and spoke extensively with them on multiple occasions at different events prior to the interview. Upon arriving at their house to interview Margo, the interviewer was surprised to learn that they were roommates. Margo is the kind of person who will never run out of things to say. As Ashley (the researcher who conducted the interviews) is similar, they spoke for hours over several dinners during the three days she visited with them. Both Margo and Beth were extremely hospitable, and Beth baked chocolate chip cookies to share while they spoke (Sullivan, 2009, pp. 85–86).

Everywhere the researcher went in search of participants for this study, people suggested that she speak to Lady Gazelle (Noy, 2008). She started a community program that specifically serves transgender people who are struggling to overcome addiction, homelessness, and other life struggles. She has become quite a household name in her local

LGBTQ community, and she has received several awards. The researcher met Lana at the event coordinated by Margo and Beth. While there, she spoke with several other women in Lady Gazelle's program. They all expressed interest in being part of the study. Ashley had anticipated that she would make appointments with each one on the day that she went to interview Lana. However, when she arrived to meet with Lana, she was told that three other women hoped to be interviewed that day as well (Noy, 2008). These interviews were all eventually conducted, though half of these particular interviews were not included in the study as they did not meet study criteria (Sullivan, 2009, p. 86).

Lady Gazelle was interviewed at her program on two separate occasions. Maria and Lana were also interviewed at Lady Gazelle's program site. At the request of Lana and Lady Gazelle, most of the interviews took place at a picnic table behind the building. The women often have differences of opinion, and occasionally a disagreement would occur because one or more people had ventured into the sacred and private interview space (though public area) during the audio recording process (Sullivan, 2009, p. 86).

Maria, the final research partner, was extremely tentative about sharing her story (Nguyen et al., 2008). She began the discussion by explaining that she did not intend to divulge anything personal. When asked questions about her childhood, she would respond with generalities, "Many transgender children experience..." About a half an hour into the interview, as the researcher shared some things about herself, Maria began to open up. The interview with Maria was by far the most challenging. The researcher was a virtual stranger, and she had to make her feel comfortable so she knew that the researcher was trustworthy (Nguyen et al., 2008). Before the researcher left, Maria offered her a hug. The researcher believes that they did establish a bond during their short time together (Sullivan, 2009, p. 87).

So, a Straight and a Gay Walk into a Research Project: Philosophical Dilemmas

One of the deepest struggles we have faced in regard to this project is that both of us are cisgender. Laurie identifies as a straight ally. Ashley identifies as a lesbian and thus can empathize with some (but not all) of the challenges faced by the partners. She has endured coming out, homophobia, familial rejection, discrimination, and life in a heterosexist society. However related, the difficulties are not the same. One of the research partners reminded us that, "Gay people understand trans people as much as straight people do, which isn't much" and "Transgender people have a much more difficult time in society than gay people do." At a Day of Remembrance for transgender victims of violence in the southwestern U.S. city where the study took place, one of the keynote speakers (an FTM, female to male, trans individual) told of being raped by a gay man after he came out to him at a bar (Sullivan, 2009, p. 84).

And so, we were particularly cognizant to reduce the harm present in other studies where the researcher is not part of the cultural "ingroup" (Pillow, 2002). We continually asked ourselves, "Who has the power in this situation?" (Foucault, 1995 [1975]). We then adjusted things accordingly to balance the power as much as possible (Cannella & Viruru, 2004). The choice to interview adults (in a reflective format) as opposed to children was deliberate and linked to unresolved ethical quandaries about the power that adults have over children (Bondi et al., 2002; Sullivan, 2009, p. 81).

Pulling from Charlton's work in disability studies, we operated under the creed, "Nothing about us without us" (Charlton, 1998). We aimed to engage in "socially just" and collaborative methodologies (DePalma, 2010). Early in the project, a decision was made that those interviewed for inclusion in the study would be considered research partners, rather than subjects or participants (Gower, n.d.; Pole et al., 1999; Whiteford & Wright-St Clair, 2005). These stories were theirs, and not ours. We interviewed twelve individuals, and ten of these interviews were included in the text. Many others were incorporated in differing ways. Prior to conducting interviews, other transgender individuals gave feedback regarding the research and interview questions (Creswell & Miller, 2000). Several interview items were adjusted as a result. Many of the research partners reviewed the manuscript for this book before its publication. They offered suggestions, made corrections, and gave updates. This member-checking was a valuable part of the process (Manning, 1997). We wanted to ensure that to the largest extent possible we were acting primarily as a vessel to bring forth their stories. This work truly belongs to the brave, resilient, and generous research partners who offered their private lives to the world for the purpose of educating others about the struggles faced by transgender children throughout the United States (Bondi et al., 2002; Sullivan, 2009, p. 81; 2014, p. 16).

We problematized the peculiar sense that we are helping strangers peer into the lives of people they would not have privy to otherwise. It felt almost voyeuristic, and we were the ones exposing their secrets, often painfully raw (Lather, 2007). We reminded ourselves that the stories were indeed gifted, and there is a profound good in utilizing and appreciating those gifts. A teacher who reads this book may be able to better serve, protect, and support her trans student after reading the stories held sacred within these pages. And also, who are we to decide if the stories should be shared? They do not belong to us after all (Sullivan, 2009, pp. 81–82).

It is important to note that while dominant *conservative* Christian religions are critiqued, we do not assert all Christianity is harmful. There are inclusive churches, several of which are located in the Southwestern region where our research partners lived. We recognize that several of the partners are quite religious. For some, particularly Mary, it is their faith in God that has allowed them to survive despite living in an often unforgiving world. We highly respect her belief system and the belief systems of all of the research partners (Sullivan, 2009, pp. 94–95).

The partners were interviewed about experiences that occurred in their early childhood. At the time of the interviews, these occurrences were a decade ago for some and decades ago for others. We do not assert that each of their memories are "accurate" but rather that they are valid (Gubrium & Holstein, 2001). Although in some cases a partner may have confused one teacher with another or been unsure of the exact phrasing of someone's words, by and large, the memories were incredibly detailed. This is likely because early childhood was an important time for the partners, and some of their experiences were so pleasant or so jarring, they are ingrained in memory even years later (Sullivan, 2009, p. 96).

References

Barnes, R. (2018, November 23). Trump administration asks Supreme Court to immediately take up transgender military ban. Retrieved December 1, 2018, from https://www.washingtonpost.com/politics/courts_law/trump-administration-asks-supreme-court-to-immediately-take-up-transgender-military-ban/2018/11/23/6cf11b32-ef39-11e8-8679-934a2b33be52_story.html?utm_term=.f0482ea08113.

Berli, J. U., Knudson, G., Fraser, L., Tangpricha, V., Ettner, R., Ettner, F. M., & Schechter, L. (2017). What surgeons need to know about gender confirmation surgery when providing care for transgender individuals: A review. *JAMA Surgery.* Published online February 8, 2017. https://doi.org/10.1001/jamasurg.2016.5549.

Blest, P. (2017). How much damage has North Carolina's bathroom bill done in 1 year? *The Nation.* Retrieved from https://www.thenation.com/article/how-much-damage-has-north-carolinas-bathroom-bill-done-in-1-year/.

Bondi, L., Avis, H., Bankey, R., Bingley, A., Davidson, J., Duffy, R., et al. (2002). *Subjectivities, knowledges, and feminist geographies: The subjects and the ethics of social research.* Lanham, MD: Rowman & Littlefield.

Brayboy, B., & Deyhle, D. (2000). Insider-outsider: Researcher in American Indian communities. *Theory into Practice, 39*(3), 163–169.

Cannella, G., & Viruru, R. (2004). *Childhood and postcolonization.* New York, NY: Routledge.

Capper, C. (1992). A feminist poststructural analysis of nontraditional approaches in educational administration. *Educational Administration Quarterly, 28*(1), 103–124.

Casper, V., & Schultz, S. B. (1999). *Gay parents/straight schools: Building communication and trust.* New York: Teachers College Press.

Chalabi, M. (2014, July 29). Why we don't know the size of the transgender population. *Fivethirtyeight.* Retrieved from https://fivethirtyeight.com/features/why-we-dont-know-the-size-of-the-transgender-population/.

Charlton, J. I. (1998). *Nothing about us without us: Disability oppression and empowerment* (1st ed.). Berkeley: University of California Press.

Creswell, J. (1998). *Qualitative inquiry and research design.* Thousand Oaks, CA: Sage.

Creswell, J., & Miller, D. (2000). Determining validity in qualitative inquiry. *Theory into Practice, 39*(3), 124–130.

DePalma, R. (2010). Socially just research for social justice: Negotiating consent and safety in a participatory action research project. *International Journal of Research & Method in Education, 33*(3), 215–227.

Flores, A. R., Herman, J. L., Gates, G. J., & Brown, T. N. T. (2016). *How many adults identify as transgender in the United States?* Los Angeles, CA: The Williams Institute.

Foucault, M. (1995 [1975]). *Discipline and punish: The birth of the prison* (A. Sheridan, trans.). New York, NY: Vintage Books.

Gender Wiki. (2016). *Gender wiki.* Retrieved December 23, 2016, from http://gender.wikia.com/wiki/Gender_Wiki/.

GLAAD Media Reference Guide-Transgender. (n.d.). Retrieved from https://www.glaad.org/reference/transgender.

Gordon, M., Price, M. S., & Peralta, K. (2016, March 26). Understanding HB2: North Carolina's newest law solidifies state's role in defining discrimination. *The Charlotte Observer.* Retrieved from http://www.charlotteobserver.com/news/politicsgovernment/article68401147.html.

Gower, G. (n.d.). *Ethical research in indigenous contexts and the practical implementation of it: Guidelines for ethical research versus the practice of research.* Australia: Edith Cowan University. Retrieved April 28, 2008, from http://www.aare.edu.au/03pap/gow03579.pdf.

Green, E., Benner, K., & Pear, R. (2018). 'Transgender' could be defined out of existence under trump administration [online]. Nytimes.com. Retrieved from https://www.nytimes.com/2018/10/21/us/politics/transgender-trump-administration-sex-definition.html. Accessed 26 Nov 2018.

Gubrium, J., & Holstein, J. (2001). *Handbook of interview research: Context and method.* Thousand Oaks, CA: Sage.

Hale, A., Snow-Gerono, J., & Morales, F. (2008). Transformative education for culturally diverse learners through narrative and ethnography. *Teaching and Teacher Education: An International Journal of Research and Studies, 24*(6), 1413–1425.

Hoffman, J. (2016, May 17). As attention grows, transgender children's numbers are elusive. *The New York Times.* Retrieved from https://www.nytimes.com/2016/05/18/science/transgender-children.html?_r=2.

Human Rights Campaign. (n.d.). *Violence against the transgender community in 2018.* Retrieved from https://www.hrc.org/resources/violence-against-the-transgender-community-in-2018.

Jaggar, A. M., & Bordo, S. R. (1989). *Gender/body/knowledge: Feminist reconstructions of being and knowing.* New Brunswick, NJ: Rutgers University Press.

Johnson, A. (2007). Unintended consequences: How science professors discourage women of color. *Science Education, 91*(5), 805–821.

Kohlberg, L. (1966). A cognitive-developmental analysis of children's sex-role concepts and attitudes. In E. E. Maccoby (Ed.), *The development of sex differences* (pp. 82–173). Stanford, CA: Stanford University Press.

Lather, P. (2007). *Getting lost: Feminist efforts toward a double (d) science.* New York, NY: State University of New York Press.

Manning, K. (1997). Authenticity in constructivist inquiry: Methodological considerations without prescription. *Qualitative Inquiry, 3*(1), 93–115.

Miller, H. (2017). *100 anti-LGBTQ bills introduced in 2017 | Human Rights Campaign* [online]. Human Rights Campaign. Retrieved from https://www.hrc.org/blog/100-anti-lgbtq-bills-introduced-in-2017. Accessed 26 Nov 2018.

Nguyen, T., Tanjasiri, S., Kagawa-Singer, M., Tran, J., & Foo, M. (2008). Community navigators for breast- and cervical-cancer screening among Cambodian and Laotian women: Intervention strategies and relationship-building processes. *Health Promotion Practice, 9*(4), 356–367.

Noy, C. (2008). Sampling knowledge: The hermeneutics of snowball sampling in qualitative research. *International Journal of Social Research Methodology*, *11*(4), 327–344.

Pillow, W. (2002). When a man does feminism should he dress in drag? *Qualitative Studies in Education*, *15*(5), 545–554.

Pole, C., Mizen, P., & Bolton, A. (1999). Realising children's agency in research: Partners and participants? *International Journal of Social Research Methodology*, *2*(1), 39–54.

Sammons, A. (n.d.). *Gender: Cognitive theory*. psychotron.org.uk. Retrieved from http://www.psychlotron.org.uk/newResources/developmental/AS_AQB_ender_CognitiveBasics.pdf.

Schmider, A. (2016). 2016 was the deadliest year on record for transgender people. *GLAAD*. Retrieved from http://www.glaad.org/blog/2016-was-deadliest-year-record-transgender-people.

Silva, D. (2017). *North Carolina repeals controversial "bathroom bill"* [online]. NBC News. Retrieved from https://www.nbcnews.com/news/us-news/hb2-repeal-north-carolina-legislature-votes-overturn-controversial-bathroom-bill-n740546. Accessed 26 Nov 2018.

Sirois, M. (2016). Gender creative life-definitions. Retrieved December 23, 2017 from https://gendercreativelife.com/definitions/.

Sullivan, A. L. (2009). *Hiding in the open: Navigating education at the gender poles: A study of transgender children in early childhood* (Order No. 3361853). Available from ProQuest Dissertations and Theses A&I. (304843384). Retrieved from http://ezaccess.libraries.psu.edu/login?url=https://search-proquest-com.ezaccess.libraries.psu.edu/docview/304843384?accountid=13158.

Sullivan, A. (2014). Seeking solace in the music room: Normalized physical spaces in the early childhood environment and the resulting impact on transgender children. *Gender, Education, Music, and Society*, *7*(2), 12–24. Retrieved from https://ojs.library.queensu.ca/index.php/gems/article/view/5168.

The NCES Fast Facts Tool provides quick answers to many education questions (National Center for Education Statistics). (n.d.). Retrieved December 1, 2018, from https://nces.ed.gov/fastfacts/display.asp?id=372.

Ura, A. (2017, March 8). *Committee sends Texas "bathroom bill" to full Senate*. Texas Tribune. Retrieved from https://www.texastribune.org/2017/03/08/senate-committee-advances-texas-bathroom-bill/.

Weber, P. (2014, February 21). Confused by all the new Facebook genders? Here's what they mean. *Slate*. Retrieved from http://www.slate.com/blogs/lexicon_valley/2014/02/21/gender_facebook_now_has_56_categories_to_choose_from_including_cisgender.html.

Welcoming Schools. (2019). Retrieved from https://assets2.hrc.org/welcoming-schools/documents/WS_LGBTQ_Definitions_for_Students.pdf.

Whiteford, G., & Wright-St Clair, V. (2005). *Occupation & practice in context*. Sydney: Elsevier.

Wiseman, M., & Davidson, S. (2012). Problems with binary gender discourse: Using context to promote flexibility and connection in gender identity. *Clinical Child Psychology and Psychiatry, 17*(4), 528–537. https://doi.org/10.1177/1359104511424991.

CHAPTER 2

Being Young and Trans in School

PINK OR BLUE? PICK A SIDE ALREADY! GENDER IDENTITY DEVELOPMENT IN YOUNG CHILDREN

Stacee, a transwoman, writes, "… I was fit to exist in a culture that had despised me as an effeminate male, and that had no room for a gender experience that existed in some purple space between pink and blue…" (Minichiello & Kottler, 2010). According to Smith, "Being transgender guarantees you will upset someone. People get upset with transgender people who choose to inhabit a third gender space rather than 'pick a side'" (2010, p. 26). Theorist Judith Butler (2006) describes what she calls the 'heterosexual matrix': those discourses that attempt to define and articulate homosexuality through a heterosexual binary or lens, meaning that, even when non-hegemonic genders exist, they will be explained and molded to fit the 'heterosexual matrix.' This may be extrapolated to include not only gay discourses but also other non-heteronormative gender ontologies, especially, for this project, transgender ontologies. Unfortunately, when it comes to an educational framework, administrators and educators inadvertently reinforce and reproduce the 'heterosexual matrix' on a daily basis, leaving little to no room for non-heteronormative articulations of gender to exist or thrive.

Early childhood education settings with rigid gender normative environments can have far-reaching ramifications for our youngest transgender students. The paucity of such a self-affirming, 'third' space for transgender individuals commences in the womb. Ultrasound equipment can now allow most expectant parents (with financial resources and access) to know the sex of their unborn baby (Basow, 2006). The way the child is addressed, adorned, and handled, as well as preparations for the child's future, begins after the life altering statement, "It's a girl," or "It's a boy" (Basow, 2006). It is quite disturbing that the first part of this phrase refers to the child as an "it" prior to the assignment of a gender. To be gendered is to be human, to move from object to subject, abstract to concrete, imagined to real, and incomplete to whole.

Studies suggest that infants and toddlers "develop the abilities to discriminate the sexes and learn the attributes correlated with sex" (Martin, Ruble, & Szkrybalo, 2002, p. 903). At around two or three years of age, children begin to comprehend gender roles (Yip, 2006; Martin et al., 2002). As young children begin to understand themselves and how they fit into the world, they commence external expression of their internal concepts of gender. This can be observed through "gender identity self labeling, sex-of-playmate preference, toy and activity interests, role in fantasy play, forms of social interactive behavior (e.g., propensity for aggressive and rough-and-tumble play vs. non-aggressive play), parental rehearsal play, and so on" (Fridell, Owen-Anderson, Johnson, Bradley, & Zucker, 2006, p. 729). During these early developmental stages, two to four year old transgender children may begin to exhibit signs that they do not identify with their assigned birth sex (Zucker et al., 1999). Most children, both transgender and cisgender, begin to self-label as either a "girl" or a "boy" (Zucker et al., 1999). It is at this phase that children develop Kohlberg's concept of gender constancy, or the knowledge that "gender is an invariant part of the self" (Zucker et al., 1999). Studies have found that gender "nonconforming" children had less of a concept of gender constancy than a control group as measured by assessing gender identity, gender stability, and gender consistency (Sullivan, 2009, pp. 25–26; Zucker et al., 1999).

Cracks in the Foundation: Cisnormative Educational Settings

Cisnormative education settings are environments that reinforce a presumed natural match between one's gender identity and how an individual was assigned at birth based on appearance of genitalia. These spaces inadvertently binarize individuals from a young age. As very young children (including infants) are socially pressured to 'pick' between only two genders, 'boy,' or 'girl,' the incongruity between what they internally feel and process, and what external society dictates when it comes to their gender, can only serve to abrogate those children's internal incipient feelings and identities. The lack of settings that promote and encourage diversity in early childhood further isolates the transgender child.

Heterosexism is the "unconscious or conscious exclusion of non-heterosexual individuals and their realities" (Blackburn, 2004, p. 103). Although heterosexism does not by definition describe oppression of transgender individuals, it is a very important concept to explore in relation to this population. One reason for the link is that transgender people are often mistaken as being gay or lesbian (which they may or may not be). A heterosexist school climate would thus place transgender human beings at a stark disadvantage. United States "schools are typically heterosexist and homophobic institutions" (Blackburn, 2004, p. 103; Sullivan, 2009, pp. 53–54; 2014, pp. 14–15).

Heterosexism is reinforced and, as Foucault and other theorists have explained, 'institutionalized,' in school-age children from a very young age (Foucault, 1990 [1978]). DePalma and Atkinson (2010) explain that, "children learn homophobia and transphobia at a very early age: 'gay' can mean anything that is ugly or doesn't work properly, that gay and lesbian family members are best kept secret, [and] that there are 'boy' activities and 'girl' activities" (p. 1670).

Many schools do not include transgender youth in their anti-discrimination policies. Partially as a result, transgender students are constantly at risk for teasing, harassment, discrimination, exclusion, and oppression (Kosciw, Greytak, Giga, Villenas, & Danischewski, 2016; Markow & Fein, 2005). Bullying of transgender human beings typically occurs because their gender expression is non-cisgender (Markow & Fein, 2005). However, some students, faculty, and administrators (although not all) refuse to accept that heterosexism and homophobia exist at school, and refute the need for inclusive anti-discrimination policies (Blackburn, 2004). Perhaps some individuals are idealistic while others are secretly or overtly homophobic and/or transphobic and do not want to provide written protections for transgender individuals. Whatever the reason, the misconception that heterosexism does not occur increases the difficulty of implementing all inclusive non-discrimination policies. Higgins (2016) cites the 2015 GLSEN School Climate Survey findings that 83% of teachers feel a responsibility to foster a learning environment that is safe and inclusive for LGBTQ students. Anti-discrimination policies would be the most helpful way to achieve this (Markow & Fein, 2005). Teachers who personally know a student who is lesbian, gay, bisexual or transgender (LGBT) are more likely to endorse this view (Markow & Fein, 2005; Sullivan, 2009, pp. 54–55).

Another reason why heterosexism applies is that, as transgender individuals are struggling with gender identity, many may grapple with their sexual orientation as well. In addition, institutions that hold heterosexuality as the norm (and as a result force normative sexual values on students) may be more likely to foist gender norms on children as well (further instantiating Butler's 'heterosexual matrix' theory). Heterosexism and transphobia are inextricably and irrevocably linked (Sullivan, 2009, p. 37).

Nationally, there is an absence of civil protections in educational statutes for trans students (Russo, 2006). Discrimination of any type, "including harassment based on gender identity," should not be tolerated in educational settings (Russo, 2006, p. 116). Anti-LGBT language as well as bullying based on gender identity or expression is rampant in U.S. schools (Kosciw et al., 2016). When transphobia and homophobia are transformed into verbal assailment (bullying/hate speech), they can be magnified by teacher apathy regarding the behavior of the aggressor(s). Such a laissez-faire attitude greatly shapes the school climate. Ignoring remarks like, "that's so gay," "you're so gay," or "you're a fag," places value on homophobic remarks that are akin to comments such as "that's so stupid" or "you're so dumb" (Markow & Fein, 2005). GLSEN reports that 95.8% of students have heard homophobic comments such as "dyke" or "faggot" and 98.1% of students heard the word "gay" used disparagingly (Higgins, 2016). Students are more likely to hear such homophobic comments at school when adults are not present (Kosciw et al., 2016). However, when present, teachers and other school staff often failed to react (Kosciw et al., 2016). In addition, 56.2% of students report hearing homophobic remarks from teachers or other school staff, and 63.5% of students report hearing negative comments from teachers or other school staff regarding gender expression (Kosciw et al., 2016). How can transgender students feel safe in an environment when the adults who are supposed to protect them turn a blind eye or intensify the problem? (Sullivan, 2009, pp. 53–54; 2014, p. 15).

Punctured Pedagogies: Teacher Educator Training

According to the U.S. Census Bureau, approximately fourteen million children are being raised in LGBTQ families, with the number steadily growing (Kintner-Duffy, Vardell, Lower, & Cassidy, 2012). Nonetheless, the early childhood education teacher preparation field has historically ignored or viewed with negativity the struggles and concomitant needs of LGBTQ children and families in educational settings (Kintner-Duffy et al., 2012). As Robinson (2002) notes, although efforts in teacher education training have gained more ground recently in increased awareness and encouraged inclusion of LGBTQ families, how these issues are presented and discussed varies greatly (Kintner-Duffy et al., 2012).

The dearth of proper teacher training with regard to LGBTQ youth has far too often resulted in the inability of those educators to become effective allies for what is clearly a vulnerable population; in addition, even when LGBTQ training for educators exists, transgender issues are frequently minimized or ignored altogether (Case & Meier, 2014). For so many of these transgender children who are already self-identifying as trans by the time they start elementary school, they thus experience a disconnect when it comes to the policies and procedures espoused by school administration and educators. The presence of LGBTQ topics as a whole in elementary educator training receives less attention than areas of other types of diversity (such as racial, economic, etc.) (Payne & Smith, 2014).

There are few professional development opportunities for educators on LGBTQ student experiences (Payne & Smith, 2014). Although nearly ten million Americans (approximately 4%) identify as LGBTQ as of 2017, with 7.3% of millennials (born between 1980 and 1998) identifying as LGBTQ (Gates, 2017), Sherwin and Jennings (2006) show that 72.5% of teacher preparation programs list the sexual orientation of students as among the lowest of importance regarding issues of diversity (Payne & Smith, 2014). For teacher preparation programs that did provide training on LGBTQ issues, "the content was usually isolated in social foundations courses while other forms of diversity were more widely integrated across the curriculum" (Payne & Smith, 2014, p. 400).

Thus, the deficits in LGBTQ issues in early childhood training can and do affect children as young as three to six years. In the U.S., this age group typically enters school for the first time (either at preschool or kindergarten). In addition to markers, glue, and scissors, transgender children in early childhood settings bring to school struggles related to gender identity. McGuire, Anderson, Toomey, and Russell (2010) summarize studies on the angst that transgender children have felt in early childhood education settings when the training for teachers has marked deficits, specifically citing how educators "use students' given [birth] names rather than their preferred [identified gender] names" (p. 1176), even reporting students being 'coached' by educators to act in a manner concordant with the sex assigned them at birth. Those same educators sometimes justify the bullying and abuse aimed toward transgender children at school since a gender expression that does not match assigned birth sex instantiates students 'bringing it on themselves' (p. 1177) (Sullivan, 2014, p. 14).

When LGBTQ issues are present in multicultural education textbooks used for teacher training, Jennings and Macgillivray (2011) discuss their shortcomings, demonstrating that, with textbooks in the fields of psychology, health, or human sexuality, LGBTQ individuals are missing altogether or presented in such ways that, as mentioned earlier, serve to further pathologize and reinforce stereotypical presentations. When LGBTQ individuals were present in textbooks, far too often, the only representations of them were as victims of bullying, depressed, and prone to self-destructive behaviors such as suicide (Jennings & Macgillivray, 2011).

Furthermore, textbooks containing LGBTQ issues used in teacher training programs often misrepresent or mis-define phrases such as 'gender identity' and 'sexual orientation,' frequently conflating the terms (Jennings & Macgillivray, 2011), even going so far as to define the 'T' in LGBTQ as 'transsexual' (Jennings & Macgillivray, 2011). The term transsexual is viewed as an outdated and pejorative term by many in the transgender community. This can augment the confusion for teachers in training. While the term 'transgender' is slowly finding its way into more and more teacher training textbooks, the 'T' in LGBTQ is rarely parsed out to reveal findings specifically for trans individuals (Rands, 2009). In addition, the pedagogical thrust in teacher training programs has historically directed more toward LGBTQ adults, with far less information on transgender children (Rands, 2009).

Nonetheless, there are some guidelines that may assist with teacher educator sensitivity to LGBTQ-related issues. Jennings and Macgillivray cite suggestions for inclusion of non-cisgender/heterosexual topics in the teacher preparation classroom with regard to curriculum, specifically choosing textbooks that offer distinct chapters on LGBTQ issues.

The chapters should specify and articulate LGBTQ issues and realities and shift the perception and presentation of LGBTQ individuals from a 'victim narrative' to one that is more affirmative (Jennings & Macgillivray, 2011). As Bishop and Atlas claim, "an inclusive curriculum has been shown to enhance the school experiences of LGBT students by decreasing homophobic remarks, lessening victimization, creating a greater sense of belonging in the school community, and making it easier for students to talk with teachers about LGBT issues" (2013, p. 768).

For Blackburn (2004), "It is the job of educators to tap into students' agency (the ability to exert power) for the good of the students, and to create school communities that allow students to be themselves and work for social change" (p. 102). Education for future teachers, as well as continuing educator training, should address how to adequately support and nurture the educational experiences of gender expansive students. Some examples of important topics that may be incorporated into teacher education training are as follows:

- Learning how to appropriately respond to transphobic remarks made in the classroom and the hallway (Henquinet, Phibbs & Skoglund, 2000; Markow & Fein, 2005).
- Learning how to incorporate transgender history and current struggles into curriculum in a manner that reduces stereotypes.
- Learning how to improve school climate so that transgender students feel comfortable discussing issues that arise with their teachers in the same manner as cisgender students are able (Henquinet et al., 2000; Sullivan, 2009, pp. 60–61).

Thus, transgender children and their schooling experiences are issues critical to the profession of early childhood education. Far too often, teacher training and teacher responses to bullying and harassment either ignore LGBTQ issues, or trivialize them, resulting in further victimization of the transgender child. In addition, historically, the pedagogical approaches to teacher training programs have elided LGBTQ issues, often times aggregating data and findings of transgender student experiences along with lesbian and gay student experiences, when they are different and unique. While transgender children could benefit from more attention and respect afforded them in educator training and practices, regrettably, such preparation of their future teachers does not regularly occur. While some recent strides have been made, there still is a great need for adequate instructional based resources in order to sufficiently prepare future educators to understand and advocate for to transgender and other LGBQ+ issues.

Trapped in the Box: Absence of Trans Youth in Early Childhood Education Curricula

As the ultimate goal for educational curricula is to inculcate the values of tolerance and citizenship into all individuals, many schools place primacy on the inclusion of minority studies in their instruction (Bishop & Atlas, 2015). Nonetheless, while multicultural education has successfully included studies on racial, socioeconomic, and cultural differences, there has been far less inclusion of LGBTQ issues and individuals (Bishop & Atlas, 2015). Even with the incorporation of instruction that examines the melange of families that form today's society, including single-parent, blended, and stepfamilies, there is little to no emphasis given to LGBTQ families (Bishop & Atlas, 2015). When LGBTQ information is present in student textbooks, frequently what results is an 'othering' of trans youth within those very textbooks, as trans individuals are often presented exclusively in sections on suicide, depression, or STDs (Payne & Smith, 2014), thus reinforcing the victim discourse for LGBTQ individuals. Hence, far too often, transgender children and their experiential realities are often ignored or portrayed in an inferior light in early childhood education curricula.

Bishop and Atlas (2015) summarize studies that document why educators eschew LGBTQ families and issues in school curricula. For example, educators may ascribe to a belief that it is inappropriate for children to engage in conversations about same-sex love or gender expansive identities, asserting that children are far too young for such discussions. Also, educators may be inexperienced or misinformed (and feel unqualified to teach about this subject), or they may possess opinions that are heterosexist, homophobic, or anti-LGBTQ. Additionally, they may fear that they would be viewed as part of the LGBTQ community if they support such discussions. They also may worry that dialoguing about LGBTQ persons violates administrative policies, or that parents would object to such topics being discussed (Bishop & Atlas, 2015).

The reality for transgender individuals in early childhood education is quite stark. Just about every early childhood curriculum utilized in the United States (re)enforces gender norms (Bishop & Atlas, 2015).

This is true of both the formal and the hidden curriculum. The normalizing forces are sometimes overt and sometimes quite subtle. Teachers will frequently encourage female assigned children to assume more culturally feminine roles in the classroom, such as encouraging girls to play "like ladies," giving girls pink objects to work with, and providing dresses for use in dramatic play. If a boy decided to wear a dress, drink pretend tea from a pink and purple cup, or draw himself with long hair, he may be at risk of being reprimanded by the instructor and other students (Quinn, 2002; Sullivan, 2009, p. 59).

In addition, much of the literature provided for children to read in preschool and kindergarten reinforces gender and heterosexist norms. While over 20,000 children's books are published each year in the United States, a miniscule amount of those texts contain transgender characters (Sullivan & Urraro, 2017). In 2014, 0.015% of published children's picture books contained non-cisgender characters (Sullivan & Urraro, 2017). Furthermore, transgender curricular issues are also elided. Specifically, Bishop and Atlas cite a 2008 study on curricular research undertaken by Kosciw and Diaz that surveyed almost 600 LGBT parents and over 150 children of LGBT parents and found that only 27% of students and 29% of parents reported a presence of LGBT families in the school curricula (Bishop & Atlas, 2013). According to DePalma and Atkinson, "teachers and non-teachers alike tended to assume that parents would disapprove of activities such as using picture books that depicted gay and lesbian headed families" (2010, p. 1671). This reluctance to include non-cisgender gender identities in the curriculum marks another attempt to 'heteronormalize' educational topics and practices. Nonetheless, research suggests that finding instructional ways to present gender in more complex and non-binarized ways will change the gendered 'scripts' that both teachers and cisgender students traditionally ascribe to in classroom settings (Ryan, Patraw, & Bednar, 2013).

Regrettably, as most schools do not incorporate gender identity education into their curriculum, students can be quite misinformed about transgender individuals (Frankfurt, 2000, p. 64). For Quinn, "Silence around these issues illustrates the message that something is wrong with GLBTQ teens. Guilt, fear, alienation, isolation, and shame are typical responses to this message" (2002, p. 919). Lack of teacher education regarding transgender issues in addition to little to no curriculum exploration of gender identity can lead to discrimination and homophobic attitudes in schools. According to Quinn, "The education system teaches a curriculum of heterosexuality by not discussing other sexual orientations" (2002, p. 919). Providing a supportive environment for transgender children must be woven into every facet of the educational experience, including curriculum (Bishop & Atlas, 2013). To quote Singh and Jackson (2012), "Educators and youth activists can begin advocacy to develop safer environments in their school settings for queer and transgender youth by ensuring that sexual orientation and gender identity and expression are enumerated or listed as protected categories in school policy" (p. 180) (Sullivan, 2009, pp. 58–59).

Despite the resistance, the inclusion of LGBTQ narratives in curricula for very young children is possible (*It's Elementary—Talking About Gay Issues in School*, 1996; DePalma & Atkinson, 2009; Miller, 2016; Gender and Sexual Identity, n.d.; Lesson Plans on Bullying, Bias, and Diversity, n.d.). Also, the outcomes of inclusionary practices demonstrate marked success, including the reduction of normalizing discourses (for both teachers and students), a decrease in bullying, a greater understanding of the gender spectrum, and an increase in inclusion (*It's Still Elementary*, 2015; DePalma & Atkinson, 2009).

One of the means by which this can be accomplished is explained in the award-winning documentary film *It's Elementary—Talking About Gay Issues in School*. The film, its accompanying guide to community organizing, and the follow-up documentary *It's Still Elementary*, offer strategies, lesson plans, resources, and real-life outcomes of teaching this content in primary schools (Chasnoff, Chung, Courville, & Respect for All Project, 2008; *It's Elementary—Talking About Gay Issues in School*, 1996). The initial film served as the first of its kind to deal with anti-gay discrimination by providing educators with tools by which to combat intolerance and bias toward gay, and, arguably, all LGBTQ individuals (Groundspark, n.d.). Since its airing in the late 1990s, *It's Elementary* has been acquired by more than 3000 educational institutions, has won multiple awards, and has received positive critical acclaim both from educators and from the viewing public (Groundspark, n.d.). The documentaries have succeeded in fomenting educational activism and advocacy for lesbian and gay issues and individuals in schools (Groundspark, n.d.). A more recent documentary, *Creating Gender Inclusive Schools* (2016), provides a model for how gender inclusive pedagogies can be successfully implemented with young children.

Another example of advocacy for LGBTQ individuals in educational settings is the *No Outsiders Project*. This project, spearheaded by educational researchers Renée DePalma and Elizabeth Atkinson, used drama, film, art, and children's literature to instruct early childhood aged children about LGBTQ individuals (DePalma & Atkinson, 2009; DePalma, 2010). The project examined the means by which heteronormativity functions in primary schools and classrooms in the UK (DePalma & Atkinson, 2009; DePalma, 2010), seeking to establish means of challenging hegemonic modes of praxis in elementary schools in order to actualize change (DePalma & Atkinson, 2009). Consequently, the project yielded multiple transformative results. It succeeded in connecting with and receiving support from local school administration, who invited the project team to hold more workshops and events. Several special interest groups have formed in the wake of the project, including the Queer Studies Special Interest Group of the American Educational Research Association (AERA) and the British Educational Research Association (BERA) (Brace, 2009). The *No Outsiders Project* serves as a prime example of a concerted and collective effort to address LGBTQ equality in UK primary schools. It seeks to educate a mostly cisgender audience on the importance of the multivocality of children's gender expressions and identities. Such a project could easily be replicated elsewhere in the world (Sullivan, 2009, pp. 73–74).

In *Strategy, Identity, Writing* (1990), post-structuralist and feminist theorist Gayatri Spivak states "what I really want to learn about is what I have called the unlearning of one's privilege" (Hutnyk, 1990, p. 42). In posing such a question, Spivak addresses the notion that gender normative and heteronormative educational institutions (and educators) must recognize the privilege they possess. They ought to bear this in mind when addressing the issues, struggles, and realities that affect LGBTQ individuals. This should drive the need for curricula of inclusion and transparency of queer gender ontologies. The education profession must recognize the systemic hegemony that bequeaths privilege to dominant ideological mechanisms, for perseverant norms help the powerful to remain as such. Likewise, the profession must be cognizant of the treatment of trans and LGBTQ topics in its curricula, which, as we have noted, are often relegated to a secondary or invisible status. Educational institutions and the development of curricula should espouse a queer theoretical perspective, with an eye aimed toward 'alterity,' which, as Britzman states, "begins with acknowledgement of difference as the precondition for the self" (Britzman, 2012, p. 303).

A Game of Dodgeball: Social Interactions of Trans Youth

The rules of dodgeball state that, "the objective of dodgeball is to eliminate all players of the opposing team by throwing one of four game balls and hitting the opposing player below the shoulders on the fly" (Dodgeball Team Sport Rules, 2017). There are many ways to be labeled 'out' in a dodgeball game. These include throwing a ball that is caught by the other team, getting hit by a ball thrown by the other team, and crossing the center line that divides the court in half (Dodgeball Team Sport Rules, 2017). Much like the game of dodgeball, far too often trans and other LGBQ children are required to take their place on one of only two possible teams, and are often times forced 'out' by someone of the opposing team. The action of being 'outed,' at times, occurs through an act of bullying, harassment, doxing, or violence. Although we have used a metaphor here, one cannot ignore the analogous comparisons that occur between a game of dodgeball and the transgender child in an early childhood educational setting. These negative social interactions can bear great weight on the mental health and physical well-being of transgender children.

Classmate relationships can support or harm a transgender child's school success. A 2015 School Climate Survey by GLSEN noted that "students who feel safe and affirmed have better educational outcomes. LGBTQ students who have LGBTQ-related school resources, report better school experiences and academic success" (Kosciw et al., 2016, p. xix). For example, students at schools with a Gay-Straight Alliance (GSA) were 59.3% less likely than other students to hear gender slurs (such as 'gay') and were 51% less likely to hear homophobic comments (such as 'fag' or 'dyke'). Trans students at these schools were 35.9% less likely to hear negative comments related to gender expression, and reported a higher number of supportive school staff and peers who accepted them (Kosciw et al., 2016). It is important to understand that the word gay (when used to denigrate), is considered a gender slur because it is often used because of the victim's gender expression, not their sexual orientation.

When transgender students identify themselves as such, they may lose friends. This can be due to lack of acceptance for their gender identity and expression (Quinn, 2002). This is quite true for early childhood aged children. Students as young as preschool are capable of deliberate discrimination of a peer based on sexual orientation and gender differences

(Henning-Stout, 1994). Quinn explains that, "The cultural norm of heterocentricity causes many LGBTQ teens to hide their identity to fit into peer group expectations" (2002, p. 918). Cisgender peers can provide emotional and instrumental support, however it may be limited (Muñoz-Plaza, Quinn, & Rounds, 2002). Peers who also identify as transgender can provide valuable support (Muñoz-Plaza et al., 2002). As being a transgender child in most U.S. schools is an experience fraught with difficulties and struggles, no one understands this nearly as much as other transgender children (Sullivan, 2009, pp. 56–57).

With regard to school climate, according to GLSEN's School Climate Report, the situation for LGBTQ individuals has improved in the last few years. However, it can still be deemed oppressive and negative for LGBTQ persons. In 2015, LGBTQ individuals saw a marked decrease in hearing homophobic comments. 60% of students experienced these comments, compared to 80% in 2001. The 2015 study reported a diachronic drop in the frequency with which the comment "that's so gay" has been utilized (Kosciw et al., 2016). Nonetheless, LGBTQ students in 2015 cited a higher occurrence of disparaging comments related to gender expression (as compared to 2013), in addition to a decrease in the responsiveness and intervention by educators and staff when witness to homophobic comments (Kosciw et al., 2016).

Teachers especially need to be cognizant of the type of language used in the elementary school. DePalma and Jennett (2010) reported on a 2009 study by Stonewall. The findings show that 75% of primary school teachers regularly hear the gender slur 'gay' used disparagingly. As this term frequently went unchallenged by teachers who overheard it, LGBTQ students believed that the comment was deemed 'acceptable' by instructors (p. 17). Transgender students in particular, report that teachers do not respond to their requests for help and appear indifferent toward any bias or bullying directed at them. They also cite lack of teacher intervention when trans students are being assaulted (Case & Meier, 2014). In addition, educators will often times blame trans students when they attempt to bring their concerns to teachers, suggesting that their "violation of gender norms" legitimated the harassment or bullying (Case & Meier, 2014).

Most studies related to how school climate affects LGBT persons are primarily conducted with LGBT participants (Brown, 2004). Rarely are non-LGBT students included. A variety of studies have provided guidelines for improving school climate for transgender youth.

In *A Place for Everyone*, Kate Frankfurt makes several suggestions in relation to this topic (Frankfurt, 2000).

- Encourage positive peer relationships.
- Send a message of support for transgender students.
- Perform a climate survey to assess the number of transgender students on campus as well as to explore areas of school strengths and weaknesses.
- Invite transgender guest speakers to answer questions and dispel myths.
- Include transgender students in leadership activities (Frankfurt, 2000; Sullivan, 2009, p. 57).

There are several currently existing programs that are working to improve the school climate for transgender students. Trainings offered by such organizations can increase awareness, understanding, support of transgender human beings, and curriculum resources (Henquinet et al., 2000). Although the programs emphasize issues that are critical to equality for all, they frequently (but not always) focus primarily on lesbian and gay individuals. Listed below are examples of some of the existing programs that include or could be modified to include support of early childhood aged transgender students and their families. This is a sampling of programs, but not an exhaustive list (Sullivan, 2009, p. 57).

- GLSEN—The Gay Lesbian Straight Education Network (GLSEN) offers free online K-12 curricula that addresses LGBT issues (Educator Resources: LGBT Inclusive Curriculum, 2017).
- Safe Schools—A Massachusetts Department of Education program that "provides training, technical assistance, and professional development to school administrators and staff on topics related to gender identity, sexual orientation, and school climate." Safe Schools also "houses the Massachusetts GSA Leadership Council, which supports students in developing leadership skills, making statewide connections with LGBTQ students and allies, and improving school climate." In addition, safe school hosts an annual GSA Leadership Summit (Safe Schools, 2017).
- Safe Zone Project—The organization offers free online resources (curricula, activities, website links etc.) for supporting LGBT inclusion and ally training. These resources (typically, though not always,

utilized at a university level) have been utilized to train thousands of educators around the world. Those who complete formal Safe Zone training are given Safe Zone stickers to display on classroom or office doors. These stickers allow students and their families to know that the educator is an ally, and that it is a safe space to come out (Curriculum, 2017; Consortium of Higher Education LGBT Resource Professionals, 2017).
- Teaching Tolerance—This goal is a project from the Southern Poverty Law Center. If offers free classroom resources for teachers on a variety of social justice topics, including trans youth. There are five lessons on Gender Expression. They are differentiated based on age (pre-k and k, 1–2, or 3–5). (Gender Expression, 2017).
- *Teaching, Affirming, and Recognizing Trans and Gender Creative Youth, A Queer Literacy Framework*—This book, edited by sj Miller, acts as a guide for literacy instructors. It offers lesson plans and activity suggestions that challenge the gender binary and can be utilized with early childhood aged children (Miller, 2016; Sullivan, 2016).
- QuERI—"The Queering Education Research Institute© (QuERI) is an independent think-tank, qualitative research, policy, and training center dedicated to bridging the gap between research and practice in the teaching of LGBTQ students and the creation of LGBTQ youth affirming school environments" (What We Do, 2017).
- The Youth Project—A Nova Scotia based program that provides "a variety of programs and services including support groups, referrals, supportive counselling, a resource library, educational workshops, social activities" (About the Youth Project, 2017; Sullivan, 2009, p. 57).

According to the GLSEN School Climate Survey, although more work needs to be done, there are some encouraging statistics with regard to trans individuals in the school system. For these students, participation in extracurricular activities, including a GSA, "is related to a number of positive outcomes, such as academic achievement and greater school engagement" (Kosciw et al., 2016, p. 82). Supportive groups such as GSAs or Queer Student Alliances can provide LGBTQ students in particular with a safe and affirming space within a school environment that they may otherwise experience as hostile (Kosciw et al., 2016). GSAs may also provide leadership opportunities for students and potential avenues for creating a positive change in schools (Kosciw et al., 2016). In addition, "Learning about LGBT historical events and positive role models may enhance LGBTQ students' engagement with the school community and provide valuable information about the LGBTQ community" (Kosciw et al., 2016, p. 54). Research shows that support from administration is an extremely crucial resource for LGBTQ students (Meyer, Tilland-Stafford, & Airton, 2016). Individuals such as health providers and therapists sensitive to issues faced by transgender students, social and peer support groups, support groups for parents and families, and advocacy organizations such as Parents/Friends of Lesbians and Gays (PFLAG), Gay Lesbian and Straight Education Network (GLSEN), Trans Youth Family and Allies (TYFA), and GSA for Safe Schools (Luecke, 2011) all may provide services and resources available to LGBTQ individuals.

Another example of support is instantiated by the Parent Services Project, which, in 2005, created a groundbreaking early childhood curriculum titled *Making Room in the Circle* (Klinger-Lesser, Burt, & Gelnaw, 2005). The lessons and subsequent exercises and videos are intended to facilitate nurturance and understanding of LGBTQ families and children. This curriculum addresses core issues. In a manner reflecting the age of the students, it does not exclude important topics that even some high school educators might be reluctant to discuss. Because they have had fewer years of learning discrimination from adults, young children are often more open minded and receptive to gender variations than older children (Klinger-Lesser et al., 2005). Just a few of the topics covered include: exploring the differences between gender identity and sexual orientation, understanding children with lesbian and gay parents, and recognizing heterosexual privilege (Klinger-Lesser et al., 2005). This curriculum was cited as a resource by Early Head Start National Resource Center in 2013 (Early Head Start National Resource Center, 2013). Although this curriculum is an excellent tool, it primarily focuses on lesbian and gay related topics. However, it could be expanded to be more inclusive of transgender students. The curriculum is broken down into six units, which are as follows:

1. Building Relationship with All Families.
2. Looking at the Bigger Picture (Historical, Legal, and Social Conditions).
3. Exploring Lives and Experiences and LGBT Families: Commonalities and Differences.
4. Navigating Different Landscapes: The Impact of Homophobia and Straight Privilege.

5. Creating Inclusive Environments: Policies, Practices, and Curriculum.
6. Continuing the Journey: Taking Responsibility for Change (Klinger-Lesser et al., 2005; Sullivan, 2009, pp. 59–60).

Gender theorist Kate Bornstein (1994), explains what she refers to as the "artificial amalgam" of the perceived (or forced) heteronormative gender binary (p. 38). For her, "The choice between two of something is not a choice at all, but rather the opportunity to subscribe to the value system which holds the two presented choices as mutually exclusive alternatives. Once we choose one or the other, we've bought into the system that perpetuates the binary" (Bornstein, 1994, p. 101). One of the means by which LGBTQ students have been able to mitigate the hegemony of the gender binary is to participate in social experiences that foment understand and encouragement of their gender(s), such as inclusive activities and clubs and organizations, supportive staff and administration, as well as acceptance and inclusion by peers. As research demonstrates, LGBTQ students experienced a more positive and safer school atmosphere when student support clubs (such as GSAs) were present and utilized, when they received instruction containing positive representations of LGBTQ individuals, when staff and school personnel were supportive, and when the school enforced an anti-bullying and harassment policy to protect individuals based on gender identity and expression (Kosciw et al., 2016).

The Charade: Gender Performativity and Survival

In *Gender Outlaw* (1994), trans scholar Kate Bornstein explains that, "We perform our identities, which include gender, and we perform our relationships, which include sex. Transgender is simply identity and more consciously performed on the infrequently used playing field of gender" (p. 124). In Judith Butler's seminal text *Gender Trouble* (2006), she identifies the 'heterosexual matrix.' As previously mentioned, the heterosexual matrix is the means by which society perpetuates heteronormativity through the simultaneous recognition and exclusion (annihilation) of all that is homosexual and all that does not ascribe to heterormativity. "In other words, for heterosexuality to remain intact as a distinct social form, it 'requires' an intelligible conception of homosexuality and also requires the prohibition of that conception in rendering it culturally unintelligible" (p. 98). Thus, as Bornstein and Butler have elucidated, many transgender individuals in the early education classroom (both students and instructors), must 'perform' what society expects of them with regard to their gender. If they refuse to engage in this performativity, they face negative consequences and ramifications.

Atkinson and DePalma (2009) explain that, for those LGBTQ instructors in the elementary classroom, their inability to be openly 'out' can often times lead to a self-censoring, or, as postmodern theorist Foucault would argue, a panoptic self-policing, "an active process of 'passing' rather than a passive process of silence or conformity" (p. 20) (Foucault, 1995 [1975]). Another performative incidence occurs when LGBTQ staff or faculty are assumed (sometimes incorrectly) to be 'experts' with regards to LGBTQ issues and student. There is the presupposition of a homogenous and uniform LGBTQ gender identity. This instatiantes what Butler refers to as 'institutionalization' of gender, that "the substantive effect of gender is performatively produced and compelled by the regulatory practices of gender coherence" (Meyer et al., 2016; Butler, 2006, p. 32). In other words, there is a supposition that all LGBTQ individuals are endowed with knowledge of how best to mitigate issues with other LGBTQ individuals, a clearly flawed assumption. Meyer et al. (2016) noted that "several [LGBTQ] participants [were seen] as experts on any LGBTQ-related issue regardless of their own level of knowledge and experience with transgender and gender diversity issues" (p. 13). As one self-proclaimed gay participant in the study conducted by Meyer et al. (2016) states, "'They tend to lump, you know, gay and lesbian, bisexual issues together with gender identity, so they figured that I would have all the answers to this because I'm a gay man' [laughs]" (p. 13).

For the children in early education settings, as DePalma explains, the thrust seems to be "fixing children into reassuring gender categories based on categories of biological sex" (2013, p. 5). At times, even with children who may be deemed gender creative, exhibiting or identifying with a gender that that does not match feminine or masculine norms, the emphasis from school officials and/or teachers may be to 'change' that individual's gender expression. In fact, those students more than likely do not wish to be changed. As Singh and Burnes (2009) have noted, incorrect terminology when addressing trans or gender-variant/gender-nonconforming youth can lead to isolation and discomfort in such individuals. Therefore, even within the LGBTQ community, there are often are still misnomers, resulting in the reality that "many transgender youth often have to negotiate with people using incorrect language, pronouns, and/or names" (Singh & Burnes, 2009, p. 218).

Utilization of proper pronouns and adjectives is paramount for transgender individuals. Some trans individuals who identify as MTF (male to female) may choose "she/her/hers" pronouns and adjectives, while others who identify as FTM (female to male) may choose "he/him/his" pronouns and adjectives. It should never be assumed which adjectives and pronouns should be assigned to an individual. Some trans individuals switch between pronoun and adjective use, sometimes using "she/her/hers" and "he/him/his," while others use gender neutral pronouns such as "they/them/their," "ze," or even "hir." Some individuals do not use pronouns at all, instead preferring that their name is used in every instance that a pronoun or adjective would be utilized.

Another phenomenon that can occur within the elementary education school setting is what Meyer et al. (2016) deem the 'sacrificial lamb' scenario. This is a situation in which LGBTQ students are seen as "singular sites of all learning and change" (p. 17). They are forced to make public all of their private experiences of being LGBTQ for the sake of the cisgender/heterosexual individuals around them for didactic purposes. In outwardly and openly performing their gender, such individuals "were...sacrificed in order to ensure that gender boxes on forms were changed, in-services addressing gender diversity topics were offered, and policies were fully implemented to improve the school's overall approach to gender diversity" (Meyer et al., 2016, p. 17). Thus, such individuals not only performed what could be interpreted as a 'unified' or 'homogenous' non-hegemonic gender identity, but also were called upon to publicize all of their private experiences as LGBTQ for the sake of educational didacticism directed toward cisgender individuals. Occasionally, LGBTQ persons may be asked to present on panels. Those in the community jokingly refer to this service as "gay jury duty." Even for individuals expressing gender expansive gender identities, there can be the perception of uniformity which they are expected to perform. Meyer et al. (2016) state that, "the identity development and expression process for transgender and gender-creative youth can challenge and easily run afoul of normative expectations for appropriate behavior," even when those expectations fall into the category of LGBTQ ones (p. 19).

In Butler's 2009 article *Performativity, Precarity, and Sexual Politics*, she explains that "the theory of gender performativity presupposes that norms are acting on us before we have a chance to act at all, and when we do act, we recapitulate the norms that act upon us" (p. xi). For so many individuals, perhaps without them even knowing it, they are performing a gender that in one way or another funnels them into a strainer of normalcy and heteronormativity. While, for many LGBTQ youth (and even school staff and administrators) in early educational settings, performing a gender that is contrary to their internal identity can constitute one type of survival in order to avoid bullying and a slew of other harassing practices. For others, it instantiates yet another prevarication: that of the expert in possession of all the requisite knowledge and experiences of being 'other.' Thus, in a strange twist of circumstances, the transgender person 'normalizes' their 'non-normative' ontology through gender performance.

REFERENCES

About the Youth Project. (2017, March 26). *Youth project*. Retrieved March 26, 2017, from http://www.youthproject.ns.ca/Page11.htm http://youthproject.ns.ca/about-us/.

Atkinson, E., & DePalma, R. (2009). Un-believing the matrix: Queering consensual heteronormativity. *Gender and Education, 21*(1), 17–29. https://doi.org/10.1080/09540250802213149.

Basow, S. A. (2006). Gender role and gender identity development. In J. Worell & C. Goodheart (Eds.), *Handbook of girls' and womens' psychological health* (pp. 242–251). New York, NY: Oxford University Press.

Bishop, C. M., & Atlas, J. G. (2013). School curriculum, policies, and practices regarding lesbian, gay, bisexual, and transgender families. *Education and Urban Society, 47*(7), 766–784. https://doi.org/10.1177/0013124513508580.

Bishop, C. M., & Atlas, J. G. (2015). School curriculum, policies, and practices regarding lesbian, gay, bisexual, and transgender families. *Education and Urban Society, 47*(7), 766–784. https://doi.org/10.1177/0013124513508580.

Blackburn, M. V. (2004). Understanding agency beyond school sanctioned activities. *Theory into Practice, 43*(2), 102–110.

Bornstein, K. (1994). *Gender outlaw: On men, women, and the rest of us*. New York, NY: Routledge.

Brace, E. (2009). No outsiders: Exploring transformations at the intersections of communities of practice. In R. DePalma & E. Atkinson (Eds.), *Interrogating heteronormativity in primary schools: The no outsiders project* (pp. 133–150). Stoke on Trent, UK: Trentham Books.

Britzman, D. (2012). Chapter twenty-seven: Queer pedagogy and its strange techniques. *Counterpoints, 367,* 292–308.

Brown, R. D. (2004). Assessing the campus climate for gay, lesbian, bisexual, and transgender (GLBT) students using a multiple perspectives approach. *Journal of College Student Development, 45*(1), 8–26.

Butler, J. (2006). *Gender trouble*. New York, NY: Routledge.
Butler, J. (2009). Performativity, precarity and sexual politics. *Antropólogos Iberoamericanos En Red, 4*(3), I–XIII. https://doi.org/10.11156/aibr.040303e.
Case, K. A., & Meier, S. C. (2014). Developing allies to transgender and gender-nonconforming youth: Training for counselors and educators. *Journal of LGBT Youth, 11*(1), 62–82. https://doi.org/10.1080/19361653.2014.840764.
Chasnoff, D., Chung, C., Courville, M., & Respect for All Project. (2008). *It's elementary: Talking about gay issues in school: A guide for community organizing, professional development and K-8 curriculum*. San Francisco, CA: Respect for All Project.
Consortium of Higher Education LGBT Resource Professionals. (2017, March 26). Retrieved March 26, 2017, from http://www.lgbtcampus.org/.
Creating Gender Inclusive Schools. Skurnik, J., Kanopy (Firm) and New Day Films (Directors). (2016). [Video/DVD]. San Francisco, CA, USA: New Day Films.
Curriculum. (2017, March 26). *The safe zone project*. Retrieved March 26, 2017, from http://thesafezoneproject.com/curriculum/.
DePalma, R. (2010). The no outsiders project: In search of queer primary pedagogies. *Transformations, 21*(2), 47.
DePalma, R. (2013). Choosing to lose our gender expertise: Queering sex/gender in school settings. *Sex Education, 13*(1), 1–15.
DePalma, R., & Atkinson, E. (2009). Introduction. In R. DePalma & E. Atkinson (Eds.), *Interrogating heteronormativity in primary schools: The work of the no outsiders project* (pp. vii–xi). Stoke on Trent, UK: Trentham Books.
DePalma, R., & Atkinson, E. (2010). The nature of institutional heteronormativity in primary schools and practice-based responses. *Teaching and Teacher Education, 26*(8), 1669–1676. https://doi.org/10.1016/j.tate.2010.06.018.
DePalma, R., & Jennett, M. (2010). Homophobia, transphobia and culture: Deconstructing heteronormativity in English primary schools. *Intercultural Education, 21*(1), 15–26. https://doi.org/10.1080/14675980903491858.
Dodgeball Team Sport Rules. (2017, March 10). Retrieved October 3, 2017, from http://web.mst.edu/~ima/Rules/dodgeballrules.html.
Early Head Start National Resource Center. (2013, May 15–16). *Parent plenary final report-expert work group-LGBT families served by early head start program*. Retrieved from https://eclkc.ohs.acf.hhs.gov/hslc/tta-system/ehsnrc/btt/docs/parent-plenary-final-report-ewg-lgbt-families-served-ehs-programs.pdf.
Educator Resources: LGBT Inclusive Curriculum. (2017, March 26). *GLSEN*. https://www.glsen.org/educate/resources/curriculum.
Foucault, M. (1990 [1978]). *The history of sexuality, an introduction: Volume I* (R. Hurley, Trans.). New York, NY: Vintage Books.
Foucault, M. (1995 [1975]). *Discipline and punish: The birth of the prison* (A. Sheridan, Trans.). New York, NY: Vintage Books.
Frankfurt, K. (2000). A place for everyone. *Principal Leadership, 1*(2), 64–67.

Fridell, S., Owen-Anderson, A., Johnson, L., Bradley, S., & Zucker, K. (2006). The playmate and play style preferences structured interview: A comparison of children with gender identity disorder and controls. *Archives of Sexual Behavior,* 35(6), 729–737.

Gates, G. J. (2017, January 11). *In US, more adults identifying as LGBT.* Retrieved from http://www.gallup.com/poll/201731/lgbt-identification-rises.aspx.

Gender Expression. (2017, March 26). *Teaching tolerance.* Retrieved from http://www.tolerance.org/gender-expression.

Gender and Sexual Identity. (n.d.). Retrieved December 2, 2018, from https://www.tolerance.org/topics/gender-sexual-identity.

Groundspark. (n.d.). It's elementary. *Groundspark: Igniting change through film.* Retrieved from http://groundspark.org/our-films-and-campaigns/elementary.

Henning-Stout, M. (1994). *Responsive assessment: A new way of thinking about learning* (1st ed.). San Francisco: Jossey-Bass.

Henquinet, J., Phibbs, A., & Skoglund, B. (2000). Supporting our gay, lesbian, bisexual, and transgender students. *About Campus,* 5(5), 24–26.

Higgins, M. (2016, October 18). LGBT students are not safe at school. *The Atlantic.* Retrieved from https://www.theatlantic.com/education/archive/2016/10/school-is-still-not-safe-for-lgbt-students/504368/.

Hutnyk, J. (1990). *Strategy, identity, writing.* New York: Routledge.

It's Elementary—Talking About Gay Issues in School. New Day Films (Firm), and Kanopy (Firm) (Directors). (1996). [Video/DVD]. Unites States: New Day Films.

It's Still Elementary. Chasnoff, D., & Kanopy (Firm) (Directors). (2015). [Video/DVD]. United States: Kanopy Streaming.

Jennings, T., & Macgillivray, I. K. (2011). A content analysis of lesbian, gay, bisexual, and transgender topics in multicultural education textbooks. *Teaching Education,* 22(1), 39–62. https://doi.org/10.1080/10476210.2010.538474.

Kintner-Duffy, V. L., Vardell, R., Lower, J. K., & Cassidy, D. J. (2012). "The changers and the changed": Preparing early childhood teachers to work with lesbian, gay, bisexual, and transgender families. *Journal of Early Childhood Teacher Education,* 33(3), 208–223. https://doi.org/10.1080/10901027.2012.705806.

Klinger-Lesser, L., Burt, T., & Gelnaw, A. (2005). *Making room in the circle: Lesbian, gay, bisexual and transgender families in early childhood settings.* San Rafael, CA: Parent Services Project.

Kosciw, J. G., Greytak, E. A., Giga, N. M., Villenas, C., & Danischewski, D. J. (2016). *The 2015 national school climate survey: The experiences of lesbian, gay, bisexual, transgender, and queer youth in our nation's schools.* New York: GLSEN.

Lesson Plans on Bullying, Bias, and Diversity. (n.d.). Retrieved December 2, 2018, from https://www.glsen.org/educate/resources/lesson-plans.

Luecke, J. C. (2011). Working with transgender children and their classmates in pre-adolescence: Just be supportive. *Journal of LGBT Youth,* 8(2), 116–156.

Markow, D., & Fein, J. (2005). *From teasing to torment: School climate in America: A survey of students and teachers.* Retrieved from http://www.glsen.org/sites/default/files/From%20Teasing%20to%20Torment%20Full%20Report.pdf.

Martin, C., Ruble, D., & Szkrybalo, J. (2002). Cognitive theories of early gender development. *Psychological Bulletin, 28*(6), 903–933.

McGuire, J. K., Anderson, C. R., Toomey, R. B., & Russell, S. T. (2010). School climate for transgender youth: A mixed method investigation of student experiences and school responses. *Journal of Youth and Adolescence, 39*(10), 1175–1188. https://doi.org/10.1007/s10964-010-9540-7.

Meyer, E. J., Tilland-Stafford, A., & Airton, L. (2016). Transgender and gender-creative students in PK-12 schools: What we can learn from their teachers. *Teachers College Record, 118*(8), 1.

Miller, s. j. (2016). *Teaching, affirming, and recognizing trans and gender creative youth: A queer literacy framework.* London, UK: Palgrave Macmillan.

Minichiello, V., & Kottler, J. A. (2010). A transgender's qualitative journey: deconstructing gender-based social opprobrium. In V. Minichiello & J. A. Kottler (Eds.), *Qualitative journeys: Student and mentor experiences with research* (pp. 193–206). Thousand Oaks, CA: Sage.

Muñoz-Plaza, C., Quinn, S. C., & Rounds, K. A. (2002). Lesbian, gay, bisexual and transgender students: Perceived social support in the high school environment. *High School Journal, 85*(4), 52–63.

Payne, E., & Smith, M. (2014). The big freak out: Educator fear in response to the presence of transgender elementary school students. *Journal of Homosexuality, 61*(3), 399–418. https://doi.org/10.1080/00918369.2013.842430.

Quinn, T. L. (2002). Sexual orientation and gender identity: An administrative approach to diversity. *Child Welfare Journal, 81*(6), 913–928.

Rands, K. E. (2009). Considering transgender people in education: A gender-complex approach. *Journal of Teacher Education, 60*(4), 419–431. https://doi.org/10.1177/0022487109341475.

Robinson, K. H. (2002). Making the invisible visible: Gay and lesbian issues in early childhood education. *Contemporary Issues in Early Childhood, 3*(3), 415–434.

Russo, R. G. (2006). The extent of public education nondiscrimination policy protections for lesbian, gay, bisexual, and transgender students: A national study. *Urban Education, 41*(2), 115–150.

Ryan, C. L., Patraw, J. M., & Bednar, M. (2013). Discussing princess boys and pregnant men: Teaching about gender diversity and transgender experiences within an elementary school curriculum. *Journal of LGBT Youth, 10*(1–2), 83–105.

Safe Schools. (2017, March 26). *The Safe Schools program for gay and lesbian students.* Retrieved from http://www.doe.mass.edu/sfs/lgbtq/.

Sherwin, G., & Jennings, T. (2006). Feared, forgotten, or forbidden: Sexual orientation topics in secondary teacher preparation programs in the U.S.A. *Teaching Education, 17*(3), 207–223.

Singh, A. A., & Burnes, T. R. (2009). Creating developmentally-appropriate, safe-counseling environments for transgender youth: The critical role of school counselors. *Journal of LGBT Issues in Counseling, 3*(3/4), 215–234.

Singh, A. A., & Jackson, K. (2012). Queer and transgender youth: Education and liberation in our schools. In E. R. Meiners & T. Quinn (Eds.), *Sexualities ineducation: A reader* (pp. 175–186). New York, NY: Peter Lang.

Smith, G. A. (2010). We're all someone's freak. In K. Bornstein & S. B. Bergman (Eds.), *Gender Outlaws* (pp. 26–30). Berkeley, CA: Seal Press.

Sullivan, A. L. (2009). *Hiding in the open: Navigating education at the gender poles: A study of transgender children in early childhood* (Order No. 3361853). Available from ProQuest Dissertations and Theses A&I. (304843384). Retrieved from http://ezaccess.libraries.psu.edu/login?url=https://search-proquest-com.ezaccess.libraries.psu.edu/docview/304843384?accountid=13158.

Sullivan, A. (2014). Seeking solace in the music room: Normalized physical spaces in the early childhood environment and the resulting Impact on transgender children. *Gender, Education, Music, and Society, 7*(2), 12–24. Retrieved from https://ojs.library.queensu.ca/index.php/gems/article/view/5168.

Sullivan, A. L. (2016). Kindergartners studying trans* issues through I am Jazz. In S. Miller (Ed.), *Teaching affirming, and recognizing trans and gender creative youth: A queer literacy framework*. New York, NY: Routledge.

Sullivan, A. L., & Urraro, L. (2017). Missing person's report! Where are the transgender characters in children's picture books? *Bank Street Occasional Paper Series, 37*. Retrieved from https://www.bankstreet.edu/occasional-paper-series/37/part-i/transgender-childrens-books/.

What We Do. (2017, March 26). *The Queering Education Research Institute*. Retrieved from http://www.queeringeducation.org/.

Yip, K. (2006). *Psychology of gender identity: An international perspective*. New York: Nova Science Publishers.

Zucker, K., Bradley, S. J., Kuksis, M., Pecore, K., Birkenfeld-Adams, A., Doering, R. W., et al. (1999). Gender constancy judgments in children with gender identity disorder: Evidence for a developmental lag. *Archives of Sexual Behavior, 28*(6), 475–502.

CHAPTER 3

Theory, History, and Realities of Transgender Individuals

QUEERLY SPEAKING

As we analyze the means by which the research partners in our study negotiated the spaces of the school, it is helpful to understand the underlying theories that elucidate the struggles and obstacles they faced. Queer theory offers a theoretical means of understanding a less bifurcated and more fluid gender constitution. First emerging in the 1990s, queer theory was born of postmodern theory as a response to socio-political events and currents from previous decades (as well as psychosocial and psychological studies of the self). Queer theory posits that gender is fluid and socially constructed, inveighing against what it refers to as 'artificial' binaries of 'male' or 'female,' and arguing instead that gender is multiple and fluid. Postmodern theorists such as Judith Butler (2006), Monique Wittig (1992), and Kate Bornstein (1994) stress the focus of locating and defining gender in the margins, where interstitial gender ontologies are positioned and negotiated. This enables the possibility and legitimacy of non-cisgender subjectivities that do not always subscribe to the established heterosexual binaries so prevalent in society.

Queer theory explores what is meant by the term "normal" and how this concept is often used to harm, oppress, and control. At its core, queer theory aims to challenge accepted constructions of the body and gender. Butler explains, "If gender is a norm, it is not the same as a model that individuals seek to approximate. On the contrary, it is a form of social power that produces the intelligible field of subjects, and an apparatus by which the gender binary is instituted" (2006, p. 48). Gender seeks to de-binarize perceived 'true' notions of what is 'male' or 'female,' 'masculine' or 'feminine' (Sullivan, 2009, pp. 8–9).

Post-structuralism has also stemmed from postmodernism. Like postmodernism, post-structuralism rejects the binary oppositions that constitute so many structures in society (gender being one of them). It argues instead for a deconstruction of the systems of knowledge that form the illusion of essential meaning (Derrida, 1997). Among post-structuralism's tenets are the beliefs that European and U.S. norms often assumed as reality should be exposed, assertions of absolute truth rejected, the "self" understood not as a rational and independent entity, but rather as comprised of a myriad of (occasionally competing) identities through which the world is viewed, that knowledge production should be studied, and that the meaning of a text derived from the reader is more important than that of the author (MacNaughton, 2005). Michel Foucault, a post-structuralist researcher, offered the primary framework for data interpretation. His writings, including *The Hermeneutics of the Subject* (2005 [1981–1982]) and *The History of Sexuality volumes I–III* (1990 [1976]; 1990 [1978]; 1990 [1985]), were of particular relevance in the analyses. In *The History of Sexuality*, Foucault explored how individuals internalize norms regarding their sexuality and exert effort to conform to these norms. Though people are mostly unaware that this occurs, and especially to what degree, it provides an advantage to those in power. There are likely many transgender children who endure this struggle (Sullivan, 2009, p. 9).

Discipline and Punish: The Birth of the Prison (1995 [1975]) served as the most influential text for exploring the purpose and process in which institutions develop and implement rigid rules for accepted behavior. In this publication, Foucault meticulously explored the concept of normalization—the imposition of society's norms upon an individual or groups of people. He explained how this is used as a form of control in an attempt to gain power. Foucault primarily focused his study of normalization within the contexts of the body, which he identified as a societal construct and not a physical reality. We are interested in how United States society (through European influences) came to normalize bodies and the impact that this has on transgender children. Foucault's genealogies of related topics (institutions, the subject, education, the construction of childhood, gender) detailed a variety of societal influences including media images, economics, laws and policies, politics, medicine, and child development. The utilization of his theories, in concert with those of Butler (2006) and Feinberg (1998), created the framework for an analysis of the academic realities of classroom space and curriculum (intended, hidden, and experienced) as told by the transgender persons who existed within such environments (Sullivan, 2009, pp. 9–10).

Let's Talk About Sex, Baby!: Sex v. Gender v. Sexual Orientation

In order to be conversant about the terminology related to this study, it is necessary to elucidate the significations of certain words and phrases. Several different theorists have proffered varying definitions of the distinctions between 'sex' and 'gender.' In 2006, Lori B. Girshick reconceptualized the sex, gender, and sexual orientation continuum. She offered a layered view of sex (biological/medical assignment), gender identity (sense of being male, female, or both), gender expression (external characteristics and behaviors), and sexual orientation. Previous attempts to construct such a visual understanding (including the Whalley Continua) were more static and binary and allowed only for the placement along a single line with male at one end and female at the other end (Reicherzer & Anderson, 2006). Girshick's conceptualization has increased the understanding of persons with diverse gender identities. Sexual orientation, however, is unique and not reliant on either sex or gender identity. Just as cisgender people vary in their sexual orientations, transgender individuals may fall at any point on the sexual orientation spectrums and identify as lesbian, straight, gay, queer, or bisexual. Girshick's continuum is offered below, with individuals able to identify where they may fit in on the spectrum (see Fig. 3.1) (Sullivan, 2009, pp. 13–14).

Theories About Sex and Gender

Many have separated the notion of 'sex' from that of 'gender.' Psychologist John Money and his associates in the 1950s utilized the term 'sex' to describe one's physical characteristics and 'gender' to refer to one's psychology and behavior (Muehlenhard & Peterson, 2011). Later, in the 1970s, Rhoda Unger posited that 'sex' was biological, while 'gender' was more socially constructed (Muehlenhard & Peterson, 2011).

Sex (Biological/Medical Assignment)

Less male	More male
Less female	More female

Gender Identity (Internal Sense)

Not-Man	Man
Not-Woman	Woman

Gender Expression (Presentation)

Less masculine	More masculine
Less feminine	More feminine

Sexual Orientation (Affection/Attraction)

Less toward males/men	More toward males/men
Less toward females/women	More toward females/women
Less toward trans	More toward trans

Sexual Orientation (Behaviors)

Less with male/bodied	More with male-bodied
Less with female-bodied	More with female-bodied
Less with transgender-bodied or intersex	More with transgender-bodied or intersex

Fig. 3.1 Sex, gender, and sexual orientation continuum (Sullivan, 2009, pp. 14–15)

Thus, she posed an argument that 'sex' denotes an organic, physical-biological means to determine that which is 'male' or that which is 'female,' while 'gender' usually denotes something psychological, socially constructed, or perhaps 'acquired.' Sex can therefore be defined as both the biological anatomy that one is born with, as well as the act of sexual intercourse itself. Nonetheless, despite the perceived 'static' view of the term 'sex,' it can and has been inextricably connected to gender. Many postmodern and feminist theorists such as Butler argue that sex and gender should be seen as bound up in each other, and the term 'sex' sometimes can be inclusive of elements such as gender. 'Sexual orientation' refers to the preferred sex of one's partner(s), such as someone who is heterosexual, preferring the opposite sex, homosexual, preferring the same sex, bisexual, preferring both sexes, pansexual, preferring all types of sexes, or asexual, preferring no partner(s) of any sex. 'Sex' is often articulated through a myriad of ways, and should not be delineated as a static term. For example, Kitzinger examines how intersexuality challenges notions of biological sex as 'given' or 'natural,' arguing instead that, like gender, the term 'sex' too, is socially constructed (1999). Intersex people, therefore, should not just be defined biologically or chromosomally (as there are many ways that intersexuality is expressed in humans), but instead should be seen as a legitimate ontology bound up in cultural, historical, and social forces as well (Kitzinger, 1999).

Thus, just as theorists like Kate Bornstein view gender as a dynamic, changing process constantly in evolution, the term 'sex' should likewise be viewed in a similar vein. Even when considering the term in regard to its physical capacities, the 'sex' of individuals can be multiple and/or varied. Intersex individuals may possess sexual anatomy, chromosomes, and/or sex organs not defined as either male or female (Weber, 2014), but they may identify as male, female, both, or neither. In addition, one's 'sex' may be changed or altered due to Gender Confirmation Surgery (GCS), a surgical procedure to alter one's physical body in order for it to, for some, match up to their internal sense of gender identity. Statistics show that, although difficult to determine the exact number per year, as many as 500 individuals in the United States undergo GCS (Bernstein, 2015).

Like sex, 'gender' can also be viewed as having a variety of significations, including gender assignment (how others view someone with regard to gender or sex), gender role (the expectations of a certain culture toward a particular gender), gender identity (how each individual psychologically conceives of him/herself), and gender attribution (how society judges others when they are seen or viewed) (Bornstein, 1994). While traditional notions of 'sex' and perhaps even 'gender' are often static and one-dimensional, both theory and practice have shown that the terms, whether alone or co-articulated through and by each other, are variant, polyvalent, and multi-dimensional. Such terms do not necessarily signify the same thing for everyone, so it becomes important and often times essential to keep in mind the myriad of significations that such terms proffer.

ASSIGNED, DESIGNED, REFINED: PSYCHOLOGICAL TREATMENT OF TRANS CHILDREN AND YOUTH

The American Psychiatric Association (APA) has assigned the term Gender Dysphoria (GD) to transgender individuals. The "symptoms" of GD are detailed in the Diagnostic and Statistical Manual (DSM) 5 (American Psychiatric Association, 2013). Prior to the release of the DSM 5 in 2013, GD was referred to as Gender Identity Disorder (GID). As GID was deemed pejorative and stigmatizing, there was a great push for a change in terminology (Cantor, 2002; Beredjick, 2012).

For one to be "diagnosed" with GD, that individual must exhibit a "strong and persistent cross-gender identification (not merely a desire for any perceived cultural advantages of being the other sex)" (Bressert, 2016). For children, diagnosis would include at least six or more of the following during at least a six-month period (American Psychiatric Association, 2013):

- Repeatedly stated desire to be, or insistence that he or she is, the other sex
- In boys, preference for cross-dressing or simulating female attire; in girls, insistence on wearing only stereotypical masculine clothing
- Strong and persistent preferences for cross-sex roles in make-believe play or persistent fantasies of being the other sex
- A strong rejection of typical toys and/or games typically played by one's sex
- Intense desire to participate in the stereotypical games and pastimes of the other sex
- Strong preference for playmates of the other sex
- A strong dislike of one's sexual anatomy

- A strong desire for the primary (e.g., penis, vagina) or secondary (e.g., menstruation) sex characteristics of the other gender (American Psychiatric Association, 2013).

For children, manifestation of "symptoms" may include: children labeled as boys asserting that their penises or testes bring them disgust or that that they would rather not have them, or an anathema to male stereotypical toys, games, and activities. In children labeled as girls, this may manifest as discomfort with urinating in a sitting position, claims that they have or will grow a penis, aversion to growing breasts or menstruation, as well as avoidance of stereotypically feminine clothing (American Psychiatric Association, 2013).

For adolescents and adults, diagnosis would occur via "symptoms" such as: a desire to be a different sex, the ability and frequency of passing as a different sex, a desire to be treated and live as a different sex, or the belief that the individual has similar feelings and reactions of a different sex. These must occur alongside consistent discomfort with one's own sex or feeling of inappropriateness while occupying the gender role associated with that sex. More manifestation of symptoms in adults include a concern with ridding oneself of primary and secondary sex characteristics (through means of surgery, procedures to physically alter one's sexual characteristics to make them more like that of a different sex, and/or request for hormones), or the belief that they/he/she was born as the wrong sex (American Psychiatric Association, 2013).

Branding any child with a "disorder" or "dysphoria" can have long lasting effects. They may be treated differently by friends and loved ones, viewed as mentally ill and/or in need of aid. In an article entitled *An Attack on Our Most Vulnerable: The Use and Abuse of Gender Identity Disorder* (1997) Duncan Osborne explores some of the problems associated with labeling. He offers that a number of children diagnosed with GID will grow up to be gay or lesbian and not transgender (Osborne, 1997). It is suspected that this is a way for homophobic clinicians to diagnose and treat lesbian and gay children (Osborne, 1997). The APA first included GID in the DSM in 1980, just seven years after homosexuality was eliminated as an acceptable diagnosis (Osborne, 1997). Consistent with some of the positivist literature, Osborne states that transgender children are labeled with a disorder "because their behavior defies social convention" (Osborne, 1997, p. 2; Sullivan, 2009, pp. 17–18).

The dominant view in the medical community is that children 'become' transgender due to fetal exposure to sex steroids, in other words, an in utero increase in the sex hormones typically associated with a different chromosomal presentation (Lee & Houk, 2005; Slabbekoorn, Van Goozen, Sanders, Gooren, & Cohen-Kettenis, 2000). Giordano and Giusti (1995) conducted a comprehensive literature review of 228 pieces of literature regarding the link between hormones and transgender gender identities. They found that "hormonal factors (gonadal and adrenal hormones, hormone receptors, transduction mechanism of the hormonal signal, neurosteroids, neurotransmitters, etc.) play a determining role in the formation of gender identity" (p. 165). We assert that as educators of our youngest students, causation is of no consequence. The field of early childhood education has a responsibility to act in the most ethically manner possible, and perseverating on causality further pathologizes young transgender bodies. The above is presented merely to inform the reader of the current state of affairs, and to highlight the absurdity of assigning diagnoses to children who are not cisgender (Sullivan, 2009, pp. 19–20).

The fields of medicine and psychology have also provided options for remedying incongruities between physical bodies and gender identity and expression. Older transgender children and adolescents can benefit from hormones that halt puberty and the development of secondary sex characteristics (Gooren & Delemarre-van de Waal, 1996; Stevens, Gomez-Lobo, & Pine-Twaddell, 2015). These endocrine interventions, also known as puberty blockers, which have been developed for children with early puberty onset, can cease periods in young female-to-male trans individuals as well as reduce the development of facial hair and a voice deepening for adolescent male-to-female trans individuals (Gooren & Delemarre-van de Waal, 1996; Stevens et al., 2015). If puberty is halted, sex alterations will be easier for physicians later on (Sullivan, 2009, pp. 22–23).

Once they reach late adolescence, under the guidance of a pediatric endocrinologist, transgender individuals can alter their bodies with hormones. GCS is a choice that some trans people make once they become adults. This surgery allows transgender persons to transform their bodies so that they better align with their gender identities. GCS is not appropriate for all transgender individuals. However, for those who pursue it, GCS is a life-preserving set of surgeries. Individuals who seek GCS in the United States are required to follow several steps before being approved for surgery. These include therapy, living for a year as the desired gender (called the "real life test"), and approval by three psychiatrists or psychologists (Sullivan, 2009, p. 23). These requirements can cause undue financial and emotional burden for transgender persons who are eager to live in bodies that they feel comfortable in.

Unfortunately, the tendency to diagnose transgender individuals with mental illnesses happens with greater frequency than it does with cisgender persons. Occasionally, transgender individuals who seek psychological treatment may be diagnosed with more than GD. Bipolar Disorder, Depression, Obsessive Compulsive Disorder, and Attention Deficit Disorder are examples of other diagnoses that may accompany GD. There is a "considerable psychiatric comorbidity, resulting from both the direct effects of the internal gender conflict and the indirect effects caused by the social response to it" (Houk & Lee, 2006, p. 103). Some transgender people do have mental illness, as do many cisgender patients (Hansbury, 2005). However, far too often, being transgender is seen as tantamount to being ill (Hansbury, 2005). Gender theorist Monique Wittig explains this proclivity for pathologization of anyone who does not ascribe to the sexual-gender binary (there is only 'man' or 'woman,' 'masculine' or 'feminine,' 'straight' or 'not straight,' 'right' or 'wrong') in her theorizations of what she terms the 'straight mind' (those "discourses of heterosexuality [that] oppress us in the sense that they prevent us from speaking unless we speak in their terms") (1992, p. 25). Hence, the 'straight mind' would find inconceivable all that which is not heterosexual and cisgender (Sullivan, 2009, pp. 21–22).

Adolescence, though frequently difficult for all young people, is particularly frustrating for trans youth. This is due to the fact that "the hormones of puberty precisely induced the body characteristics they perceived as improper in relation to their gender identity" (Gooren & Delemarre-van de Waal, 1996, p. 1). When this occurs, it often reinforces the desire to be rid of secondary sex characteristics (Gooren & Delemarre-van de Waal, 1996). This can place some transgender adolescents at a greater risk for mental health issues (Russell, 2006). However, most transgender "youth grow up without significant impairment in mental health" (Russell, 2006, p. 213). Though there is an elevated risk, not all transgender youth are depressed, anxious, or suicidal (Russell, 2006). When such psychological problems do occur, they often result from lack of peer, parental, educator, community, and societal support and understanding. Transgender people endure other struggles as well. Gretchen P. Kenagy (2005) conducted a study with 182 transgender individuals, the majority of which were male-to-female. She found that "more than half the respondents had been forced to have sex, 56.3% had experienced violence in their homes, 51.3% had been physically abused, and 26% of respondents had been denied medical care because they were transgender" (Sullivan, 2009, p. 21).

Though studies have sought to identify an origin for transgender identities, there is no definitive evidence that invariably proves a root cause. Although there is a means by which transgender individuals may be 'diagnosed' and 'treated' with regard to GD, such means frequently result in further pathologization of the individual, often related to society's penchant for binarizing bodies, genders, and identities. Nonetheless, although some may find such psychological determinants inimical, for others, they provide the initiating event leading to transition. For most, without a GD diagnosis, puberty blockers, hormones, and GCS may be unattainable.

SOME STARK REALITIES OF TRANS CHILDREN: STRUGGLES AND BARRIERS

Although over time society has pressured children to make decisions about their gender, "young children are still actively in the process of constructing these concepts" (Casper & Schultz, 1999). LGBTQ youth have faced a great many obstacles. For example, as mentioned in chapter 2, there is a dearth of acknowledgment of trans youth in school curricula (Singh & Burnes, 2009). LGBTQ youth at school are two times as likely to be bullied than heterosexual youth, often times, are more harshly treated by schools, and have a greater risk for issues with mental health, truancy, and matriculating on to higher education (Kosciw, Greytak, Giga, Villenas, & Danischewski, 2016). As a result of such realities, LGBTQ youth are twice as likely to end up in juvenile detention, and 20% of those in the juvenile delinquent system, in fact, identify as LGBTQ. 3.2 million LGBTQ youth find themselves at risk for ultimate placement in the juvenile and criminal justice systems (Greytak & Goldberg, 2017). Transgender children are far likelier to experience such struggles due to heterosexist worldviews and inflexible gender role expectations that do not allow for alternative ontologies (DePalma & Atkinson, 2009).

When transgender children in the U.S. first develop and begin to express a gender identity that is incongruent with their assigned birth sex, they often receive resistance from parents and teachers. Gooren and Delamarre-van de Waal explain that "some children who, from the moment they can talk, show their dissatisfaction with the sex they are being raised in" often respond with the wish for a "magical solution" (1996, p. 1). For example, a parent might explain to their child, "You are a boy and you cannot play with dolls." The child might respond, "Okay, well then I want my penis to fall off so I can be a girl." This child could also hope that "Santa Claus will bring me a vagina for Christmas," or that the "Tooth Fairy will take my penis when she takes my tooth" (Sullivan, 2009, pp. 13–14).

Many preschool and kindergarten classrooms have pre-established rules and play centers that subscribe to gender norms. Such a social environment can be stressful and restrictive to transgender students (Frankfurt, 2000; Quinn, 2002). For example, it is common in U.S. elementary schools for teachers to establish rituals that reinforce gender segregation, including lining up girls and boys separately and alternating between males and females when releasing children at the conclusion of storytime (McMurray, 1998). In addition, many preschools offer a "housekeeping" or dramatic play area (containing baby dolls and cooking equipment) and a construction site (including blocks and toy power tools) (McMurray, 1998; Paley, 1986). It is frequent for children as young as three to label these divisions as the "girls' spot" and the "boys' spot" (Paley, 1986). These sexist practices are also heterosexist, cisnormative, body normative, and gender normative (Sullivan, 2009, pp. 2–3; 2014, p. 13).

The early childhood education profession has a commitment to establishing a safe, healthy, supportive and enriching environment for all children, including young children who embody a rainbow of diversity and culture. Unfortunately, such an educational climate is not always achieved. Policymakers, administrators and educators are often miseducated regarding the needs and strengths of transgender individuals (Sullivan, 2009, p. 3; 2014, p. 13).

Grant (2010) enumerates some of the challenges that thwart the rights of trans individuals:

- Research on LGBT people at the federal and state levels is almost nonexistent, and so the specific needs of LGBT [individuals] remain largely invisible and unaddressed.
- Significant health disparities persist, with no federal commitment to identifying or addressing them.
- With no federal prohibition against anti-LGBT workplace discrimination in place, income inequalities across the lifespan persist for LGBT wage-earners (p. 6).

Even though Title IX offers student protections from sex discrimination for those programs that receive federal money, this law has waxed and waned with regards to whether these protections extend to transgender children. In 2017, the Trump administration withdrew protective measures for trans students put in place the previous year by the Obama administration (Hersher, 2017). This move may have cripplingly devastating effects, as a recent national survey by GLSEN shows that "75% of transgender youth feel unsafe at school, and those who are able to persevere had significantly lower GPAs, were more likely to miss school out of concern for their safety, and were less likely to plan on continuing their education" (Youth & Students, 2017). In addition, "59% of trans students have been denied access to restrooms consistent with their gender identity" (Youth & Students, 2017). Consequently, concern still persists for the social experiences of those children who do not fit gender molds in early childhood education settings.

Stories for Sale: Mass Media and the Telling of Transgender Tales

With transgender bodies as the focus of current national legislation, and a topic of controversy in U.S. society today, one may query how visual culture has affected the struggles and obstacles facing modern transfolk. There is no doubt that film and television are genres that are often preferred for dissemination of information related to trans issues, due to the fact that audiences today are more and more interested in visual consumption of the transgender body on-screen (Keegan, 2013). On one hand, trans individuals have gained more visibility and, some may argue, more understanding and exposure of their identities and struggles. On television, recent programs such as *I Am Jazz* (2015) and *I Am Cait* (2015) document the transition process of both a male to female transgender adolescent (Jazz Jennings) coming into her own as well as a male to female former Olympian (Bruce Jenner, now Caitlyn Jenner) struggling with societal reactions to a perceived hyper-masculine individual now as a woman (James & Tarantino, 2015; Metz, 2015). Other shows such as the comedy *Transparent* (2014) feature the familial repercussions of a father (Mort) coming out to her family as a woman (Maura), or the musical drama *Glee* (2009), that documents the transition of Coach Beiste from 'Shannon' to 'Sheldon' (Brennan & Buecker, 2009; Sperling & Hsu, 2014).

In a similar vein, many recent films and documentaries evidence the struggles of transgender individuals living in a dichotomous, gender normative society that expects them to conform to the social guidelines established for them prior to birth. Films such as *Transamerica* (2005) demonstrate the complexity of relationships that develop when a pre-operative male to female trans individual (Bree) takes a journey with her teenage son (Moran, Bastian, Dungan, & Tucker, 2006). Movie productions also highlight the significance of gender identity in children. In the movie *Tomboy* (2011), a young child who was assigned female at birth (Laurie) lives his truth as a boy (Mikhael) when meeting neighborhood kids. Documentaries such as *Becoming Chaz* (2011) and *Boy I Am* (2006) follow transgender and misgendered persons through their voyage of transformation to a physical body that matches their internal gender identity, oftentimes fraught with resistance and ridicule (Bailey & Barbato, 2011; Burah, Couvreur, Perin, & Sciamma, 2011; Feder & Hollar, 2006). *Gender Revolution*, a 2017 documentary hosted by Katie Couric, disseminates the narratives of a trans child, a trans adult, an intersex child, an intersex adult, and gender non-conforming university students (Bailey et al., 2017).

Unfortunately, not all visual portrayals of trans individuals in the television and film industries aid in countering hegemonic, cisnormative, transphobic myths and stereotypes. As Keegan explains (2013):

> Trans difference has been typified in Western culture as a question of "feeling bad" about one's body or gender, particularly because transness itself has no as-yet discovered biological etiology. In both medical and fictional literature, transgender identity has been sutured to specific forms of negative affect–rage, sorrow, wishfulness, denial-as both 'instrument[s] of pathologization' (Butler 76) and expressions of what is imagined to be an inherently dysphoric ontology. The fictional transgender figure has traditionally been marked as vulnerable to or productive of extreme emotional states, portrayed either as the emotive center of a narrative (*The Crying Game*), as disturbed, erratic, or unstable (*Silence of the Lambs, Ticked-Off Trannies with Knives*), or psychotically violent (*Dressed to Kill, Sleepaway Camp*). [p. 3]

Far too often, the representation of trans individuals results in a further pathologization and serves to vitiate any positive epistemological associations within society.

The 2000 film *Boys Don't Cry* details the life and violent murder of Brandon, formerly Teena, a FTM transgender teenager (Sharp & Pierce, 1999). Other films likewise relay the stark and dangerous realities facing trans individuals today, such as the 2006 TV movie *A Girl Like Me: The Gwen Araujo Story*, about a young trans woman brutally murdered in 2002 by four men (Allred, Braun, Krupp, & Holland, 2006). The 2013 HBO documentary *Valentine Road*, relays the story of a fifteen-year-old gender- nonconforming child, Lawrence King, who was shot in the back of the head by a classmate in 2008 (Alpert, Cunningham, Goldschein, & Cunningham, 2013). The seminal 1990 film *Paris is Burning*, a celebrated documentary about transgender performers and drag queens, portrays the multiple modalities of performing gender as drag both on and off stage (Finch, Lacy, & Livingston, 1990). One of the performers in the film was strangled to death shortly after her appearance in the film. These documentary films and movies lay bare the unfortunate and often dangerous realities for so many transgender individuals, forced to dress and behave in a manner expected based on their sex assigned at birth, teased, assaulted or killed, labeled as mentally ill, medicated, and viewed as if they are 'sick' or 'crazy.'

In conclusion, many transgender individuals have faced and will continue to face struggles and obstacles in society. The often harsh treatment of trans children and adolescents in schools has been known to lead to depression, incarceration, homelessness, and suicide (Haas, Rodgers, & Herman, 2014). Forcing children to choose a gender when engaged in play in school settings and lack of parental support at home can lead to serious psychological difficulties for the children. Queer theory has made some inroads in diversifying traditional notions of 'gender,' but history has often times relegated trans individuals to a pathologizing status. And, although there have been more documentaries and films dedicated to explaining and normalizing transgender experiences of both children and adults, many others serve only to pathologize and render the interpretations of transfolk as violent, mentally ill, and unstable (Haas et al., 2014). Even while presenting visual narratives that demonstrate the horrors and violence directed toward trans individuals, some may argue that such presentations render the transgender body on film as just another commodity to be consumed for entertainment and profit by a cisgender, heteronormative, hegemonic society (Keegan, 2013).

References

Allred, G., Braun, Z., Krupp, P. (Producers), & Holland, A. (Director). (2006). *A Girl Like Me: The Gwen Araujo Story* [TV Movie]. United States: Braun Entertainment Group.

Alpert, S., Cunningham, M., Goldschein, G. (Producers), & Cunningham, M. (Director). (2013). *Valentine Road* [Motion picture]. United States: Bunim-Murray Productions.

American Psychiatric Association. (2013). *Diagnostic and statistical manual of mental disorders: DSM-5*. Washington, DC: American Psychiatric Association.

Bailey, F., & Barbato, R. (Producers). (2011, May 10). *Becoming Chaz* [Television broadcast]. Los Angeles, CA: World of Wonder Productions.

Bailey, F., Barbato, R., Couric, K., Hasler, J., Semel, M., & Simmons, J. (Executive Producers). (2017, February 6). *Gender Revolution* [Television broadcast]. World of Wonder Productions (Production Company). Los Angeles, CA: National Geographic Channel.

Beredjick, C. (2012, July 23). DSM-V to rename gender identity disorder gender dysphoria. *Advocate*. Retrieved March 23, 2017, from http://www.advocate.com/politics/transgender/2012/07/23/dsm-replaces-gender-identity-disorder-gender-dysphoria.

Bernstein, L. (2015, February 9). Here's how sex reassignment surgery works. *The Washington Post*. Retrieved February 20, 2017, from https://www.washingtonpost.com/news/to-your-health/wp/2015/02/09/heres-how-sex-reassignment-surgery-works/?utm_term=.816dc47176da.

Bornstein, K. (1994). *Gender outlaw: On men, women, and the rest of us*. New York, NY: Routledge.

Brennan, I., & Buecker, B. (Producers). (2009). *Glee* [Television series]. Los Angeles, CA: 20th Century Fox Television.

Bressert, S. (2016). Gender dysphoria symptoms. *Psych Central*. Retrieved March 7, 2017, from https://psychcentral.com/disorders/gender-dysphoria-symptoms/.

Burah, R., Couvreur, B., Perin, T. (Producers), & Sciamma, C. (Director). (2011). *Tomboy* [Motion picture]. United States: Hold Up Films.

Butler, J. (2006). *Gender trouble*. New York, NY: Routledge.

Cantor, C. (2002). Transsexualism—need it always be a DSM-IV disorder. *Australian & New Zealand Journal of Psychiatry, 36*(1), 141.

Casper, V., & Schultz, S. B. (1999). *Gay parents/straight schools: Building communication and trust*. New York: Teachers College Press.

DePalma, R., & Atkinson, E. (2009). Permission to talk about it: Narratives of sexual equality in the primary classroom. *Qualitative Inquiry, 15*(5), 876–892. https://doi.org/10.1177/1077800409332763.

Derrida, J. (1997). *Of grammatology*. Baltimore: The Johns Hopkins University Press.
Feder, S., Hollar, J. (Producers), Feder, S., & Hollar, J. (Directors). (2006). *Boy I Am* [Motion picture]. United States: Women Make Movies.
Feinberg, L. (1998). I can't afford to get sick. *TV-TS Tapestry, 36*(84).
Finch, N., Lacy, M. D. (Producers), & Livingston, J. (Director). (1990). *Paris is burning* [Motion picture]. United States: Miramax.
Foucault, M. (1990 [1976]). *The care of the self: The history of sexuality, volume III* (R. Hurley, Trans.). New York, NY: Pantheon.
Foucault, M. (1990 [1978]). *The history of sexuality, an introduction: volume I* (R. Hurley, Trans.). New York, NY: Vintage Books.
Foucault, M. (1990 [1985]). *The use of pleasure: The history of sexuality, volume II* (R. Hurley, Trans.). New York, NY: Vintage Books.
Foucault, M. (1995 [1975]). *Discipline and punish: The birth of the prison* (A. Sheridan, Trans.). New York, NY: Vintage Books.
Foucault, M. (2005 [1981–1982]). *The hermeneutics of the subject* (G. Burchell, Trans.). New York, NY: Palgrave Macmillan.
Frankfurt, K. (2000). A place for everyone. *Principal Leadership, 1*(2), 64–67.
Giordano, G., & Giusti, M. (1995). Hormones and psychosexual differentiation. *Minerva Endocrinologica, 20*(3), 165–193.
Girshick, L. (2006). *New sex, gender, and sexual orientation continuum*. Retrieved April 28, 2008, from http://www.loribgirshick.com/gender_work.html.
Gooren, L., & Delemarre-van de Waal, H. (1996). The feasibility of endocrine interventions in juvenile transsexuals. *Journal of Psychology & Human Sexuality, 8*(4), 69–74.
Grant, J. M. (2010). *Outing age 2010: Public policy issues affecting lesbian, gay, bisexual, and transgender elders*. Retrieved from http://www.thetaskforce.org/static_html/downloads/reports/reports/outingage_final.pdf.
Greytak, E., & Goldberg, N. (2017). *For LGBTQ youth, schools' failures may mean higher risk of criminalization*. New York: GLSEN. Retrieved from http://www.glsen.org/blog/lgbtq-youth-schools%E2%80%99-failures-may-mean-higher-risk-criminalization.
Haas, A. P., Rodgers, P. L., & Herman, J. L. (2014). *Suicide attempts among transgender and gender non-conforming adults: Findings of the national transgender discrimination survey*. Retrieved from https://williamsinstitute.law.ucla.edu/wp-content/uploads/AFSP-Williams-Suicide-Report-Final.pdf.
Hansbury, G. (2005). Mourning the loss of the idealized self: A transsexual passage. *Psychoanalytic Social Work, 12*(1), 19–35.
Hersher, R. (2017). *Trump administration rescinds Obama rule on transgender students' bathroom use*. Washington: NPR.

Houk, C. P., & Lee, P. A. (2006). The diagnosis and care of transsexual children and adolescents: A pediatric endocrinologists' perspective. *Journal of Pediatric Endocrinology & Metabolism: JPEM, 19*(2), 103.
James, A., & Tarantino, J. (Producers). (2015). *I Am Jazz* [Television series]. United States: TLC.
Keegan, C. M. (2013). *Moving bodies: Sympathetic migrations in transgender narrativity.* Retrieved from https://www.thefreelibrary.com/Moving+bodies%3a+sympathetic+migrations+in+transgender+narrativity. -a0324981029.
Kenagy, G. P. (2005). The health and social service needs of transgender people in Philadelphia. *International Journal of Transgederism, 8*(2–3). https://doi.org/10.1300/J485v08n02_05.
Kitzinger, C. (1999). Intersexuality: Deconstructing the sex/gender binary. *Feminism & Psychology, 9*(4), 493–498. https://doi.org/10.1177/0959353599009004016.
Kosciw, J. G., Greytak, E. A., Giga, N. M., Villenas, C., & Danischewski, D. J. (2016). *The 2015 National School Climate Survey: The experiences of lesbian, gay, bisexual, transgender, and queer youth in our nation's schools.* New York: GLSEN.
Lee, P., & Houk, C. (2005). *Impact of environment upon gender identity and sexual orientation: A lesson for parents of children with intersex or gender confusion* [Electronic version]. 18, 625–630.
MacNaughton, G. (2005). *Doing Foucault in early childhood studies.* New York, NY: Routledge.
McMurray, P. (1998). Gender behaviors in an early childhood classroom through an ethnographic lens. *International Journal of Qualitative Studies in Education, 11*(2), 271–290.
Metz, A. (Producer). (2015). *I Am Cait* [Television series]. Los Angeles, CA: E! Entertainment Television.
Moran, L., Bastian, R., Dungan, S. (Producers), & Tucker, D. (Director). (2006). *Transamerica* [Motion picture]. United States: Genius Products.
Muehlenhard, C. L., & Peterson, Z. D. (2011). Distinguishing between sex and gender: History, current conceptualizations, and implications. *Sex Roles, 64*(11), 791–803. https://doi.org/10.1007/s11199-011-9932-5.
Osborne, D. (1997). An attack on our most vulnerable: The use and abuse of gender identity disorder. *LGNY.* Retrieved October 20, 2006, from http://www.antijen.org/Duncan/Duncan.html.
Paley, V. (1986). *Boys and girls: Superheroes in the doll corner.* Chicago, IL: University of Chicago Press.
Quinn, T. L. (2002). Sexual orientation and gender identity: An administrative approach to diversity. *Child Welfare Journal, 81*(6), 913–928.

Reicherzer, S., & Anderson, J. (2006). *Ethics and the gender continuum: A lifespan approach*. Retrieved October 20, 2006, from https://www.counseling.org/resources/library/Selected%20Topics/Ethics/Reicherzer.htm.
Russell, S. T. (2006). *Critical mental health issues from sexual minority adolescents* [Electronic version]. 213–238.
Sharp, J. (Producer), & Pierce, K. (Director). (1999). *Boys don't cry* [Motion picture]. United States: Twentieth Century Fox.
Singh, A. A., & Burnes, T. R. (2009). Creating developmentally-appropriate, safe counseling environments for transgender youth: The critical role of school counselors. *Journal of LGBTQ Issues in Counseling, 3*(3–4), 215–234.
Slabbekoorn, D., Van Goozen, S., Sanders, G., Gooren, L., & Cohen-Kettenis, P. (2000). The dermatoglyphics characteristics of transsexuals: Is there evidence for an organizing effect of sex hormones. *Psychoneuroendocrinology, 25*(4), 365–375.
Sperling, A., & Hsu, V. (Producers). (2014). *Transparent* [Television series]. Los Angeles, CA: Amazon Studios.
Stevens, J., Gomez-Lobo, V., & Pine-Twaddell, E. (2015). Insurance coverage of puberty blocker for transgender youth. *Pediatrics, 136*(6), 1030.
Sullivan, A. L. (2009). *Hiding in the open: Navigating education at the gender poles: A study of transgender children in early childhood* (Order No. 3361853). Available from ProQuest Dissertations and Theses A&I. (304843384). Retrieved from http://ezaccess.libraries.psu.edu/login?url=https://search-proquest-com.ezaccess.libraries.psu.edu/docview/304843384?accountid=13158.
Sullivan, A. (2014). Seeking solace in the music room: Normalized physical spaces in the early childhood environment and the resulting impact on transgender children. *Gender, Education, Music, and Society, 7*(2), 12–24. Retrieved from https://ojs.library.queensu.ca/index.php/gems/article/view/5168.
Weber, P. (2014, February 21). Confused by all the new Facebook genders? Here's what they mean. *Slate*. Retrieved from http://www.slate.com/blogs/lexicon_valley/2014/02/21/gender_facebook_now_has_56_categories_to_choose_from_including_cisgender.html.
Wittig, M. (1992). *The straight mind and other essays*. Boston, MA: Beacon Press.
Youth & Students. (2017). Retrieved from http://www.transequality.org/issues/youth-students.

CHAPTER 4

Hiding in the Open: Portraits of Trans Partners (Birth-Age Eight)

Ten research partners were interviewed for this study. The partners ranged in age, race, gender identity, socioeconomic status, location of origin, and setting of early childhood education (public, private, or home) attended. As a means to explore their unique stories and introduce them to the reader, individual portraits of each partner were created. The portraits primarily focus on their out of school experiences: their personalities, families, interests, and lives at home (educational experiences will be discussed later). As all children are different, transgender children are similarly unique. Although the partners in this study shared that as young children they had an incongruence with assigned birth gender, and many of their educational and social experiences were similar, this seems to be the consequence of growing up in a common society with common values. This is not the result of all transgender children fitting a pre-assigned mold, complemented with stereotypical assumptions. Some of the children were shy, others were outgoing; some liked to play with toys, while others used their imaginations to create games using natural materials. Several of the partners performed well in school while others struggled. Some had a supportive adult or family member, though this was not the case for all (Sullivan, 2009, p. 97).

As it would be impossible to deduce an individual's life story to a few pages, the portraits are not meant to be comprehensive. They are merely glimpses into the experiences of these unique children. There was a great deal of interesting information that was not included.

© The Author(s) 2019
A. L. Sullivan and L. L. Urraro, *Voices of Transgender Children in Early Childhood Education*, Critical Cultural Studies of Childhood,
https://doi.org/10.1007/978-3-030-13483-9_4

Family histories and almost all occurrences after age eight were not incorporated into the portraits. However, of the data available and relevant to the research questions, as much was included as possible to accurately represent the partners' stories. In addition, in an attempt to stay as true to the intended meanings as possible, direct quotes were used extensively to elucidate the partners' perspectives (Sullivan, 2009, pp. 97–98). The ages and years provided in the portraits were those that were accurate at the time of the interviews.

Aidan

> Kids will figure it out, because guess what? They pay attention. (Sullivan, 2009, p. 98)

Aidan is a 26-year-old white male. He was raised in Minnesota, and received both a public and a private education. He did not attend preschool. Ashley (the researcher) has been friends with Aidan for about four years now. She met him shortly before he went on hormones and she observed his transition. The changes were striking. His appearance is quite different from that of his former self. He is tall, and this helped with his transition. Aidan has a deep voice and a great deal of facial hair that he has shaped into a goatee. He has completed gender confirmation surgery and presents as a male. Aidan is a college graduate. He is well-read, opinionated, and outspoken (Sullivan, 2009, p. 98).

Aidan was born "two months preemie, (with a) collapsed lung and a half working immune system." He had a variety of medical conditions. "I mean, I was just, you, shit you name it, I probably suffered from it. You know, horrifying stuff really." Both of his parents are doctors, his mother is a neurosurgeon. He feels that as a child his parents were extremely aware of any potential medical or psychological differences about him due to their profession. This included his masculine behaviors. Their attentiveness has led Aidan to believe that, "I swear to god, maybe it was Munchausen by Proxy, I don't know" (Sullivan, 2009, pp. 98–99).

As a young child, his parents bought him a tank, "because I demanded it for my birthday, threw a fit. It was like, you made it a little fort tank, a little flash piping. It was a GI Joe tank. I was really big into 'GI Joes' when I was a kid, and my parents got it for me. There's a picture of me popping up in a little manhole with the 'Rambo' thing and the knife." As a result of his "utter defiance to conform to female life," Aidan's parents had him extensively tested by physicians and psychiatrists. His recollection of these incidents has recently resurfaced with the aid of documentation he obtained in adulthood:

> I have some memory now. When I got them (the documents), I forced the doctor to send them to me. And they, I was on different medication regimens to try and speed up stuff, and make different things happen so I wasn't feeling that way (like a boy). And there's some question as to whether or not I have some congenital issues with testosterone manufacturing and testosterone production. 'Cause I was always very hairy. There were always just different aspects, and why would they put me on different hormone shots and stuff when I was a kid? (Sullivan, 2009, p. 99)

He began hormone shots at, "like six, six/seven."

One of his earliest realizations of living in a gender dichotomous society was when, "I used to go play with my friends, and I'd be like, 'But I want to take my shirt off. Why can't I take my shirt off? He gets to take his shirt off. I'm just like him. Why can't I take my shirt off?'" He describes life during his early childhood years as:

> …Chaos. Because by the time you become able to realize, okay, I don't really fit in, you shut off. And you let everything go on autopilot. At first, you try to struggle, and you try to be what everybody expects you to be. But, you realize pretty darn quickly around the ages of like four or five…you know, when you start kindergarten, and you have to start to socially integrate with people who are not related to you…that you're not going to fit in. And so now, you go into survival mode. (Sullivan, 2009, pp. 99–100)

Aidan has always been aware of the fact that he is male:

> I don't ever remember not knowing. Now, let's define knowing though. There's a difference between certain knowing, when you're like yup okay, that's me right there. I am [trans], I'm three, but I'm [trans] ya know. There's a complete difference between knowing and having the knowledge to put a label on it. And you look back, and you're like, oh yeah, well that's what I was thinking. I didn't know what I was thinking, but that was it. (Sullivan, 2009, p. 100)

Aidan describes his feelings about his body as, "an acceptance. That's just what I'm supposed to be. 'Cause I never said, 'Mommy when's my penis gonna grow?'" Instead, he felt that having a penis looked:

> Like a lot more fun. I never walked around saying, 'can I have a penis?' I never did that. I kind of walked around going, 'well, that's how it should be, and this is what it is, but it's supposed to be like that.' I know that that's what it's supposed to be like. I don't have that yet, but whatever, it'll come. (Sullivan, 2009, p. 100)

School presented a variety of struggles for Aidan. He greatly disliked his first-grade teacher:

> I would sit down and do something that everyone else would take an hour on, I would do in about fifteen minutes. And I would have it all correct, and then I'd go out and play; do whatever I wanted to do. And she didn't like that. So, she deemed me mentally retarded, and emotionally and mentally underdeveloped, and sent me back to kindergarten. (Sullivan, 2009, p. 101)

He was forced to move schools frequently:

> I went to a Catholic kindergarten, a Catholic first grade, and then back to Catholic kindergarten, and then to a public first grade and second grade, then to a different public third grade, and then to a private fourth grade, and then a Catholic high school.

Aidan explained that he was being bullied and he frequently switched schools to protect his safety. He stated simply: "I would get the shit beat out of me" (Sullivan, 2009, p. 101).

As a teenager, his parents found out that he was, "gay, and they sent me to reparative therapy." He wore makeup and competed as a model in an attempt to conform. As an adult he joined the military and married a gay man to help further conceal his gender identity. He left the military and was divorced. Three years ago he began his transition, and he recently married Erin, his college sweetheart. After several painful and difficult surgeries (during one of which he awoke), he has now completed his transition and legally changed his gender. In 2009, Aidan and his wife Erin (also a research partner) no longer considered themselves to be part of the transgender community, and they were living happily with their dogs in a Midwestern state (Sullivan, 2009, pp. 101–102).

Beth

I think the more we can get the information out there, it will have a snowball effect. More teachers and counselors will understand. They will not only be there for the transgender children, but the next generation of teachers. (Sullivan, 2009, p. 102)

Beth is a 62-year-old Caucasian female. Her demeanor is kind and soft-spoken. She always appears quite calm and makes all around her feel at ease. As she is a physician, this characteristic must give her an excellent bedside manner with her patients. Beth is tall and she has a true regal beauty complimented by deep blue eyes. She is friendly, patient, reserved, and intelligent (Sullivan, 2009, p. 102).

Beth was an:

> Only child. My parents were 37 years old, the same age, when I was born. Mother had miscarried a couple of times before becoming pregnant with me and I was born at the end of 1946. And Daddy had been in the war. He didn't go overseas but he was ready to ship out to Japan when the war ended. And so he came home and he and mother moved from Tampa, Florida where they had been stationed, to a tiny town in Louisiana. He had a job opportunity but that didn't work out so his brother owned a dry cleaning plant in a little town in Mississippi. And it was a town of about 20,000 people, had a good hospital, and when they found out mother was pregnant again they wanted her to be around very good doctors and turned out that [name of town] had some of those. So that's where they moved and that's where I was born. Mother did well with that third pregnancy. (Sullivan, 2009, pp. 102–103)

As a family, they were not considered:

> The social elite in town. Daddy drove a delivery truck and mother was a nurse who happened to be not working. This didn't fit in with the bankers, lawyers, and the wealthy planters (farmers) in the Delta. And so the country club set if you will. (Sullivan, 2009, p. 103)

Until attending public school for grade two, Beth's mother homeschooled her from preschool through the first grade. As a result, she was primarily raised around adults:

I had no brothers or sisters in the house. My cousins were many years older than I was and while we did live close to them, they clearly weren't going to play games on my level. The difference was eight or ten years from most of them. So it was my parents and me and for most of the time, that Daddy was working 'til 5:00 or 6:00 every day. It was me and mother. Daddy was wonderful, but people say you know you are this way because you didn't have any influence from your father. That wasn't true at all because when he was present, he spent lots of time and cared for me a lot. But daddy was not one of these sports heroes, and he would have a little baseball and glove and toss with me. But he never coached any sports or insisted that I go out for any teams. But the fact that I grew up in those preschool years around adults I think certainly had a lot to do with my intellectual achievement level at that time. Basically, (I) had a vocabulary like they did. And I would listen to them talk and they certainly were not talking baby talk. When I learned to talk, it was as an adult with sentences. (Sullivan, 2009, pp. 103–104)

As a child, Beth enjoyed playing with:

Sets; including lots of little figures about this tall. And you have a school perhaps, with a bunch of little school children figures. Or you would have all sorts of people going to work; construction workers, doctors, and nurses. You would have cowboys and Indians and the western fort, tiny little plastic figures, kind of like army men. But I didn't have any, (this) predated GI Joe. They were some cowboy dolls. This was big. This was back in the 50s, was still the Wild West. I can remember some of these television and rodeo cowboys coming to town. One called Lash LaRue. Lash LaRue was famous because he had this bullwhip. That was his weapon and he would lash out. And he came and talked in an assembly one day and partners got to shoot straight and all that kind of stuff. Roy Rogers and Gene Autry, I do think that I had a Roy Rogers action figure. (Sullivan, 2009, p. 104)

When playing with figurines, Beth would often create make-believe families:

We really did have a number of ages there and we would have at least one child and a baby in the family, the parents. I never did enter the game and say okay, this is me. In my mind I knew that playing with someone else, you always had third person characters. Just expose a little too much of yourself. (Sullivan, 2009, p. 104)

Beth, "didn't do well in sports; I didn't do well in rough and tumble games or interactions with other boys." However, she did enjoy low impact games:

> We would do, there was a city park not too far from where I lived. And we would go down to the park and have little simple sport activities like four square, do you remember that one? And we would do that and would have jungle gyms to climb on, they had tetherball. We played marbles, Chinese checkers. I was late learning how to ride a bike- seven or nine years old. Reason for that was because when I first was taught years earlier, I fell off and skinned my knees and cried and didn't want to do that again for a while. (Sullivan, 2009, pp. 104–105)

A major influence on her childhood was her religious upbringing:

> The church was the foundation of social life in Mississippi in the 1950s. And most towns had a number of Baptist churches. There were the First Baptists churches where all the community leaders all would have memberships. We actually had membership in the First Baptist Church. For some reason, the saying went- when people moved to town, they didn't ask you if you attended church, they'd just ask you if you were Baptist or Methodist. It was just taken for granted that everything in the Bible, I mean the King James Bible, was true. And there were some things you didn't question and their interpretations were the true one. And with the Baptists, one of the big things was women were to be silent in church. They could teach children Sunday schooling or attend the choir, but they could not speak from the pulpit or they could not preach. Even now there's nothing like that in the Bible, that's just the way it was accepted. (Sullivan, 2009, p. 105)

Beth was unlike most of her peers.

> By the time I was seven, I was wearing mother's clothes after school. So there was nothing erotic about it. The church every now and then got in a dig, and this is unnatural and is a perversion you know, for man to be with man and woman to be with a woman. If ever something that you think about doing is a sin you need to ask for forgiveness and pray. And so I am here. I am thinking, maybe I need to pray. You buy into it. You know some people say, 'Well when I hear that; it made me question the church.' That's not what it made me do, it made me question myself. It was very conformist, and there are places where it still is. You were stifled; you

would fall in line with everybody else. And then you say, 'God, 'come on, come on, and please take this away.' And you don't know why it doesn't happen. (Sullivan, 2009, pp. 105–106)

She was often angry with god and she would question:

'What am I doing wrong? Am I not sincere enough? Am I not serious enough about my sorrow and my penitence? Please God, I really mean this.' You never, not even for a few days, never get over who you are, even for a few days. You just have all this guilt that I just don't want it bad enough. (Sullivan, 2009, p. 106)

After medical school, a marriage, the birth of her son, a divorce, and gender confirmation surgery, Beth is now a successful physician and author who has won several local awards. She helps to coordinate LGBTQ community events. She is a proud grandmother, and works tirelessly for her patients as well the transgender community (Sullivan, 2009, p. 106).

Chris

I think learning has always symbolized freedom, because I knew that when I got to a certain point, I'd be able to be me. (Sullivan, 2009, p. 138)

Chris is a 28-year-old Latino male who was raised in Arizona. He was homeschooled prior to attending public preschool and elementary school. As an adult, Chris appears quite masculine as a result of taking male hormones for years. He is small in stature. Chris is talkative and open. Speaking with him quickly feels like reminiscing with an old friend. At the time of the interview, Chris was a graduate student who often participated in social justice related activities. Chris is also an artist and he uses technology to enhance his craft (Sullivan, 2009, p. 138).

Prior to his birth, Chris's mother, "had some insane number of miscarriages. She had a really hard time having a child, so, she was really invested in my life." Chris spent the majority of his early years at home with his mother:

Before I went to preschool, my mom was a daycare sort of person, so she did like a home daycare. My parents got divorced when I was two, so, my mom had to kinda figure out a way to support herself, suddenly, now that my dad was gone, because she had been a stay-at-home mom. So, she became like the daycare center in the neighborhood. That allowed her to still stay home with me, although thirty other kids, too. But it was really fun. I didn't care. At that point, I didn't have any brother or sisters, so I loved it, 'Oh, there's other kids. Yes!' I was, probably, between the ages of two and four, during that time, pretty young. My dad wasn't all that involved in my life, at that point. He was getting remarried and doing all that sort of stuff. I saw him, but mostly I was being raised by my mom at that point. (Sullivan, 2009, pp. 138–139)

Chris explained that because he was so young, his mom did not mind that he behaved in a masculine manner:

She didn't really care, although, she insisted that my hair was long and insisted on trying to put in certain gender norm things. But, she was also so stressed and so tired that she didn't have a lot of time to devote to it, at that point. So, my hair was the only struggle I remember during that period of time. Oh, I hated it! It was horrible! But, she loved my long hair and I wore it to church on Sundays. I was raised Mormon, so we went to church every single Sunday. I had to wear a dress and it was really painful and horrible. That was one of the worst things of my childhood, was church. I hated church! Not because I didn't like church, but I hated what THAT meant for me on that day. (Sullivan, 2009, p. 139)

Chris's mother was aware of how he felt about his long hair:

I would scream and freak out and yell, 'Please cut my hair! I hate it!' She would say, 'Oh, but, it's so beautiful; let me brush it.' And, there was this wild child running around with crazy hair, screaming, 'No! Cut it!' I hated it. And, the dresses were a constant fight, 'I feel bad. This makes me feel bad! Oh, no,' just over and over. My parents thought it was some kind of stage. I don't know; they didn't get the message. They were really excited about having a daughter, my mom, especially; my dad, not so much. My dad was fine as long as I liked sports. I loved sports. As long as I liked things he could relate to, he said, 'Oh, whatever.' Especially when I was that little, kids don't really look all that different at that point. Let's put a baseball cap on you and go to the ballgame, and I'd say, 'Yes!' So, it was kind of intense. My mom got really invested in having a daughter and that was never anything I could really identify with, so I really didn't know what she was talking about. I really hate dresses and I really hate my hair being long.

I remember, once, I talked my dad into cutting my hair because I used to go during the summer and some holidays to his house. So one summer, I talked him into letting me get my hair cut really short, like super, super short and I was in heaven! It was the best summer ever. I ran around going to ball games, had really short hair and just being really happy about it. When I got home, my mom was so upset, like the world had ended. (Sullivan, 2009, p. 140)

After his hair was cut short, people often addressed Chris as a boy:

I remember seeing my mom getting really upset. I thought it was great. I used to wear a lot of baseball caps when I was really young, just to put my hair up because I hated it and didn't want to see it and didn't want it on my person. So, whenever I could get away with doing that stuff [I would. People would say] 'oh, he's so cute,' which would be really upsetting for my mom. (Sullivan, 2009, p. 140)

Chris was also, "pretty into Superman when I was really little. Like, I wore the Superman underoos twenty-four/seven, wouldn't take them off. My mom made me a cape so I was definitely convinced I was Superman! Something about that made me Superman." (Sullivan, 2009, p. 140)

Chris describes wearing stereotypically-feminine clothing during early childhood as being in drag:

That's the only way I can describe it to people is, basically, like being in forced drag, which isn't fun. Forced drag, not fun. I used to look for clothes, I would occasionally be able to talk my mom into buying clothes, or, go out and use whatever money I had left from working during the summer to buy something that I liked. I played a lot of sports, so that was a good reason to wear a lot of shorts; to be able to wear clothes that were, at least, androgynous. But, you know, my parents always insisted on buying really feminine clothes, but I would never wear them. I'd wear my athletic shorts, my t-shirt that was horribly stained from soccer practice over anything else. So, once I got older, I started doing my own thing. When I was younger, I started putting up so much of a struggle for dresses, and that sort of stuff, like a daily battle. Although, my mom would still shop in the girl's department, I would at least get the more gender neutral of the girls' clothing. Girls' clothing is still girls' clothing, it still feels like that. (Sullivan, 2009, pp. 140–141)

I do remember, anytime I could find something I felt comfortable in, I would just latch onto it, like the Superman underoos. When I was in second grade, I think, my mom had bought me a teddy bear, actually, a friendly, larger teddy bear that had a collared shirt that had teddy bears on it, and a red tie. I took it off the teddy bear and I wore it the rest of the year! I thought, 'This is awesome! I look so good in this tie, it's not even funny!' My mom had to peel that shirt off of me to get it cleaned. (Sullivan, 2009, p. 141)

Chris explained that he was so happy about his shirt that he wore it to school every day. His classmates:

Didn't care. Kids just wear what they want. When I was little, I was probably the strongest kid in my class, because, well, not so much as an adult, but I was really athletic, played baseball and soccer and every sport I could, so I was a fairly strong child. Plus, strength and being strong really represented masculinity to me. And, not being strong in physical ways represented more feminine things to me, so, I would try to be more masculine; be stronger. I loved playing sports because it gave me a chance to work out. (Sullivan, 2009, pp. 141–142)

From the time I was little, I remember being interested in lifting weights and that sort of stuff. I used to do pushups in my room. I tried to foster that in myself. So, when I was at school, especially at recess, you're away from parents and authority figures, so, I would just be who I was, as much as I could be. I'd still be uncomfortable in my clothes, but I'd arm wrestle, try to play football, if they'd let me in the game. (Sullivan, 2009, pp. 141–142)

One of Chris's greatest struggles was conforming to his assigned gender:

I just remember not being very good at pretending to be a girl. It's the way that people see the world. The people I was supposed to relate to and have something in common with, I didn't. It didn't make a lot of sense to me to put a lot of effort into relating. I just don't understand why that's important to you. I would just get frustrated and want to go play basketball, or I'd want to go read.

In addition to playing sports, Chris:

had a wide range of toys, because I wouldn't play with the girl toys because I didn't like them. But my mom and dad insisted on buying them for me. I would only play with boy toys, so I would beg for GI Joes and He-Man, all the different toys. And, they would get them for me, but they would also buy ten Barbies or something, to balance it out. All my Barbies were gay in my mind, the boys like the boys and the girls like the girls. Ken wore a lot of dresses, A LOT of dresses; Barbie wore a lot of suits. I cut their hair. I remodeled the Barbie Dream house, they got me one and I thought, 'This clearly needs tile.' So, I took tile from our house, took little bits and laid it into the Dream house. I painted it saying, 'Now, it looks good because it's blue! I painted the pink house blue'! (Sullivan, 2009, pp. 142–143)

Attending church was another struggle for Chris:

> It was never very fun for me. I definitely remember being taught that the only thing that's acceptable is normal, in terms of being Mormon- being straight; having lots of children. I remember lots of gender-conformity expectations. If you didn't, there were a lot of 'outsider' feelings, a lot of ostracization. I remember the focus being on, through the gender-segregated, they would segregate the boys and the girls, really early on. So, all the lessons for little girls are about being good wives and growing up to be good wives. That's just terrifying. Who does that to six-year-olds? Like, why are you talking to me about this? I don't really get it. (Sullivan, 2009, p. 143)

Chris put a lot of effort into his studies, and worked diligently through high school and college. He struggled with acceptance from his family, and has made some strides with his father. Shortly after the interview was completed, Chris relocated to a Midwestern state, where he planned to propose to his girlfriend of several years (Sullivan, 2009, p. 143).

Erin

Adults try to force an adult narrative on kids, and you know, they don't have an adult narrative. (Sullivan, 2009, p. 107)

Erin is a 23-year-old Caucasian female. She was one of several siblings born into a wealthy family. As a child, she attended a private Lutheran school. Like Aidan, Ashley has been friends with Erin for several years. Erin is brilliant and possesses a genius IQ. She has an extensive vocabulary and inserts colorful language into her unique sense of humor. She often makes jokes. Erin is extremely feminine. Looking at her, it is hard to imagine that she could have been labeled male at birth. She is quite pretty and as a result, she receives a great deal of attention in public. She is very talkative and can speak on any topic (Sullivan, 2009, p. 107).

Erin explained that some of her:

Earliest memories are just at the mall with my mom. And, you know, it used to be cool for me to help her pick out clothes and look at stuff and shop. And that was totally normal for me. You'd see kids who didn't like to do it, and you'd see kids who'd like to do it. You know, it didn't really click.

She also recollects her time in preschool:

You see a couple of games going on, and you walk over to play the one you think you'd like to play, and the teacher comes over, 'Oh, no, no, not that one. No, no, no, you don't play house. You go over here. They're playing ninja turtles. Make fake little ninja things out of paper with them.' I remember that very clearly. (Sullivan, 2009, p. 107)

Her first day of kindergarten was painful for her:

There were a couple of guys who...I didn't really fit in, obviously. And I remember one guy just walked right up to me, smacked me as hard as he could in the stomach with a closed fist, and walked away. (Sullivan, 2009, pp. 107–108)

My mom walked over and said, 'Why'd you do that?' And he said, 'Look at him.' And that was his answer. So that's when I kinda figured out that you've gotta copy, so that's when I started playing kickball and doing the 'girls are yucky' bullshit. And everybody knew that I was, I think everybody knows that you're bullshit. You know, you always get picked last for everything even though you're not bad at it. You have a very small group of friends. I was friends with the disabled kid because he was the one who didn't have any friends either. So I made friends with the asthmatic who wasn't allowed to go outside six months a year because that was kind of my...you know, I guess you kind of separate out the injured one from the herd. So that was the guy I was able to make friends with. It was actually really funny, because before he knew I transitioned, after he basically cured his asthma and he didn't have the problem anymore, he didn't want to be my friend anymore. It was really funny. (Sullivan, 2009, p. 108)

In preschool, Erin realized that she was a unique child: "You just kind of know something is horribly, horribly wrong, and you don't really know what it is."

When asked if she knew she was a girl she replied:

It's about knowing or not knowing. It's about when does your, when does the definition become active. It's like I remember, you know, going into my sister's room and trying on her clothes and getting pissed, and getting screamed at it for it, and not knowing what the deal was. Cause they were okay for her to wear. (Sullivan, 2009, pp. 108–109)

She continued to explain that:

> I remember when I was a kid, I don't remember the 'when is my vagina gonna grow?' I never did that, but I remember thinking to myself, 'having kids looks like it hurts. I don't think I'm gonna do that.' What kind of fucking boy says that to themselves?! 'Boy, having kids looks like it really hurts your vagina when they come out. I don't think I wanna do that'. (Sullivan, 2009, p. 109)

At this young age she figured that her body would eventually transition into that of an assigned female so she, "didn't really worry about it." When she was small, Erin:

> Got really good at the hula hoops, which is really odd considering I don't know where my hips are. Well, it's funny, because you move your hips like that when you're a kid, and you get told that's not something boys do. Like you know the belly dancers that can completely pop their hips all the way out and go all the way around? I used to be able to do that. And my mom used to comment on it, and have me show people until my dad said 'that's ridiculous. Don't do that anymore.' And I can't do it anymore; physically incapable. (Sullivan, 2009, p. 109)

Her father also taught her "how guys act toward girls" by watching the cartoon character Pepe Le Pew. This was her favorite character, and she watched *Looney Tunes* all the time. As a result of these lessons, Erin "used to mess with girls a lot." She was often picked on in school:

> I got my ass kicked once, and my dad put me in martial arts. Told me I was a pussy. I was in like kindergarten. He told me I was a pussy, and then I got put into martial arts. And basically, I changed schools like five or six times, moved all the time. You know, I was never in a school more than two or three years. And I would get picked on for the first month or so, and somebody would finally get the balls to take a swing, and get the shit beat out of them, and then no one would touch me for the time I was there. I was in World Federation with a nasty old Korean man, who was very nice to his students. And you know, our parents would be watching, and he'd be like, 'okay. You do the form, and you do this, and you punch like this, and you kick like this, and you block.' And the parents would leave and he'd be like, 'and if they hit you, you grab them here, and

you squeeze, and you twist, and you wait 'til they scream, and then when their scream stops, you put your knee right here.' You know, and then the parents would walk back in, okay, 'then you punch, then you kick.' You know, Master Chen was hilarious, and then Master Lee, when I went to California, he would have breaking classes. You know, wood breaking classes, and you know, you're supposed to do stationary wood with guys holding it like that, and he would make us do speed break, speed breaking. (Sullivan, 2009, pp. 109–110)

Erin eventually came out to her family and endured several strained and severed relationships as a result. She began to take hormones when she was 16, and thus never hit secondary puberty. This helped immensely with her "passability." She became active in the transgender community, often aiding others in their transition. Erin has had gender confirmation surgery and no longer considers herself a transgender woman, she is simply a woman. Erin went on to attend law school (Sullivan, 2009, pp. 110–111).

Lady Gazelle

No matter what anybody thinks or says about you, love yourself. I am a beautiful woman and I can have whatever I want in this world; but I have to be true to myself. (Sullivan, 2009, p. 111)

Lady Gazelle is a 51-year-old Black transwoman. As a child, she resided primarily in Los Angeles, California. However, she also lived in Kansas City. Her schooling consisted entirely of public education. Lady Gazelle is an active and free spirited adult. She looks quite a bit like Tina Turner. She has worked tirelessly for the transgender community, and with the creation of a program serving the local population. Lady Gazelle has a fiery personality, apparent both when pleased and when crossed. She is tall and expressive (Sullivan, 2009, p. 111).

Lady Gazelle is the:

Oldest of five brothers and sisters. My mother had five kids by five different men so every time she had a baby, a man was never around. So I had to be the mother. I had to fix breakfast for my brothers and sisters. I had to change the diapers. My brother Rodrick is a year younger than me. And he has always been jealous of me 'cause he didn't know his father and his got killed in a bank robbery attempt when Rodrick was only two years old. My father has always been very good at making things look really good and nice and appropriate. But he was a heroin addict and a pimp and he only took me when my mother insisted he come get me 'cause I was out of control for whatever reason. But my brother has always been jealous of that. (Sullivan, 2009, pp. 111–112)

When she was small, Lady Gazelle enjoyed playing dress-up. It was her "favorite game. I really wasn't physically active right then but I liked to dance. I have always loved dancing. I did some entertainment. I was the first little Black boy who did the milk commercials." She also liked baseball but she:

> Hated football 'cause the guys would like to run me the ball and tackle me and that was their game. And so I didn't like football. I liked baseball but the guys really wouldn't let me play because I was such a sissy. (Sullivan, 2009, p. 112)

The majority of her playmates were girls:

> The boys didn't want to play with me. Every time I got a chance I would play with dolls. My favorite was Susie Bake Oven (Easy Bake Oven). That was my favorite since I could remember. My father's wife, my stepmother had a sister and she always treated me like a girl. I think her name was Connie and she always treated me like a girl. One of the biggest thrills going back to Kansas City to visit was to see Connie and we would be in her room for hours playing with her Susie Bake Oven. (Sullivan, 2009, p. 112)

In addition to these pastimes, she also liked to watch the *Flintstones, I Love Lucy, Speed Racer, Soul Train* and *Gilligan's Island* on television. Her favorite shows were *I Dream of Jeannie* and *Bewitched*. Occasionally, she also watched *Superman, the Ed Sullivan Show* and *American Bandstand*. Although she did not like to play games, she did enjoy roller skating (Sullivan, 2009, p. 112).

Lady Gazelle was teased quite a bit as a child because she:

> Looked like a girl. I acted like a girl. I had hair like a girl. And I also remember my highlight, my high point in life when my parents left home left me alone and I could play in my mother's makeup and clothes and stuff like that. Of course I got the worst beatings for it but, to me it was worth it. (Sullivan, 2009, p. 113)

She explained that as a child:

> My father always dressed me. If I sat with my legs crossed he would slap me in my mouth. I was under so much stress and the only one who understood me was my grandmother. She was such a sweetheart. My grandmother understood me more than my mother and father did. My father's mother used to be a prostitute in quarters and she changed her life. She was Elizabeth [last name], she was Creole. She was like a Mexican lady with blue eyes. (Sullivan, 2009, p. 113)

As a result of her feminine behavior:

> My mother took me to a couple of therapists. The school had a really hard time with me. I was angry all the time. I would break out windows. I would grab a chair and start beating everybody in the class. Man, I had some issues honey. I did not have anybody to discuss this with me. I was a child and it was my parents' job to discuss these things with me and they didn't know how to deal with me so they just didn't talk about it. The only thing my mother told me is if I turn into, if I turn out to be a punk, she said she brought me into this world and she would take me out. (Sullivan, 2009, p. 113)

At the age of 12, Lady Gazelle was institutionalized for being transgender. Around that same time period:

> I was 12, 13 something like that. I would steal cars 'cause I hadn't left school yet and I would ride around at night and stuff like that. And I was filling the gas tank up, we ran out of gas, and I was filling it up with water. And this guy and this chick pulled up and asked me if I needed some help and told them I was out of gas. He said, 'You don't have any money?' and I said, 'No' and so he said, 'Come on.' So they put me into the car with them and they asked me if I had a place to live and I told them 'No.' And so they said they have some kids, and they had three kids and they wanted me to be a babysitter. And they would let me stay there rent free as long as I took care of their kids. They were both drug addicts. So they took me over there, and her name was Kya [last name] and they took me over there and let me stay. (Sullivan, 2009, pp. 113–114)
>
> My first real sexual experience I was raped. There was a straight bar a few blocks away and they let me go out after hours and this guy bought me a coke and a pack of cigarettes and we danced. He said he was going to this other club and he was going to take me with him and I rode with him.

He pulled into this darkest street and he was so big and I will never forget this, he ripped both sides of my mouth. And I got out of the car and I was so upset and I started walking and I was crying and another guy pulled up and he offered me a ride. And he said, 'What happened?' And I told him. So he said, 'Take a couple of these and they will make you feel better'- red devils, downers. I took them and I shouldn't have taken more than one but I took two. When I came to, I was in the hospital. Sally went out to empty her trash in the alley the next day and she found me by the dumpster passed out with my pants pulled down to my ankles. And my mother came to the hospital and the first thing she said was, 'What were you doing in an alley half naked in women's clothes?' I told her I went to a costume party. She says, 'I am going to take the car and pull it around to the side exit 'cause I don't want anyone to know that you're my child.' And that's when I decided to leave home. What she did, she didn't know how to love anybody. And the first chance I got, I was out of there. (Sullivan, 2009, pp. 114–115)

After a difficult life on the streets, Lady Gazelle is now a productive woman dedicated to helping other transgender people who have suffered through similar circumstances. Since starting a crucial program for transgender people, she has been interviewed by various media outlets and has received several accolades for her community service work. As of 2009, Lady Gazelle lived in her own home with her husband and was in the process of adopting an African American child (Sullivan, 2009, p. 115).

Lana

I made it a point to always play with the girls not the boys, despite my teachers. But that's where I felt that I belonged, I really did. (Sullivan, 2009, p. 115)

Lana is a 29-year-old Black female. She grew up in Texas, Colorado and Germany where she attended both public and private schools. Lana is tall and slender and has beautiful chocolate colored skin. She is quiet, but finds her voice when needed. She uses her natural leadership abilities to help effectively assist with Lady Gazelle's program. She is caring and was extremely helpful and accommodating during the researcher's visits to the program (Sullivan, 2009, pp. 115–116).

Lana is the second child of four; she has one older brother and two younger sisters. Although her brother was given the opportunity, Lana did not attend preschool:

> I remember I wanted to go to Head Start, but my parents thought there was something wrong with me so they would not let me go. And I remember another time I was not allowed to go 'cause I was seeing a psychiatrist. I wasn't really taught. (Sullivan, 2009, pp. 115–116)

She was sent to a psychiatrist as a result of her selective mutism:

> What I would do is okay, say like you were sitting there and you were talking to me. Unless it was something that was interesting to me, I wouldn't talk to you at all, period. I would just look at you and go 'psss.' That's really what I would do. And once they figured it out if it wasn't something of interest, I just be like 'okay bye,' and I wouldn't say anything to you period. I would go find something of interest and then I'd go occupy myself with that. So, and I knew how to talk, I just wouldn't. I don't know why, I just wouldn't talk and went, 'okay, and you're weird.' (Sullivan, 2009, p. 116)

During her early childhood years, Lana would only speak with her mother:

> 'Cause during the time my brother was in preschool, my mother volunteered for preschool she was also teaching me stuff. So I was learning. That's the reason I was more willing to engage with her, because I felt like I don't know if she was doing something to benefit me or whatever. I just knew it was fun when she was teaching me stuff. That's the reason I connected with her. So that's probably the reason why, like, my dad worked a lot. And it wasn't like he wasn't there, he just worked a lot. You know, so we had somebody that had to pay the bills. My mom worked a lot but she always made sure she was there. (Sullivan, 2009, pp. 116–117)

Lana explained that at the age of three and four years, she had a strong personality and an "attitude." When she started school at age five:

> They thought I was retarded, and I had to go through all of this and start seeing psychiatrists and being analyzed with all of this, it was just insane. I went through all of this testing of this and that, and they couldn't find

out what it was, and I was very advanced. So far advanced what happened was, I went, well starting in Colorado I was in kindergarten and then I moved to Germany. After they found out how advanced I was, (they sent me) to go and be tested on a worldwide level. 'Cause on a national level I was tested in the top five percentile. Then once they found that out, they were like, 'wow, okay so well maybe she's, he's not retarded.' (Sullivan, 2009, p. 117)

When Lana was in second grade, her family relocated to Germany and enrolled her in a private school for American children. Prior to this move, and placement in a gifted program, Lana felt gravely misunderstood (Sullivan, 2009, p. 117).

She has always known that she is a girl. This initially created conflicts when the first child assigned female at birth was born into the family:

I remember I was so jealous when um, let me see, my mom had my sister. I was probably around, let me see, she had my sister we were we were in Germany. She had my sister right before we went to Germany so it's around the time I was in kindergarten. I remember she got all these girl toys and stuff and she was the only person I had to play with girl toys, 'cause they wouldn't buy me any of my own. I would have to go to my cousin's, Allison's house and play with her girl toys. And see, my aunt didn't mind. She's always, she'll be like, 'go play,' and I would. I had a cousin, a boy cousin and girl cousin. We're both a year apart. So we were all three pretty much the same age. I would go play with her (the girl) because of her toys and I could be myself. And we would play house and stuff and I would be the mom. So that was that. When I had my sister I was very jealous. I was like 'uhh.' And then I was like okay, maybe I shouldn't be jealous. That means there will be girl toys and I won't have to go anywhere. So it was good and bad. (Sullivan, 2009, pp. 117–118)

I remember when my mom, I got really excited when she decked out the room in Rainbow Brite. I was like, 'oh, okay, this is wonderful.' You know 'cause they, that's what I used to watch in the morning is my Rainbow Brite, my Strawberry Shortcake. My, I was always into Madonna, Janet Jackson, Prince. I mean, come on now. But I would always dress up because I liked their outfits. That's why I liked them. And then Boy George, when he came out, that was it! That was my world because he was a boy and he wore makeup and it was around that time. I was like, let me see, how old was I? I can't remember exactly but it was the first time I could relate to somebody, because it was a man on television that would dress up. (Sullivan, 2009, p. 118)

In addition to Rainbow Brite and Strawberry Shortcake, Lana:

> Liked to knit, and play in my mom's makeup. Um, I would draw a lot. Draw or write a lot. Other than that it was pretty much Barbie and my roller skates. I used to love roller skating a lot. I used to be able to do splits on skates actually. It used to be fun. And skate backwards, that was our thing. Our school would take us and we would go skating every, like it was either once a month or every Friday. But we would go skating, roller skating. So that was my release. I could be, you know what I mean. The other girls were, that's how I learned how to do what the other girls were doing on skates. (Sullivan, 2009, pp. 118–119)

Lana's father responded to her desire to play with toys intended for girls by enrolling her in football:

> That was horrible. One time before a game he kept trying to get me out on the field and I scratched him all up 'cause I refused to play and I just didn't want to. It wasn't what I liked. I mean I enjoyed sports as far as I love volleyball, running, um, I later picked up basketball. So I figured out (how to be) masculine enough to pacify him. Actually I ended up enjoying it a lot, but never really liked football. And he tried to put me in baseball with my brother. His solution was (to) make me do activities with my brother and maybe that would help me be more masculine; but it kind of propelled me in the other direction. (Sullivan, 2009, p. 119)

It is also interesting to note that Lana was living in Germany during:

> The time when the Berlin Wall was falling. That was insanity. I've seen gas stations blowing up, people catch on fire. My mother was actually pregnant and she used to check under cars in the morning to see if there were any bombs while my dad was at work, it was sheer insanity. I remember bomb threats at two and three in the morning. We would say to my mother, 'Mom there is someone on the phone saying they are going to blow up the building,' and she would start to freak out and drag us all into the middle of the streets and the apartment complexes would all be vacated. (Sullivan, 2009, p. 119)

After several years in Germany, Lana moved back to the United States where she continued her education in the public school system. She graduated from high school at the age of 15 and dedicated herself to community service until the age of 19. She moved to California and enlisted in the military. She became addicted to drugs which reached its apogee when her parents and sister were killed in a train crash in Colorado. She is now sober and holds a leadership position within Lady Gazelle's program (Sullivan, 2009, pp. 119–120).

LLUVY RAE

> It's like you can't really be yourself unless you're alone in your own space…So it's sort of like suffering just being alone, feeling like you're the only one in the world that has these problems, being called names because they don't understand. (Sullivan, 2009, p. 154)

Lluvy Rae (pronounced You-Vee Ray) is a 28-year-old MTF trans person. She is Native American and Mexican. She grew up on the Navajo Reservation in Arizona. During early childhood she attended public school. Lluvy Rae is a relatively reserved person. She has Navajo facial features and long, thick, shiny hair. She has a favorite sweater that she wears all of the time, even in the summer. Lluvy Rae is very helpful and she goes out of her way to assist those around her. When Ashley met with her, she was quite accommodating, even making photocopies for her. She is dedicated to the LGBTQ community (Sullivan, 2009, p. 120).

Lluvy Rae's mother was a single parent. Her father passed away when she was four years old. Her mother:

> Had at the time, there were eight of us; three brothers, three sisters and me; there were seven. And we were all like, I have two younger than me. I have my younger sister and younger brother. And then I have at that time two older sisters and two older brothers. We were all a few grades apart.

When describing her early years, Lluvy Rae used the terms "pain," "no love," "hurt," and "I'm not happy" (Sullivan, 2009, pp. 120–121).

During early childhood, she struggled with being transgender and living within cultural limitations:

> But that early, preschool to third grade, we also had different cultural events; like in the fall and in the spring we had Native American Culture Week or whatever. And when we do culture week, like that there's dances and stuff that we have to perform and I hated that. I seriously hated that. That was like the worst part. We had to, like the guys had to participate in this cultural dance where you have to wear a mask and no shirt and

just like jeans or jean short pants and you have, I guess you would call them maracas, only we don't call them maracas. They're made of squash and they have corn inside, I forget what it's called, like rattles. Then the females wear the dresses and stuff. I was uncomfortable when I don't have a shirt on, but I didn't have a choice. If I didn't participate, I didn't pass the class. Even in kick ball, in P.E. classes we had separate changing areas and I would not change into what I was supposed to because I felt uncomfortable even at that age. So I think events like that it was just another thing that made me feel uncomfortable. The attitude made me uncomfortable. (Sullivan, 2009, p. 121)

Lluvy Rae was a shy child who was teased for being different. She internalized the way she was treated and this reduced her self-esteem:

Oh, about the confidence. About being self confident about your emotions; about always being looked at. You're obviously different, but the way they acknowledge it is kind of rude now. It's always, 'you can't, you can't.' Like the school plays and stuff, I wanted to try out for the female part and they were like, 'Oh, you can't. It's for a girl.' And they were like, 'maybe you want to....' I was really artistic. I didn't know how to draw very well, but I was really creative, that's what I would think. And they would be like, 'oh, why don't you be over here?' Why don't you paint this for us?' I was kind of in the neutral, like the setup of the play. Like the back part of it. I did eventually, later on, passed the third grade. I like drama and I participated in drama and plays and stuff. I think I've just been kind of, 'ok I just want to do it, this is what I'm interested in, so I'll just do the male role if that's what they want to give me.' So that's all I'll try out for. So, I think the emotions and stuff and the confidence definitely affects you later because I know I've spoken to other transwomen who you know said, 'I didn't get that love when I was younger.' (Sullivan, 2009, p. 122)

Lluvy Rae kept a small bag of trinkets that she would bring to school. She collected items that would be considered feminine, including flavored ChapStick. When a teacher caught her with the ChapStick, she was reprimanded (Sullivan, 2009, p. 122).

So, there were a few times when they did contact my mom. She'd get a letter and I'd get home and, actually they didn't send it; they'd give it to me to give to my mom. I'd give it to my mom and she'd be like, or they'd put the ChapStick in with the letter, seal it and give it to me and I'd have my mom sign it and I'd just bring it back. The first few times it happened

I actually took it to my aunt who understood, who was okay with me being, with me playing with her clothes, with me playing with her daughters and stuff. I took it to her. I'd cry and say, 'I got in trouble because I took my sister's ChapStick to school and they want my mom to sign this.' So she would sign it in my mom's signature and I would take it back. I did that several times and then we had a parent teacher meeting and they would bring all this stuff, not only grades but issues that we had in class; they brought up so my mom was like, 'I never got those.' I'm like, 'Oh, my God, I'm going to get in trouble.' But my mom never, she understood. She knew I was different, she knew that I wasn't going to, I think she knew that I was eventually, I was more feminine than I was masculine. She knew that more than likely I was going to be gay. I don't think trans was in the question because at that time trans wasn't really out. It was coming, like I'm speaking about on the reservation, no one really knew what transgender was or any aspect of it. I think then in the 80s it was more about gay and AIDS. That was what was in the media, nothing really about trans. So, I think she knew that there was no way I was going to get married and have kids and be with a woman. I think that was clearest in her mind at a very, very early age for me. The teachers did address, you know, that this happened, but my mom really didn't say anything until we got home and she was like, 'who was signing those papers for me and what are you not bringing back to me?' And I'm like, 'Oh my God, my Aunty Lizzie did.' (Sullivan, 2009, p. 124)

She didn't have a problem with it; she thought it was a little ridiculous. It's ChapStick and it's flavored, what's the big deal? Mom seriously did not have a problem with it whatsoever. If it would have been something like my sister's shirt or something, maybe then she would have had an issue with it, but even then I don't think it would have been. Nothing was ever a big deal to my mom. I think in her mind, as a single parent working two jobs, she kind of was like, 'if it's not a big deal I don't have to worry about it.' Like the ChapStick thing, she's like, 'whatever.' There's a few times that I actually, we would go to Kmart or something and she'd be like, 'what do you want to buy?' And I would want to buy the flavored lipsticks and because we were alone and not with any of my other siblings, she would buy them. And it was like, she never said it, but we can buy it, but don't ever use it around them. And I knew. So I had my own little compartment that I had everything stashed in it that, terrified that I would take to school in my bag and then get confiscated. So she wasn't really surprised that I was wearing lipstick or flavored ChapStick or whatever. It was just funny how the teachers made a big deal about it. I was just like, 'it's for your lips,' you know, 'what's the big deal?' I could understand if it was something attention grabbing like a clothing item. (Sullivan, 2009, p. 124)

As Lluvy Rae grew, she was sent to a private school out of state. There she was placed in the gifted program and she flourished. She was given more freedom to be herself. Lluvy Rae no longer lives on the reservation, though she knows that some of her high school peers are transgender and have also transitioned. Today, she is using her kind and nurturing spirit to help others in the transgender community (Sullivan, 2009, pp. 124–125).

Maria

Life is like a book 'cause every time you don't enjoy life or something occurs respectively, you burn the pages. (Sullivan, 2009, p. 125)

Maria is a 21-year-old woman who identifies herself as both Mexican and Hispanic. She is petite and has olive colored skin. She is skilled at make-up application, appears quite feminine, and passes extremely well. Maria is a bit tentative at first around new people. She is passionate about her relationship with her grandmother above most other things. She is a deeply thoughtful person, constantly assessing situations that affect her life. 'Philosopher' and 'poet' would be appropriate words to describe this energetic young woman (Sullivan, 2009, p. 125).

During her early years, Maria moved multiple times. However she has always remained in the North American southwest. She was born in Tucson, Arizona and relocated to Nogales, Sonora, Mexico. She left Mexico to attend school in Texas before moving back to Arizona. She lived at times with her mother and stepfather, and at other times resided with her grandparents (Sullivan, 2009, p. 125).

As a child, she was:

Not a fan of toys. I was more a fan of water sports. I loved water. I loved like, water balls and I used to do games that were more creative and like more original, like hide and seek or playing building the castle or treehouse. I remember that was the game that was very popular back then when I was a young. It wasn't like today, you (play) video games and you're always stuck. No, back then it was more creational. I used to enjoy the walkie talkies and pretending I was a detective or a, sometimes a princess and I was in a castle or sometimes cooking those little toys that you use to cook. When was younger I would I always ask my grandma, 'I want the Santa Claus to bring me the Easy Bake Oven.' And every time Santa Claus brought me those presents I was very happy. (Sullivan, 2009, pp. 125–126)

She also loved talking and gossiping with elderly women, a pastime she still enjoys today. Maria was assigned male at birth and she knew from a very young age that she was different from boys her age:

> It's an internal feeling that you have when you're a transgender. It's a natural thing that you are born with. It's like when you feel hungry or when you have to go to the bathroom, it's the same thing…oh I feel different.
>
> Her relationship with her mother was strained and she endured physical abuse from both her mother and stepfather. She did not feel that she could have an open and productive dialogue about her gender identity with her parents: "I couldn't tell my mom 'cause my mom would beat me up really bad." (Sullivan, 2009, p. 126)
>
> My mom knew I was gay but she didn't accept it, but my mom, especially my step-dad. He was the one that used to beat me up 'cause he would tell me, 'Look at the way you act. Look at the way you move. You look like a little sissy, act like a man.' And he would always hit me, slap me, punch me, pinch me, and pull my hairs and throw me against the ground, the dirt, and punch me again to make me a man. You know, there were days that I could not even walk or move 'cause I was so sore, 'cause my neck was so swollen and I was so beaten down. It got reported to the police several times. The problem with my step-dad is that he was very smart. He has never been in trouble with the law and he is very detailed in his speech and he speaks very perfect, very smart, calculated individual. (Sullivan, 2009, pp. 126–127)

Childhood presented other challenges for Maria, she explains, "You know, where I grew up I had to face everything, you know, from getting rocks thrown at…my other transgender friends getting beat up, raped." Although she mentioned that, "most of my problems did not start in my early years." She went on to explain that in first grade:

> The only time I felt safe, uh, it was either when I was next to a person that was my friend or when I was with my grandparents. Those were the only times I ever felt safe. Other than that I never felt safe. (Sullivan, 2009, p. 127)

When asked if there was a place in her classroom where she felt empowered she replied:

> No not really. No I pretty much felt hopeless and I felt impotent. I didn't see any… myself, I didn't see like, end of the tunnel. I was in the middle of the tunnel and the tunnel just kept going and going and never stopped and I was like in the universe and there was no end. (Sullivan, 2009, p. 127)

Maria was unable to socialize much with other children:

> 'Cause number one my mom didn't let me. She never, she was the kind of person that she never, she would never let me go out with anybody. She always instilled in me, I was always instilled in by my parents that you know that people were this or that. You can't go out with them 'cause this might happen to you and you are not capable of taking care of yourself, you know. I had an accident when I was young. I was very young when I had the accident and I hit myself on the forehead. So then my mom always told me, she would always tell me you can't go out with anybody the world is miserable. The world is filled with misery, it's all nothing but crime, blab, blab, blab. I guess now I realize that they were afraid that I would explore myself at an earlier age. They were afraid that…if that if I did socialize that…I would probably get ideas with it. And they were afraid I'd get ideas and then stand up for myself. And that what it is, and that's something they didn't want. Basically like being in Iraq, like being in a foreign country, like communist. You don't want people to see how the outer world is 'cause they are afraid that people are going to stand up for themselves. Keep them ignorant. But if you keep someone ignorant, you can't keep them ignorant forever. (Sullivan, 2009, pp. 127–128)

In contrast, her relationship with her maternal grandmother is extremely strong:

> My grandmother is more supportive; more open-minded to all of this then my mom. See I tell my grandma, what do you think of this project we are doing? And she says, 'I support you 100%. So as a matter of fact, I want you to teach me what it is.' And I taught her the transgender, transsexual, all that it means and she learned. Even when the guys picked on me and when one of the females spit on me, I told my grandmother about it and went and put them in their place. Trust me, she went there and yelled at them and she put them in their place. And she is very supportive and she always sticks up for me. She always defends me. And my grandmother, I can say she is my mother. She is my personal counselor, she's my teacher, she is my…grandmother. And she…she…how can I put it? She is everything, she is my medicine. She's everything. (Sullivan, 2009, pp. 128–129)

When reflecting on her early childhood experiences, Maria explained:

> If I could rewind life backwards again and be four or five, 'cause I consider myself, I always consider myself another girl, and be back four or five years old, oh little girls you know, waking up with gifts and with my grandparents and in bed with them, I would do it in a flash back. I would do it in a beat. But at the same time I won't. 'Cause all the negativity that I had to encounter in the past it has made me the person that I am now, more appreciative and more…and it has made me a better person. (Sullivan, 2009, p. 129)

Margo

> I just thought I was the only person in the world like me. (Sullivan, 2009, p. 129)

Margo is a 49-year-old Caucasian female who was assigned male at birth. She spent her early years in the southeastern United States. Margo was born in Pensacola, Florida and grew up in Jacksonville, Florida and Atlanta, Georgia. She received a public early childhood education. As an adult, Margo is full of life, energetic, and quite talkative. She works extremely hard to coordinate local transgender community events. She is very smart and amazingly artistic. Her artwork adorns most of the walls of her home. The majority of her art displays geometric shapes in a spectrum of color. This motif spills out from the bedrooms into the entire living space. Margo works as a graphic designer and she and Beth are roommates and good friends. They share their lives with a very friendly striped cat (Sullivan, 2009, p. 129).

Margo has an acute memory, and can recall many incidents from her infancy and toddlerhood, including, according to her, the ride home from the hospital when she was first born. Her earliest recollections revolve around attempts to decode complex social interactions:

> My mother was a paranoid schizophrenic and she had a number of breakdowns in various stages in my life and it took me a long time to put this together and realize that I was living with my grandparents, my mother's parents, for some time. I was being passed between my grandparents, and my mother was being hospitalized for shock therapy and stuff and I was being buffered from all that. And so I had these vague memories of these things and I think back about, on what my interpretation was at the time

versus what it really was now, that I really know now. And so that was a big period of my life because I was having to put things together and no one bothered to put it together for me to get it right. Like my mother never explained money to me, but she would ritually always buy me a Nestle Crunch Bar every time she would take me to Montgomery Ward. And that was in the impulse area, you know, at the checkout line. And then one day she didn't get me one and I just reached over and grabbed one and started to unwrap that thing in the parking lot and my mom knocked the crap out of me and made me go back into the store and return that candy bar. And it was the most humiliating experience that I had ever gone through. And it was that the idea that my mother did not explain this to me until after the fact. (Sullivan, 2009, p. 130)

Margo explained her early peer interactions:

First you play with yourself and then you play with others, you know. And it's not until you pass being a toddler that you start having social interaction with other kids. And a lot of it was predicated by where we lived. And so, and since I was born on a Naval Base, my first memory was pretty much: we're living on a base and there weren't that many other kids there. And so I lived in my head and I did a lot of make believe, you know. I would play in the dirt and play in the plants and just do a lot of things that didn't involve other kids. I was a bit of a loner until we started having neighbors. And then when I had these neighbors, that's when I started realizing there was something different about me because they weren't letting me play with the girls anymore. And they let me play with the girls in the beginning, and they stopped letting me play with the girls. After I was playing with the boys, the boys were not treating me right and so at that point I started to realize, you know, girls get treated this way and boys get treated this way. (Sullivan, 2009, pp. 130–132)

The dichotomous nature of these divisions was befuddling to Margo:

I was confused because my parents would get baby shower gifts, and so they would have some blue blankets and some pink blankets. Sometimes you feel like a nut, sometimes you don't, you know. My mother was just using whatever blanket was clean. So all this social imprinting that most kids were getting that had some consistencies, in my case, were very fragmentary, and very complicated, you know. So it wasn't until I started meeting other children that I started putting things together. So this was a very profound period for me because I got to play doctor and I realize

I am not like everyone else, I am not like the other girls, you know? And when you get told you are a boy then they make you cut your hair like a boy and they make you dress like a boy, and then they get on you about, 'Don't put your hands on your hips,' and, 'Stop dressing like a girl and stop acting like a girl.' I was under fire. I was in the dog house all the time because my mannerisms were considered feminine and so it was a very rude awakening for me, finding out that I was not a girl. Finding out that they were going to make me do what I don't want to do. And so it was very depressing, you know, to not tell anyone 'cause I just knew what would happen if I did. (Sullivan, 2009, p. 132–133)

I knew, I knew, and I knew from a very early age, I would say for sure by age four I knew (I was a girl) because my family was concerned about my development. So much so that when it was discovered that I wasn't standing up to urinate, my mother hauled me into the psychiatrist. So that was my first recollection of not fitting in, that I wasn't fitting, that I wasn't normal, that they were taking me to a psychiatrist. They would sit me on the floor and there was a bunch of toys on the floor and it was as if the psychiatrist didn't really have an agenda, you know. I was just there to see this doctor and they didn't tell me what kind of doctor. They just said he's not going to give you any shots and so I was pretty cooperative. 'Cause up to that point, every time they would take me to the doctor they were sticking needles in me. So, you know, I got to see this doctor and I don't know why I am there for but the first half of the session I am fixing all the toys that the other kids broke. And then I am just playing with stuff and I think I am grabbing the wrong toys, 'cause he would say, 'Well why don't you play with this instead.' And that was my first recollection that somebody thought something was wrong with me, and I wasn't right the way I was. I was being told, 'Don't behave this way, don't behave this way,' you know. (Sullivan, 2009, p. 133)

Because it was really weird because when I went home my parents looked like they were mad at me, and then I was told the first time I went to potty that, if I need to go potty I had to go and get a grown up. And when I went to get a grown up, usually they make me get a man and so my granddad would usually stand up and pee with me, my dad would stand up and pee with me. And if I ever got caught sitting to pee there was hell to pay. I would still do it but, it would kind of behoove me to play along 'cause they did that for at least a good year or so. They did that I would say, all the way up until I went to school pretty much.

Reflecting on her family life from her early childhood years, Margo explained:

Knowing what I know now, my mother was mentally ill. I mean she loved me, but she was mentally ill. And my father was kind of an absentee father, he re-entered the Navy after having been out. I still don't know what was involved there. I think my parents were having marital problems, you know, my grandparents were raising me. They'd practice corporal punishment, my mother didn't. I remember if I did anything bad, my grandparents forced me to go outside and pick a switch. And if I came back with one that was too scrawny, oh I would just start crying 'cause then I knew they would go out and get a bad one. Yeah that was normal shit back then. (Sullivan, 2009, p. 133)

Margo also remembers:

Forced haircuts. My grandparents made me get a haircut. So if everybody would say, 'You have such beautiful daughter, she is so cute,' they would call me over and buzz all my hair off. And it was very, very…I was acutely aware that I am on the wrong side of the tracks 'cause I couldn't do nothing right. You know, 'cause my mannerisms were wrong, my ideas were wrong, everything was wrong. So it was a pretty crappy time period. (Sullivan, 2009, pp. 133–134)

In high school, unbeknownst to her parents, Margo participated in a research study that offered her reparative therapy. This failed, of course. She began taking hormones at 18 and was "excommunicated" by much of her family because of her transition. She graduated from art school and traveled to Brussels, Belgium for Gender Confirmation Surgery. Margo is now assessing what it means to have reached middle age, while she creates her artwork and works tirelessly for the transgender community (Sullivan, 2009, p. 134).

MARY

Reach out and help and plant your seeds. Don't hide them because if you want to have a good harvest, you have to build a strong foundation. (Sullivan, 2009, p. 134)

Mary is a 56-year-old African American male-to-female trans person. She grew up in Detroit, Michigan and Chicago, Illinois. During her early childhood years, she attended a public school that primarily served African American students. Ashley greatly enjoyed her conversations with Mary. Mary is extraordinarily inspirational. Her appearance and her speech patterns are reminiscent of Maya Angelou. When she talks, she always ties the present in with historical past. Very often, she brings up the civil rights era and her experiences during that time period. She is impassioned and has recently written a book about her life and her teaching career. Mary was a special education teacher in a southwestern public school district where she was out as a trans woman. She often speaks of the "babies" (children) she has worked with throughout the years. She clearly has a deep affection for youth and acts as everyone's mother (Sullivan, 2009, pp. 134–135).

During her early years, her family lived in a predominantly white community where they were the:

> First African Americans to move into the neighborhood. There were synagogues and Jewish bakeries and liberal women with babushkas, and it was safe and we were not a threat. We were a part of the community. I guess, the token if you will. That's what we were called, and I accepted that label because it opened doors for me to be the token. It gave me parties that the other African American children did not go to. Of course, it came with, 'Oh, you want to be white. Oh, you want to be this.' I thought, 'No, it's not that at all.' There were parties and bar mitzvahs and bat mitzvahs and camping trips. Just a number of things that I had that my peers did not have, and I was blessed to have that and to be a part of that. And I shared that. And not that it made me any better. It helped me. It polished my edges. There were many times that I was the raisin in a pot of rice that sat at the table, and there were no racist jokes. I was just a part of the whole ball of wax that was there. And yet, I looked around and I thought, 'I'm the only black face in the room.' You know? (Sullivan, 2009, p. 135)

She noticed that there was something different about her when she was roughly five years old:

> I leaned toward drama of the movie stars that I saw in the movies, the dance. I also leaned toward the prostitutes that danced in the clubs, and their pretty dresses, the costumes that they wore. I leaned toward the mothers that lived under a pretense of having a home and having a family and knowing that they were not really happy with their husbands. So I guess I pulled a lot of those characters and adapted my own persona and pulled from all of those women in order to be me. (Sullivan, 2009, pp. 135–136)

At the age of seven, Mary attended a Halloween party in a wedding dress:

I coordinated the whole thing and designed the whole thing, and put it together, and stole my sister's doll's wig. I even won a prize. I don't remember, second or third. But I was criticized the next day by one or two of the girls at school. And yet, there were teachers who thought it was a creative idea, and there were students who thought it was creative. A number of people said I made a gorgeous bride. And that's all I wanted. I wanted to be a bride. And I lived my life that way, always wanted to be a bride, and never a bridesmaid. So I guess I wanted a husband and a home, and I sought that and I looked for that. I had experiences where I crossdressed and never realized that it was crossdressing. I'd take curtains and beautiful material off the clothesline of the neighbors and dance. It was a form of escape. It was also a way of expressing who I was. I felt happy when I was that girl that, the impossible girl, but I could be her for a couple of hours. Because that boy, I didn't understand. I didn't want to be him. Yet I played baseball, and I was good at all the sports, and rode bikes and did boy things. But that girl in me had a personality and it made me come alive and I couldn't hide her. She wanted to be heard, and she wanted to be recognized, and she wanted to be a part of me. And, I allowed her to be a part of me, and as I grew, I embraced her. (Sullivan, 2009, pp. 136–137)

In addition to the repercussions of being a transgender child, life in a time period marked with racial tensions presented other challenges as well:

Being African American and growing up in a Jim Crow society where you're told you're not good enough as a child, and words hurt, you start believing those things: 'You're not good enough, you'll never make things, you're Black, you can't do this, you can't do that.' That kind of pain eats at you, and I knew in my heart of hearts that I was a good person. And I knew that I prayed every night and every morning, and I asked God, 'Why? Help me.' But we don't all learn the lesson at the same time, and it was something that I had to go through. I did not ask to be born trans. I did not ask to be born African American and have the difference. I just knew that that was very painful in my youth, because people would tell me 'You're not good enough.' And I sort of believed that. I knew in my heart that it wasn't true. (Sullivan, 2009, p. 137)

As an adult, Mary has utilized her childhood challenges to create a productive life for herself while working to improve the lives of local children with special needs:

I built a strong foundation, even though its dysfunction, but I did that. And out of that, I'm very proud that I have lived it, shared it, and helped others. That's what I do. That's who I am. I know who I am now. No one can hurt me anymore by telling me who I am and what I am not. That does not belong to me. (Sullivan, 2009, p. 137)

Reference

Sullivan, A. L. (2009). *Hiding in the open: Navigating education at the gender poles: A study of transgender children in early childhood* (Order No. 3361853). Available from ProQuest Dissertations and Theses A&I (304843384). Retrieved from http://ezaccess.libraries.psu.edu/login?url=https://search-proquest-com.ezaccess.libraries.psu.edu/docview/304843384?accountid=13158.

CHAPTER 5

Spaces, Places, Faces- Erases and Embraces: Actions and Experiences of the Trans Child Within Normative Frameworks

NAVIGATING THE SOCIAL CIRCLE: TRANS CHILDREN AND THEIR RELATIONSHIPS WITH OTHERS

Gender theorist Diana Fuss problematizes the rigid dichotomization that frequently occurs not only with regard to lesbian and gay identities, but that also may be extrapolated to include all LGBTQ ontologies as well. Fuss describes the bifurcation of socially acceptable modalities of gender in terms of 'inside' and 'outside,' claiming that "inside/outside functions as the very figure for signification and the mechanisms of meaning production" (1991, p. 1). Such a dichotomization consequently involves alienation for whatever is relegated to the 'outside' of what is socially acceptable. For the individuals whose stories are expressed in this chapter, far too often it is made apparent that they are, in fact, only able to exist on that 'outside.'

The early childhood years are an important social time for all young children. Interactions with peers and adults can have lifelong implications, positively or otherwise. This chapter explores some social experiences of the transgender partners in this study. Many of the narratives are quite raw and bravely offer a glimpse into painful experiences. Others are comical. It is also quite apparent why some memories have stood fast in such striking detail, all these years later (Sullivan, 2009, p. 144).

It is also important here to explain terminology that will be utilized throughout. If a child was labeled female at birth but is transgender, that child will respectfully be described as male, their gender identity. This is not meant to confuse the reader but rather validate the authentic gender of these special children. Thus, a child referred to in this study as "she," is known to peers and adults as "a boy" and almost always treated as such. It is helpful to be cognizant of this in exploring the narratives. In addition, the words "gay" and "transgender" are occasionally used interchangeably by the partners. This is frequently because the child or someone in the child's life *assumed* that individual was gay due to gender "nonconforming" behavior, not because they are in fact gay (Sullivan, 2009, p. 144).

Friendships

Same-Gender Friendships

Interestingly, several of the partners explained that the majority of their friends were of the same gender identity and not biological sex. Most of the MTF (male to female) interviewees formed friendships with girls while the FTM (female to male) interviewees preferred spending time with other little boys. It does make sense that the children who identified with feminine toys, clothes and behavior, would feel drawn to like-minded children. When a transgender girl forms a friendship with another child with similar interests (playing dress-up, entertaining a Barbie dinner party, or cooking with Easy Bake Ovens), they are given more freedom and flexibility to act as they wish and imitate adult feminine societal roles than if they befriended a boy who enjoyed different activities (Sullivan, 2009, p. 144).

The research partners' reflections on their early childhood experiences often instantiate what theorist Lynda Hart refers to as 'acting out,' "transgressing the boundary between the imaginary and the real" (1993, p. 1), that is to say, stepping out from one's predetermined 'role' in society to gravitate toward another. As discussed by the following partners, they expressed a desire as children to engage in play with those who possess the same gender identity. Lluvy Rae felt much more comfortable around other little girls:

> I mean, girls in grade school were really super nice. They were my best friends; they wanted to hang out with me, like cool whatever. But the guys always just were upset that I was always with the girls and never wanted to

be any part of their games, like at recess time. They would have kickball and they would want me to play and I would rather go on the swings to be with the girls just because I knew they would be more friendly. The guys seemed to have a dominance, they seemed to have a mind-frame that they were more dominant and I understood that very well. They were always, like, I'm better than you, I can kick harder or I can run faster or blah, blah, blah. I just never tried. I'm like, 'why put so much energy into that when I can just be myself with the girls over here?' You know what I mean? (Sullivan, 2009, pp. 145–146)

Margo stated that:

I had mostly female friends until school. It was kind of like really weird 'cause when you're really young, they are pretty co-ed about things because they don't think you are sexually aware. No one worries about boys and girls playing. But then by the time you get to school age, there seems to be a lot of interest in segregating the sexes and segregating the grades and the ages and all of that. Whereas before school, you're exposed to kids who are younger and older than you, and you are kind of just are playing with whoever your neighbor happens to be. And so a lot of my friendships were kind of catch as catch can. 'Cause I was not in the popular group. (Sullivan, 2009, p. 146)

Chris recalls that the majority of his friendships were with boys:

Pretty much always. I remember, in the group my mom babysat, that she did daycare for, there were some older boys. They were really fun to hang out with because they were older and just awesome and I thought they were just the coolest things ever. They taught me how to climb a fence, and all sorts of things like that - boy things. (Sullivan, 2009, p. 146)

Lady Gazelle, Lana and Maria also spoke of having friendships with children of the same gender identity (Sullivan, 2009, p. 147).

As evidenced in the above narratives, in order to feel a sense of belonging and comfort, the partners purposefully associated with those individuals who shared their same gender identity. In some cases, as with Chris, the friendships yielded positive results, such as how to be more like a boy; in others, as with Lluvy Rae, associating with those of the same gender identity came at a cost–that of feeling judged by others.

Friends with the "Outcasts"

Several of the people who participated in the study explained that it was easier to befriend other children who were considered socially awkward, although frequently in different ways. They found refuge in relationships with peers who had glasses, were overweight, or suffered from medical ailments. Firstly, the ones who also did not conform to societal norms were more accepting of the transgender children behaving in ways that felt most comfortable. In some ways, they were similarly ostracized and teased by those who were more able to conform. Also, it occasionally appeared that if these children did not bond to one another, they would be entirely without school-time friends during their early childhood years (Sullivan, 2009, p. 147).

For years, Erin held a friendship with a child who suffered from severe asthma. When they entered high school and the child obtained medication that stabilized his ailment, he discontinued their relationship. Similarly, Beth explained that:

> Popularity was not something that happened very easily. I was pretty well ignored by a lot of the kids. The children with whom I did spend time were sort of the other social outcasts. There were boys who were overweight for example, or the Jewish kids because we had a nice size Jewish community. Kids can be real cruel even at a young age. And so some of the Jewish kids felt like they didn't have a lot of friends and I spent some time with them. (Sullivan, 2009, p. 147)

Beth also played with much younger children. Of the peers that were her own age, she had "a lot of casual friends. I would walk home from school and they were nice to me, but never included me in their weekend trips" (Sullivan, 2009, p. 148).

Margo had similar experiences:

> I would say I started finding that I either got along better with younger kids than me, or older kids than me. Like there was this kid, this one boy I would play with and he was a lot older than me and he was real fat and he collected real unusual animals, you know. So I would go down to the creek and catch crayfish with him and stuff, and that was the closest thing I did to boys' stuff. (Sullivan, 2009, p. 148)

Uniquely, in comparison to the other research partners, Lluvy Rae was friends with other transgender children. She had several friends her age who were also aware that their gender assignment and gender identity were in incongruence.

> There was like a group of us that were real effeminate. We would run around with the girls and stuff. And we were in all different classes. I think if we were all in one class, it would have been a big mess. We always looked forward to recess and lunch and also after school. We lived in different communities but still we hung out at school. I ended up going to a Catholic school. Some of the others dropped out because it became too much for them. And that's the funny thing. A lot of them, everyone knew since we were kids, but they still gave us a hard time. They just never gave us a break. It's not like we're going to change or even if we change, it's not being yourself. Because I did run into a few of them and they would try to act butch or try to act masculine or something. It did not sit well. It was like selling out. I don't know what their circumstances are or why they're doing it. It was probably because they wanted acceptance back from their family. I know that people in my family, especially the men, would say, 'Why don't you do that.' They just thought that what I was doing was an act in order to get attention. It really wasn't. It was just me being me. And people wouldn't accept it, which made it harder for them. There were some who would grasp it and would understand it. It was so funny, a lot of people say oh it's just a phase. There is a phase where you go away and you come back and they're like 'Wow! Oh my gosh!' (Sullivan, 2009, pp. 148–149)

For so many of the research partners, friendship was almost always a means of settling. Instead of being accepted by the 'in' crowd, the trans partners were only able to choose other 'outcasts' to befriend. Other than Lluvy Rae, who interestingly found a like-minded group of friends with regard to gender, many others were ignored or excluded by their peers.

Childhood Crushes

For most people, one of the most memorable experiences is the first individual for whom romantic feelings were experienced. This often happens during the early childhood years, as was discussed by several of the research partners. This experience is so consistent and pervasive, that many websites now use the answer to the questions, "Who was your first childhood crush?" or "Who was your first love?" to reset forgotten passwords. This momentous event however, is often experienced and/or responded to differently for LGBTQ children than for their straight peers. It is common in the United States for an adult to ask a five-year-old child assigned female at birth if she has a boyfriend, simply for the amusement that arises from the response. There is nearly always the assumption of heteronormativity and heterosexuality, even from a very young age and even from LGBTQ adults, instantiating what Butler (2006) calls the 'heterosexual matrix' and what Wittig calls the 'straight mind' (1992), explained earlier. Here, some of the partners shared these early experiences (Sullivan, 2009, p. 149).

Lana explained that:

> When I was in school I never really had problems with the girls. I had problems with the boys. Only problems I had with the girls were when they tried to date me. That just wasn't right. It wasn't, it wasn't fun at all. I remember Valentine's Day I would sneak my little Valentines to the boys. I would sneak 'em. I would never put my name, but, 'You're cute,' put it in the basket and keep going. (Sullivan, 2009, p. 150)

Lana was especially captivated by one particular child:

> I had a crush on this boy. His name was Mark, he has this little mole. It was to die for, it was so cute. I remember he was my best friend and we used to go to (small group instruction), like for some odd reason they used to take just us two. And we would go one-on-one to our lunches and our art classes together. They had one-on-one training together and that was cool. But I dare to say he was gay too. And now that I think about it, he was very feminine and the way we liked each other wasn't the way most little boys at that age liked each other. And so I think they knew that he was probably gay and I was gay. And they put us together for a reason. I know that sounds insane for me to say that, but I am dead serious. I don't know why, but I guess they thought it would be more comfortable, or I don't know what they thought they would get out of it. I remember, 'cause the first time when they did it, I thought, 'Wow he's cute but there is only us two.' And you know the class was about thirty-six students. They would just come and get Mark and me and we would just go and it was always one-on-one. Though every day I thought, 'this is odd.' I used to ask, 'Is he gay?' I used to ask my parents, 'Is he gay?' I wouldn't confess

to myself, but they knew, okay. You walk around playing with Rambo and Barbie all the time. But it is just interesting. He and I were actually really close, but I don't know what happened to him or where he went or whatever. But after that, I was always real secluded kind of, 'cause I don't think I wanted anyone to really know. (Sullivan, 2009, pp. 150–151)

Lluvy Rae was able to discuss her crushes on boys with other peers who possessed a feminine gender expression:

> So being in school with predominantly Native American kids and then knowing, like I had other friends that were just as feminine as I was. We would call each other girls. Yeah, when we were little we would like, it was the cutest little thing we would say to each other. And we would tell each other about each other's crushes on boys. I had my first crush when I was in preschool. Oh, my gosh it was intense. Oh, my gosh. It was just crazy. It's crazy for me to even know I had those feelings, to have a crush, to think you like someone that early, that's crazy, but I knew. (Sullivan, 2009, p. 151)

Lady Gazelle also recalled a childhood crush:

> I had one friend, this biracial kid. And he could fight really good. He was really cute too. And he befriended me and he used to protect me and stuff like that. He really taught me how to fight 'cause before him, I didn't know how to fight. But maybe he wanted a gay boy relationship, but he was supposed to be straight, but he didn't like me acting like a girl. As soon as I let my guard down, he put it back up. One time we were playing around and wrestling and crap and it became sexual and touching. And he stopped speaking to me, and his job was done. But he taught me how to protect myself. I hadn't thought of him in a long time. (Sullivan, 2009, p. 152)

Interestingly enough, only MTF research partners related stories about childhood crushes. Surprisingly, with the exception of Lady Gazelle (whose friendship ended abruptly as she describes), the partners reported fairly positive experiences with childhood crushes: Lana was able to (albeit surreptitiously) leave boys love notes, Lluvy Rae was able to openly discuss her crushes on boys with her peer groups, and, up until the relationship took a different turn, Lady Gazelle was protected by her crush.

Age Affecting Peer Relationships

Several of the participants discussed the impact of age on peer relationships. There seemed to be a general consensus that the younger the transgender child, the easier friendships were made. It appeared that in general, prior to attending school, there were fewer problems with peers. This is likely due to the fact that children who are four years old have had less years of exposure to the pressures of gender norms than children who are eight years old. As explained in Chapter 3, Foucault argues that heterosexism is persistently and consistently reinforced and 'institutionalized' in school-age children (1990 [1978]). This is evidenced time after time with the research partners' recollections. For most of them, difficulties with friends increased with age (Sullivan, 2009, p. 152).

Chris illuminated this when he said:

> Well, I don't remember having a lot of problems. The older I got, the shyer I got, and felt really uncomfortable. When I was younger and when we were all just kids, gender wasn't obvious, other than through self-elected things. Mostly, I felt really comfortable. I was really happy and I had friends and interacted well with the world. (Sullivan, 2009, p. 152)

Barriers to Friendship

It is well known that peer relationships greatly impact the educational experiences of young children (Mikami, 2010). Transgender children, however, have a variety of barriers to building and maintaining friendships. Their mannerisms often make them a target of ridicule, they are unhappy and frustrated with their bodies and their clothes (if not allowed to dress in the clothing they choose), they frequently feel unsafe and unable to express themselves in a way that feels comfortable, and they identify with interests and peers that do not adhere to societal norms (Mikami, 2010). As a result, they may be left with a variety of questions about the world that are painstaking to attempt to answer (Sullivan, 2009, pp. 152–153).

This phenomenon was exquisitely described by Lady Gazelle:

> The kids, they would not bother me 'cause I was new. They would not bother me right off the bat. I'd be good for a couple of months. And then once they all realized that I was different, they wanted to test me. And by then, I didn't want to be in the school anymore. You know, gays and lesbians experience this, 'do they know?' thing. But I don't think it is near as

intense as ours, you know what I mean? Do they know that I am gay? Do they know that I am a lesbian? That's one thing. You can still be a chick, you can still be a guy. But do they know that I am trans and I really want to be a girl? Do they know that I am not a boy like them? What are they going to do? How are they going to treat me? What are they going to say? Whatever they do, this is the biggest fear that they are going to put us in a box as a gay man. That's a trans' biggest fear. Because once they put you in that box, their expectations of you will be different than what you can give them. (Sullivan, 2009, p. 153)

Isolation

Occasionally these barriers to friendship lead transgender children to retreat from the building of relationships. The consequence is often loneliness and isolation. On more than one occasion, interviewees have reported that they felt as if they were the only person in the world like themselves. Thus, they believed that no one understood them, supported them, or respected them. Aidan in particular spent most of his free time in the classroom playing in the absence of his peers: "Yeah, I would just go sit in the corner somewhere, play alone." Lady Gazelle's mother once asked her, "Why you would choose the loneliest lifestyle on earth?' And I believe I chose the loneliest lifestyle on earth. So no matter how lonely I was, if I wasn't lonely, I would make myself lonely because I felt that I deserved it." Maria's experience was a bit different. She was forced into isolation: "I didn't socialize as much 'cause my Mom didn't let me" (Sullivan, 2009, pp. 153–154).

As Lluvy Rae was often scolded at school for acting in a feminine manner, she self-isolated in some cases so that she could have increased freedom of gender expression:

> It's like you can't really be yourself unless you're alone in your own space. Like your room, or you're home alone, or you're at your grandma's house playing in the backyard or something. So it's sort of like suffering just being alone, feeling like you're the only one in the world that has these problems, being called names because they don't understand. (Sullivan, 2009, p. 154)

In general, feelings of isolation and solitude were universally expressed by all of the research partners.

Economic Disparities

Margo spoke of the struggle to understand and accept the differences between herself and her peers. In recollecting her memories, Margo is unique in that she is the only partner who described in detail the economic disparities between herself and her peers. However, these financial disparities do speak to greater socioeconomic and sociocultural inequities that clearly affect the transgender community. Transgender children are cut from the diverse rainbow cloth of life, and they can fall into any variety of race, culture, religion, or economic status. Those students whose income is lower than the median income face additional challenges as they are "othered" for both economic status and gender identity. Margo recalls:

> There was another incidence where I got put into a nursery. And I accidently was wandering around the nursery and I walked into the kitchen, and they were making peanut butter sandwiches and Kool Aid. And then I walked out 'cause they ran me out of the kitchen. And then I ran into the upper crust group. They were having sodas, and they were having fast food. And then I got yelled at to go to the picnic area and they start giving us the peanut butter sandwiches and this really bad Kool Aid that was not sweetened enough. And so I put together that there is something going on here, we're not all the same. Some people get some things, some people don't, regardless. And it seems like Santa favors the people who have money. That was a big discovery for me 'cause I was like, 'If he's making a list and checking it twice, then why did the kid that is throwing dirt clogs at me get nicer stuff for Christmas than I did?' So I started putting all these things together, you know- like the Tooth Fairy, Easter Bunny, Santa Claus. And you know, all this self-awareness was me figuring out my world on my own 'cause nobody was explaining it me. Nobody ever explains anything to kids. You know, they reprimand them when they do something wrong, but no one ever explains to them why you do things.
>
> But the disparities between my home life and the other kids' home life were rudely apparent. 'Cause other kids would talk about their Thanksgiving or talk about their Christmas, or they would say, 'my step-father this or my step-father that.' 'My step-mother is,' or 'I went to my Mom's house and then went to my Dad's house.' So I was becoming very more sophisticated 'cause I realized not everyone's parents stayed together. And so school was a big rude awakening. I was finding out that there are kids whose parents are divorced; and finding out they have more money than us. Then there are people who have less money than us. And so it was a real rude awakening

'cause you had to assimilate their things in no time and just realize they have no schools for parents. And some kids get a better deal than others. And I was one of those kids that it was very clear that their parents weren't teaching them things before they came to school. And they were able to just do their academics; whereas with me, I struggle though stuff 'cause my parents weren't helping me in those areas. So school was just really about disparities and inequity. But then it was also a place of growth and a place to meet other kids 'cause we didn't always have a lot of people I could play with or entertain me. (Sullivan, 2009, pp. 154–156)

Margo's reflections on her perception of difference between her and other students provide valuable insight as to the internal strife she experienced during her childhood.

Bullying and Violence

The treatment of the trans partners as objects of ridicule, bullying, and violence can best be elucidated by Miller's theory on disgust with regard to the bullies viewing trans individuals as 'outsiders': "Disgust helps define boundaries between us and them and me and you. It helps to prevent 'our' way from being subsumed into 'their' way. Disgust… locates the bounds of the other… as something to be avoided, repelled, or attacked" (1998 [1997], p. 50). As feelings of disgust originate with the body, it is not surprising that the partners' trans bodies were targeted and ridiculed.

It is well understood that bullying can have an effect on academic performance as well as feelings of safety in school (Diaz, Kosciw, & Greytak, 2010). Every person who participated in the study spoke of being bullied as well as being physically assaulted by other children. The surprising nature of the violence is that it took place among early childhood aged students. It was often brutal and unrelenting. Several of the partners had to switch schools on multiple occasions due to extreme torment. These narratives are of particular relevance for early childhood teachers, who are the arbiters of classroom culture (Sullivan, 2009, p. 157).

Name Calling

One common experience shared by the partners was teasing. Name calling was often utilized as a means to identify these children as "different" and punish them for their non-conformity. Interestingly, although the interviewees grew up in different decades, in different parts of the country, attending varying types of educational settings, the hurtful names used to bully them were consistently the same. Although the partners are now adults, and the last person interviewed experienced early childhood in the 1980s, the cruel names still occupy a central status in the U.S. linguistic vernacular. They can still be heard echoing from playgrounds throughout the United States (Sullivan, 2009, p. 157).

Lady Gazelle recalls that she was teased:

> From kindergarten on up. Every time I even think about school, I think about the abuse I received as a child during school. School was not a good place for me to be or to go. I hated school with a passion and from my earliest to my latest memories, I could never concentrate in class for fear of what somebody was going to do me next. (Sullivan, 2009, pp. 157–158)

She explained that the bullying occurred during class time. Her peers would, "imitate my voice, make comments under their breath, laugh at me at every convenient chance. They would antagonize me." They called her a variety of names including, "'fag, punk, sissy, girl.' Those were the names that I was called on a daily basis" (Sullivan, 2009, p. 158).

When Beth first entered school:

> I was in 1st grade for two weeks and then went right into 2nd grade. I knew a few of those kids but I didn't know as many as I did in the 1st grade 'cause we were peers. I was seven when I started school. I was not athletic so when they would throw a football at me it would hit me in the face and I cried. I cried a lot. 'Cry baby cry; stick a finger in your eye'. (Sullivan, 2009, p. 158)

The children often teased her about her feminine mannerisms:

> 'Sissy' is what they would say. Again this was at the years before sexuality, so that wasn't the time they would use the word queer. These were second through fourth graders, and would say, 'little sissy.' You don't know what to do for that. You're smaller than they are. You know if you go and say you 'am not,' they're going to push you down and start the fight that you're going to lose. So just tried to ignore them and hoped recess would be over soon. (Sullivan, 2009, p. 158)

Occasionally, some children would defend her: "There were a few of the boys and they did the right thing. There are some good guys out there in elementary school. You could tell some kids didn't like to see other kids get picked on." Some of the other names that the children called each other included, "four eyes" and "lard butt" (Sullivan, 2009, pp. 158–159).

Margo discussed being bullied: "I had eczema. And I had a bad reaction to a vaccination and got bad eczema. And so that added to everything, and the kids would call me 'fungus foot' and it was no fun." There were a variety of reasons Margo believes that she was targeted: "Being skinny was the number one thing. Another one was having blonde hair. I had white blonde hair. And thinking I was a girl, 'cause I had some female mannerisms. I was getting teased and getting picked on by other kids." Maria was also teased for her feminine behavior. She was primarily bullied by boys. They called her a "fag" and a "sissy" (Sullivan, 2009, p. 159).

Lluvy Rae was called:

> Names like, 'girly boy, faggot, queer; you'll never be a girl.' You know, like, 'Why don't you be a boy, why don't you act like a boy, why don't you man up,' or whatever the term is now? Sometimes it can really affect you, your confidence level. That's what really drove me to be shy and not participate when I really, really wanted to. There was always some element when I wanted to participate, some element of dividence mode like the guys needed to do this, like the roles were broken down. The guys need to do this and the girls need to do this. So that was frustrating and it made me be this shy in the corner kind of person. Not really interacting with kids. (Sullivan, 2009, p. 159)

With the exception of a few of Beth's classmates standing up for her, the majority of the other research partners all described being bullied and harassed by their classmates.

Violence

Bullying can take on a variety of forms, from exclusion to name calling to violence. These actions are of particular concern when children are being physically assaulted, sometimes to the extent that bones are broken. Students aged three to eight are capable of inflicting pain that can cause lifelong physical and emotional scars. Unfortunately, it appears that early childhood aged trans individuals may be disproportionately targeted due to lack of understanding, education, and support (Diaz et al., 2010; Sullivan, 2009, p. 160).

Aidan remembers:

> Getting kicked in the head with balls on the playground. 'Knock it off!' So, like they're like playing dodge ball or something, and I go, 'Can I play?' And like everyone would turn and throw every single dodgeball right at me and be like, 'You're out; have a good one.' And I'd be like, 'Oh.' I was picked on. That's all. So, I would sit in the corner with my bag, and play with myself. (Sullivan, 2009, p. 160)

One of the reasons that Aidan was bullied was because of his red hair. He explained that his experience was reminiscent of the "Ginger Kids" episode from the television show "South Park." During this episode, red-haired children are considered to be subhuman and are discriminated against at school (Parker & Stone, 2005; Sullivan, 2009, p. 160).

Aidan continued to explain that in the first grade:

> I would get the shit beat out of me. Kids would like gang up and beat me. It was bad. Like, what happened with the first grade and I got sent back to kindergarten, they took me out of that school...and sent me to Oakland. And that teacher was just mean, but then Mrs. [last name] was really cool. Then we actually ended up physically moving, so I went to another third grade. And they took me out of there 'cause all the kids were ruthlessly mean to me again. That was like, they were playing basketball, and I wanted to play, and like everyone turned around and threw the basketballs at me and hit me in the head. Well, I laugh now, 'cause I'm picturing being on the street, and just watching the scene happen. And then I went to [name of school] Academy, and I was treated pretty badly. But [name of school], I made it back to a neutral ground. That was a struggle. But they also figured out I had ADHD in fifth grade, so I started medicating and ostracized myself quite readily, you know, after that. (Sullivan, 2009, pp. 160–161)

Lluvy Rae was often lived in fear of physical assault:

> I guess it's another good thing I learned to be always attentive to things because I always had to watch my back. I always had to run if mean

people would chase me like throwing rocks. I could never really enjoy my recess time because people always wanted to be jerks that day and just chase me around. They thought it would be funny to push me or something. If it resulted in me getting injured like a scraped knee or elbow or something, it was always that it was my fault that I started the situation. (Sullivan, 2009, p. 161)

That's another thing with grade school, anytime I was in trouble it was always my fault. Others' actions weren't taken into consideration. It was always me. I didn't like that. I didn't like being blamed for stuff that I really didn't do. I was picked on, I never picked. They'd say I called them this name or that name when it really wasn't true. I would say well you called me, 'fag, queer, sissy,' whatever and that was never addressed. It was just, 'Don't say that.' But if it was like, 'Oh, he called me an ass or he called me a bitch,' or something then it would be, 'Oh my God, you're getting a note home today.' And none of those words ever came out of my mouth. It was always their word against mine. That was really frustrating for me in grade school. It was always their word against mine. I never understood why a teacher never saw two sides of a story. They heard two sides of a story, but they always chose one side when it should have been mutual. When the initial thing like sitting us both down and saying, 'well, the two of you shouldn't be calling each other names.' They saw me as a troubled kid, but I never caused any of the problems. I was always the victim. (Sullivan, 2009, pp. 161–162)

Anytime I was in trouble it was because I would come in from recess or from break time with a scraped knee or something, or my pants were torn, or elbow sleeve or something. I never said anything about my injuries because I knew it was going to be my fault, unless it was hurting really bad or I was crying. And they're asking why I am crying and then they would see my elbow. They would say like, 'Well, what did you do?' 'What did I do? I got pushed by a mean kid is what happened.' They would call the kid over and say, 'what happened?' And that kid would say, 'Oh, well, they said this to me,' or, 'they did this to me,' or, 'they were throwing rocks at me,' which isn't even the case. And I had girlfriends even in grade school that would be like, 'No, that's not what happened.' 'Cause kids are honest, kids honestly say, 'that's not what happened, this is what happened.' And then it's like, 'mind your own business, this is what happened between them.' Other people have always seen the situation happening. They always saw the situation happening. They never really listened. They never really took other people's accounts. 'Who saw what was happening?' They never took that seriously either. (Sullivan, 2009, pp. 162–163)

Beth was bullied, but only by the boys. She elaborated on one particular incident:

> When I was in second grade, my nose was broken before school. The boy who was in first grade but should have been in second, he was already being held back. He was a big bully. He called me a 'sissy.' And one of the very few times I defended myself, he came up to push me and I actually hit him and turns out I bloodied his nose. Oh, that was the wrong thing to do. He came after me and got me down on the ground and started pounding me until a couple of people pulled him off. And so I broke my nose. It was actually the last physical threat that I had. (Sullivan, 2009, p. 163)

Both the MTF as well as the FTM research partners reported a history of bullying and violence and, unfortunately, little if anything was done to prevent it.

Causes of Bullying

Interestingly, when discussing bullying, several of the people who participated in the study offered explanations for why the bullies behaved in such an abhorrent manner. They explored the complexities of social relationships and proposed that the bullies were targets themselves. They suggested that they may experience violence at home. For some, offering these explanations may be a way of gaining insight and understanding into what happened to them. This can be a catalyst for healing as they move forward in their adult lives (Sullivan, 2009, pp. 163–164).

Lana recalled:

> I remember in particular there was this one kid, [name of child]. He was horrible, he was just… I went to school with him from, I left the school and I went to [name of city] and when I came back I went to the same school. But he was still there torturing me. And then finally it got to the point to where everyone said, 'You got to stick up for yourself,' you know what I mean? 'You can't just…' So when I (told on) him, he got in trouble with his dad. Then once his dad came out there, he got into trouble with him. That explained why he acted the way he did because his dad's reaction to him. His dad hit him with a stick for crying out loud in front of everybody and then started calling him 'faggot' this, that and the other. And these were all the names that he was calling me. So all the names he

was calling me he was learning from his dad. And that's when that came to me. And I was just like, I saw his dad and I remember even at that age that it was just like... And then it was good 'cause I always had my mother to speak to about all of that. Even though I would never say I was gay, but we would talk about it without putting labels on it. And I think that part of me thought that if I didn't put a label on it, it would be easier for, it would make it easier for me to talk to her. 'Cause I wanted to tell her, 'Well you know, I am gay that's why they call me faggot.' You know, she knew. (Sullivan, 2009, p. 164)

Margo explained that:

> Going to school, you know, some kids get teased and some kids don't. But a lot of times you have kids who, I don't even think know how bad they are even when they are teasing. I think a lot of the kids that tease really do have their own problems. So they deflect it, you know? So it's basically misdirection 'cause a lot of these kids, bullies in particular, are usually just like me or different. In some way they are hiding something to overcome. I got beat up by some girls too. There are a lot of tomboys that don't want to be girls, mom and dad makes them be girls and so they get a big kick out of beating up boys. 'Cause I remember I got teased on by a lot of girls. (Sullivan, 2009, p. 165)

Coping with Bullying

Each of the participants had a unique way of coping with bullying. The coping mechanisms included crying, hiding, isolation, staying close to the teacher, finding protective friends, telling adults, using humor or favors to distract the bully, and fighting back. Halberstam's notion of 'queer space' as a means to reclaim hegemonic spaces that have forced LGBTQ individuals out has been enacted by some of the research partners in the form of mechanisms utilized to survive and self-protect (2005). Some were subtle and passive, while others were active and retaliatory. Retaliation will be discussed later in this chapter. Whatever means they utilized, all seemed to aim at personal protection. Many of the coping strategies, however, distracted the partners from their studies. For some, this had an effect on their academic performance (Sullivan, 2009, p. 165).

Mary was often in self-protection mode while at school:

I thought some people will hurt you, and if you don't hurt them back, they will continue to hurt you. So that gave me the strength not to draw first blood. And I've lived my life that way. But when someone hurt me first, I get them back in double whammies, and justify it in telling myself, 'vengeance is served cold.' I would have never said this to you if you hadn't said that to me first. And I lived my life that way, and that's wrong. Because now I've realized that that's self pity, that that's a form of protection, that's a form of really not dealing with the matter. And yet I felt like if I don't do this, you are going to hurt me for whatever reason. And I don't want to be hurt. I would never hurt you. For instance a girl calls me a 'deviant.' And I didn't know what that meant. (Sullivan, 2009, pp. 165–166)

As a child, Mary was often discouraged from trying new things:

If you didn't laugh or make fun of me, I would give it a try. But if you made fun of me, or made me feel less than, I would dig in and plant. 'You wanna hurt me? How can I hurt you?' And I think I have lived my life that way. Because I look at, even in my job and career, how people would like to make themselves, ego, feel better than. And I go, 'Okay, you wanna play? I'll show you how the game is played.' And I had several teachers, and I thought, 'We're here for the children. This is no match.' And I've had a number of teachers go, 'You really got me. You really got me.' And I said, 'Well, you should've never played with me. I'm an old girl at this. I don't play fair. You drew first blood, and I had to make you bleed even more so.' So people leave me alone once they realize that I'm not going to be pushed over. And that's anger management, you know? And I've had to go to through classes for that. And they would say, 'Why did you?' And then, 'Because she cut me, I had to cut her head off.' And they would go, 'You're so graphic.' And I said, 'Who drew first blood?' 'Don't you think that's a little psychotic?' And I said, 'Don't you think it's a little psychotic for someone to put hands on, when you said no?' And then they back away. And it reminds me of, 'Don't mess with [Birth Name]. [Birth Name]'s crazy.' But I had to play that actress. But I thought, 'That's not who I am.' It's just a form of protection. But, I thought, 'I'm not responsible for what you think of me'. (Sullivan, 2009, pp. 166–167)

Lana sought refuge in friendships with other children:

I had a little group of friends that were all female, but that's the way I kept myself all protected is by hanging around all girls. Girls never really made fun of me for being feminine. But the boys, that's when I would have a problem. 'He runs like a girl, he sits like a girl, he acts like a girl,' and that kind of stuff. You know what I mean? And then they would want to challenge you 'cause they feel you are less than masculine and then want to fight you. (Sullivan, 2009, p. 167)

When asked if the repercussions that the bullies received deterred their teasing, Lana responded, "On some level yes, but for the most part no." When warned by school officials that if Lana was harassed outside of school, there would still be consequences, she:

Still had problems. But after that I had a growth spurt and I was taller than everybody, that's when I was left alone. That's when it was good for me. I had a little bit of peace. I didn't worry, I didn't harass or bother anybody. And that was my mother's real big concern too. She knew that I was not the type of person to bother anybody. I was really to myself, you know. So if I am not bothering you, you shouldn't be bothering me. And if you weren't bothering me then I wouldn't be having problems with you. I probably had more problems fighting in elementary than any other time. That was the first few years of school, probably kindergarten like up to third or fourth grade. But then like I said, in fourth grade, once in fifth grade I had that growth spurt, but I dealt with it. But it wasn't as bad, not nearly as bad. And it was a piece of cake. (Sullivan, 2009, pp. 167–168)

Margo utilized her talents, including art, to deflect the teasing. She was bullied:

A lot, a lot. That's why I didn't like school. It was really safe. The only way I was able to avoid being beaten up was to be a clown, if I made pranks and stuff like that, that seemed to get me a reprieve with the boys.

She also coped with the way she was treating by pretending to be sick so that she could leave school early or not attend at all (Sullivan, 2009, p. 168).

The research partners detailed a variety of coping mechanisms when attempting to deal with bullying. These varied from seeking comfort and solace in relationships with other children (Lana), throwing oneself into one's own interests (Margo), or besting the aggressor before that person could bully the trans partner (Mary).

Results of Bullying

Maria succinctly and beautifully summed the consequences that bullying and violence can have on its victims:

> Hatred is a disease. It's like HIV, and once that person that forms hatred attacks another person, that other person gets infected with that disease. So that hatred just spreads everywhere. And by the time you know it, you have that disease and then you are passing it on to everybody else. And that's why I want justice to be understood. Every time you make fun of a transgender, or every time you let a student make fun of a transgender, or not just make fun, but beat a transgender and don't do anything just think twice. 'Cause you never know, you may one day (hear), 'Mommy, Daddy, guess what? I am this…' What are you going to do then? (Sullivan, 2009, p. 168)

In summation, the recollections expressed by the research partners with regard to the treatment by their peers almost always relate to Fausto-Sterling's theory on the social necessity of establishing divisions in gender: "…to maintain gender divisions, we must control those bodies that are so unruly as to blur the borders" (2000, p. 8). Although they did, in fact, detail some positive interactions and relationships forged with peers, far too often, the research partners were treated with denigration and calumniation.

TEACHER RELATIONSHIPS: POSITIVE

The interactions of the research partners with others around them reinforce the notion theorized by Foucault (1995 [1975]) of docile bodies. Despite the fact that some of the partners did rebel and fight back against bullies by peers, it may be said that their bodies were being manipulated, shaped, trained, and molded to 'act' according to their assigned birth genders. To quote Foucault, "A body is docile that may be subjected, used, transformed and improved" (1995 [1975], p. 136). This is not to say that the research partners did not experience support and love from their teachers; as we shall see, however, this sentiment is in the minority. Constantly acting upon these individuals was "a policy of coercions that act upon the body, a calculated manipulation of its elements, its gestures, its behavior" (Foucault, 1995 [1975], p. 138).

Many of the research partners carry fond memories of their early childhood teachers. They offered safety, initiated a love of learning, and provided a comfortable atmosphere where they enjoyed the classroom activities. Certain memories of tender moments are vivid. As they spoke of their first teachers, the partners' eyes would frequently soften as they shared recollections of this special time (Sullivan, 2009, p. 169).

Preschool and Kindergarten

Beth deeply enjoyed her time in preschool and kindergarten, particularly because this meant that she was able to spend time at home where she felt comfortable and loved:

> Another influence on my life as a preschooler was the fact that my mother stayed home. She was a nurse and she went back to nursing when I entered the first grade. Before that she schooled me and that was before people called it home schooling but that's what she did. Basically she taught me most everything that I would have learned in first grade anyway. (Sullivan, 2009, p. 169)

Like Beth, Aidan felt safe with his kindergarten teacher: "I liked my kindergarten teacher; she was good, you know. If I wasn't in my corner, I was usually pretty close to her." Lana's recollections are not as clear, but still positive:

> I can't remember my kindergarten teacher's name though, but I don't think I was treated differently because they knew I was transgender. I would say when I was (treated differently), it was really noticeable when I went to private school in second grade. (Sullivan, 2009, p. 170)

Chris described his early experiences with educators:

> I remember my kindergarten teacher. She was a rock star; her name was Mrs. C. She was really cool and I liked her a lot. I liked her classroom a lot because she always had a lot of stuff in it. On the holidays, she'd have a Christmas tree and she was extremely fun. She taught us songs in different languages. She was cool.

He describes kindergarten as an important time in his life:

> I remember being around her and feeling independent, first of all because I was a big kid at school, and being really, really proud of that; and, being really excited about going to school every day. I remember meeting all sorts of new kids and being happy about that, instead of just (being) around the same group of kids all the time. (Sullivan, 2009, p. 170)

Lluvy Rae fondly recalls an enjoyable weekly activity that her preschool teacher facilitated.

> On Fridays we had a time where we had different games and stuff. And there was this game we used to play where the teachers had a suitcase full of clothes. And we had relay races and you would have to pick up the suitcase and run it to the other room and put on whatever clothes were in there. Anytime we would do that I always looked for all the feminine clothes, like the women's clothes and run back. I always looked forward to Fridays. I knew it was a game that it was kind of accepted and it was fun. It was kind of like gender neutral. Sometimes we did boys against girls. Sometimes the girls would want me on their teams. (Sullivan, 2009, pp. 170–171)

First–Third Grade

Maria did not feel a strong need to elaborate on positive experiences: "(My) first grade teacher, her name was Mrs. [name]. She was nice. Most of my problems did not start in my early years." Chris also spoke of his first grade teacher:

> Mrs. G. And I remember my Kindergarten teacher, Mrs. C., because they were really good teachers. I remember being afraid of Mrs. G because there were rumors she was a really hard teacher. But she was really awesome! She was a really great teacher. It was different than kindergarten, there wasn't as much singing. It was more strenuous for a first grader, but it was very exciting because it was about learning. It made me feel more grown up. Each grade that I got to made me feel more grown up. I remember feeling proud of that. (Sullivan, 2009, p. 171)

Beth detailed her first grade homeschooling activities:

> I can remember some of the readers and it was all the basics, *See Spot Run, See Jane Run*, that started off. And then there were little books that were like childhood adventure mystery things. I can't remember if *Nancy Drew* was one but it was like that. Mother would start me off and I can remember learning to write and the alphabet, print form rather than cursive first. The ruled paper where you would make your capital letters very tall with three lines, and one little letter over one line and the g would go below the baseline. And mother had all that. She would do it first and then say you do it. I was a real people pleaser. It really gave me a lot of happiness to hear mother say, 'That was really good. You did so well.' Not sure why they didn't send me to kindergarten in [name of town], but she opted to keep me home for one year and she wanted me to learn things right. And it's interesting because sometimes in this day and age you think of homeschooling as a place where kids get a lot of religious education. So we used secular textbooks. (Sullivan, 2009, pp. 171–172)

Beth began to attend public school in first grade. After two weeks in a first grade class, she was moved to a second grade class because she was so advanced. She recalled her time in second grade:

> I remember we would have a play, a drama every year. Each class would have a drama every year. The teacher would choose characters and would look at their list of elementary school dramas and pick out a play. Or, if they were really industrious, they would write their own plays, but most of ours were canned. Ms.[name], she seemed old to be a teacher, but she was only 25 or 26. She selected a play and ours was to be given in December. And it was about Rudolph the Red Nosed Reindeer and Santa was going to get in trouble because his nose was frozen and his light didn't shine. His red light nose wasn't working. All of Santa's elves had to figure out how to unfreeze Rudolph's nose. Well obviously, the lead character of this play was Rudolph. And guess who got picked to be Rudolph the Red Nose Reindeer? I had lines to memorize and I did a good job on it. It probably didn't help my social standing any, the new kid who came in who isn't supposed to be in second grade anyway and here they are taking the lead in the class play. I guess she knew I would memorize my lines; imagine that. That's something I remember from second grade. Costume was kind of big. Antlers were big. In third grade, I played a frog. I had to wear this green suit and mother had to dye it green. I remember that. Had this little froggy mask thing to wear. I remember walking over to the auditorium

from the classroom and all the kids who were not in the play and were looking at those kids who were in the play and pointing and laughing, like, 'You're idiots.' I remember also that we would have certain programs in which we would have children's choirs and being able to sing. I was in the choir and we would have little robes, and in my mind looked like a dress. We would wear a robe. And it was a white robe that had this big red bow on the front of it. I wish I had some of those pictures from then because I think I looked like I was really happy. (Sullivan, 2009, pp. 172–173)

Aidan had a good relationship with his second grade teacher:

My second grade teacher, Mrs. [name], she was the bomb. I think she like of realized that I was kind of like the root, the tree root that I was telling you about (the root that I would sit on in the playground during recess so as not to be bullied by the other children). That was her in second grade. She would always just kind of protect me. You know, keep me out of harm's way. (Sullivan, 2009, p. 173)

Lana had a unique second grade experience. Her parents moved to Germany so that she could attend a private school:

I was glad that we moved to Germany. So this school was, I can't understand it, of course they never explained it to me. But when I got to Germany they never explained to me why we moved to Germany. We moved to Germany because I scored so high on the national level of the United States. Once you go overseas they test you again, but they test you on the international level. Which I scored higher on the international level then I did in the national level. So once they found that out, okay we have to make changes to whatever.... (Sullivan, 2009, p. 174)

Lana enjoyed her new educational environment:

because the teachers were really in tune with me. And I think that was the first point where my parents were actually forced to take a look at the fact that I was probably transgender. And I don't think they really knew I was transgender but they knew I was gay...I don't think they accepted; that's when they knew. You see accepted, that came later in life. (Sullivan, 2009, p. 174)

After leaving Germany, Lana returned to the United States and to public school:

> When I was in public school, and somehow I am not sure how they did it, but they either had lots of teachers come in from colleges to work with me or go to colleges to work with me. Or, I would go to community colleges and do work there. So that was awesome. Even when we were living in Texas, when we lived Colorado where ever it was, I always had that opportunity. It was this really unique opportunity. It allowed me to get an education. And the good thing about that is I am well educated on some level. (Sullivan, 2009, pp. 174–175)

Mary distinctly remembers her third grade teacher:

> She recognized my differences. Mrs. [name], God bless her. She was the music teacher and she taught me scales. She also lived in the neighborhood. I say a prayer for her today, because she recognized the feminine in me that I didn't realize that I had. And I embraced that. And I got As in her class. I never failed her class. (Sullivan, 2009, p. 175)

All of the research partners who recall positive experiences with elementary education teachers describe either feelings of safety with them, or the ability for them to engage in fun or special activities. Additionally, all of the partners chronicled the 'special bond' felt for these individuals. One common thread throughout all of these experiences is that the portrayals of the positive treatment by these teachers all allowed the research partners to feel a sense of normalcy and importance.

A Special Bond

There are a variety of reasons that a teacher may touch a student's heart in a way that is memorably life changing. Consistently, the partners mentioned caring, nurturing teachers who acknowledged their potential and showed them how to explore the realms of possibilities that education has to offer. They respected the teachers that took time for them, listened to them, guided them, and supported them (Sullivan, 2009, p. 175).

Beth consistently had positive relationships with her teachers. She spoke extensively to this effect:

> I didn't do well in rough and tumble games or interactions with other boys. But what I did very well in is academics and so other kids said how much they hated school and I never understood that. And I was certainly very much the teachers' pet, I think by any stretch of the definition. You know, you could look at my school experience and certainly make that assumption. (Sullivan, 2009, pp. 175–176)

Lady Gazelle spoke specifically about how a single interaction with a teacher altered her relationship with him:

> Mr. [name], he was my first male teacher. He looked like some actor or something with blonde hair and blue eyes. And this guy was so sweet and he was a teacher. And I remember the first girl that ever hit on me, her name was Lexi. She was the biggest tomboy in the school and nobody liked Lexi. And so she let me hang around her in school and she protected me and all of that. And Lexi hit me one day 'cause I wouldn't have sex with her. And I was too embarrassed to tell anybody. And my balls were swollen and I was only nine years old when this happened. Finally, it was hurting so bad I had to tell my mother. So my mother took me to the hospital and they told me they couldn't do anything about it until the swelling went down. And the pain was so excruciating I just fell to the ground in the playground and this man picked me up and carried me to the nurse's office. And after the nurse's office he gave me a ride home. I was totally in love ever since. (Sullivan, 2009, p. 176)

Mary also discussed a supportive teacher:

> Fifth grade teacher, Miss [name], I believe she was before her time. She taught modern dance. She taught English. She taught history. She made me realize that I had talent. I just had to dig within my soul and pull it out. She made me look at my art. She made me realize that, 'You can dance; you have grace. You can move, and you move better than a number of the girls here.' I embraced that. She encouraged that. She gave talent shows. I made sure that I was a part of the talent show. She allowed me to be me. (Sullivan, 2009, pp. 176–177)

The overwhelming evidence of supportive teachers were deemed so by the research partners as these individuals spent quality time with the partners, engaged them in positive and productive activities that the partners found interesting or enjoyable, were kind and often nurturing toward them. To paraphrase Mary, the teachers 'let them be who they were,' sans judgment or ridicule.

Teacher Relationships: Negative

Unfortunately, the research partners offered almost double the amount of data regarding negative interactions with teachers as opposed to positive interactions. Their recollections are often startling and shameful of the education profession. Although some of the teaching practices have changed over time (the use of corporal punishment is now more infrequent than when most of the partners were children), and children and parents have gained more control over students' educational paths, other pedagogical approaches remain stagnantly unaltered. Among these are restrictive and regimented curriculum methods, extreme control over developing bodies, and racism (although racist practices may appear in subtler forms) (Sullivan, 2009, p. 177).

Curriculum Methods

While describing her kindergarten classroom as she sketched it, Erin recalled that:

> We had this big case in the middle with those big fat pencils in them. And I remember that because they were trying to make us learn how to write. And I hated those pencils because I wanted to hold it like this, and they wanted me to hold it like some other fucking way. And, yeah, I still to this day cannot write correctly. My handwriting sucks, I've been told. Anyway, this was the blackboard, then the flag. 'Cause we had to stand up and listen to our bible verse and salute the flag every day. It was a Lutheran school. And then this is where they would do stories. Only our teacher was kind of a bitch, so that didn't happen very often. I had a mean kindergarten teacher. I didn't think they allowed mean kindergarten teachers. (Sullivan, 2009, pp. 177–178)

In general, Lluvy Rae recalls adverse contact with her teachers.

> Interaction with teachers was like just telling me, 'Oh that's not for you, that's a girl's (item).' Like I would take my sister's favorite ChapSticks to school and wear them. And they'd be like, 'oh that's for a girl,' and take it away from me. And I'm like, okay. And they'd take it away for the day and they'd say, 'come to me after school and you can get it back' or they'd write my name on the chalkboard. It was always a system where if you did something bad your name went on the board and you had to come in after school and then they'd call your parents and they'd tell your parents. Well I didn't have a phone so the only way to contact my mom was by letter. I remember there was something about my sister's stuff at school, like her ChapSticks and stuff and they would take them and then I would go and try to get them back and they would basically tell me, just lecture me, 'you're a boy you shouldn't be playing with these.' I don't need to hear that at school. I already hear it at home. I'm really there just to learn. I'm not there to be told who or what I am. They were like, you know, 'don't bring it again; if you do it again I'm going to tell the principal,' blah, blah, blah. I still did it. It was so funny because I would bring it and use it knowing that I wasn't supposed to have it. But I would like ask to go to the bathroom, go to the bathroom, put it on and come back. And then one of the boys would tell on me. 'He's wearing...it smells like chocolate or strawberry,' or whatever, 'Oh, he's wearing girls' lipstick.' The attention I guess it caused is what the teachers didn't like. (Sullivan, 2009, pp. 178–179)

Margo always had a deep love for all things scientific. She had an inquisitive mind about the way the world around her operated. When asked why she did not grow up to become a scientist, she replied:

> It's funny you should say that. I think I would have if I hadn't had such an adverse experience in school. 'Cause you know, school's all about standardization and so teachers don't take an interest in you personally. So if you have difficulty in any given subject you know, you're kinda left to screw up on your own. And I think my parents just didn't have the time to help me with my homework. We were transitioning from traditional math skills to something called the V math. It was a really idiosyncratic way of doing arithmetic. And it was synthetic, and it was not an organic way of doing math. And so it was a way of putting a wedge between generations because you couldn't go home and have your parents help you with your homework 'cause they didn't understand it. 'Cause they were like, 'Well

we did division and we did it this way.' So I would go to school if I had help from my parents and get a shitty grade 'cause my parents didn't know what the fuck the teacher wanted. And so I think that also had a lot to do with me and my parents not getting along. Because I resented my parents 'cause other kids' parents you know, were doing their science projects for them. (Sullivan, 2009, pp. 179–180)

Like this kid named Bobby, his dad brought this fantastic volcano to school. It was like this tall, made out of plaster, detailed. And I was like, 'Whoa this is so cool!' I tried to do the same project and my dad would just half ass shit with baking soda and vinegar. And I was like 'man, I'm getting fucked over.' You know, 'cause the other kids were getting it done right. So again it came back to disparities. You know, 'cause my parents weren't as capable of helping me with my schoolwork as the other kids, so they were doing better in school than me. So I think that had a lot to do with me not being able to make it into the hard sciences, you know? I think I have a natural knack for doing math. But if I have to do it a way a certain teacher wants, I have a hard time of testing. So you know, I think that had a lot to do with me not going to academic schools as opposed to going to art school. Some have a knack for taking tests and some don't. There's a psychology to it and I realize that you know, they kinda weed people out. And it's almost as if we want to get rid of independent thinkers, you know? So the more creative you are, the more independent thinker you are, the more you're under fire. 'Cause they designed the test to work for people that take instructions, but if you are an inventor type, you will not get it right. 'Cause if you're an inventor you'll be able to have free answers and you'll try your best to guess what the teacher wants and you'll never get it. She's always telling me 'well, they're not out to do that to you, you just do it to yourself.' I'm like, 'No, you really don't get it. There really is more than one answer.' You know, but that's not what you're taught. School's all about standardized learning. So I think I just got it into my head at an early age that I wasn't going to have it very easy. I tried to go, 'cause I wanted to be a physician you know later in life. And before that I wanted to be an astronaut. But I didn't have the chops for it in terms of what they were looking for. I know I could do it, but I just know that's the way the system was made. It didn't favor me. (Sullivan, 2009, pp. 180–181)

Margo offered another example of a time when her teacher instructed in a way that was different from how her parents were teaching her at home:

I had homework. My dad said, 'Well you make an A like this and my dad does this,' which is a correct way in Art school for instance. But I went to class and got into trouble 'cause I didn't do this. 'Oh no,' this is what you're supposed to do. You're supposed to do this. That is was the teacher wanted. And if you did any one of these, you got a bad grade, but each one of these is correct. So that was my crash course in the fact of it ain't got nothing to do with how smart you are. It's a question of- 'Are you what they are looking for?' 'Cause they have to buy us, they wrote the book, tells it their way. So it was like, the first thing I remember…in school was having to do things their way, even though my way isn't about being bad. But that's how I remember the rest of the classes. 'Cause you were required to sit at your desk with your hands folded. And I remember the teacher had put masking tape on everyone's desk, a strip of masking tape. And so the first thing you were supposed to do was take one of your crayons and write your name on your desk, which I remember doing. And so between that and the fact that you always looked straight ahead, 'cause the teacher had her desk in the front, and every time they would write something on the board we had to repeat in unison. It was so B.S. Skinner. It really was like dog training when I went to school. Now they have all these visual aids and they use televisions in the classroom. They used TV in the classroom sparsely when I was in school. For the most part it was drills and repeating whatever the teacher would say. And then the teacher would say something and you would say, 'Yes Ma'am,' in unison. I could tell the difference what the Soviet Union was and what we were. I was like, 'Why are we at war?' 'They are Communists,' and they would describe it. And, 'they are not like us, they're are not, they're not free.' And I am not free here. I have to wait for a bell to ring and raise my hand to go to the bathroom, and then they are telling us how the Russians are bad. (Sullivan, 2009, pp. 181–182)

Many of the research partners' negative recollections of their teachers ascribe to Foucault's theorization of docile bodies (mentioned earlier), specifically with regard to the stripping of any power these individuals may have possessed. The type of 'discipline' exerted on the partners' bodies by teachers took various forms such as criticism for playing with the 'wrong' toys or objects, always attempting to correct the 'anomaly' that was the perceived aberrant (with regard to gender) comportment of the research partners. Discipline, for the teachers described above, "was a procedure… aimed at knowing, mastering and using. Discipline organizes [a]… space" (1995 [1975], p. 143).

Body Normalization—Maximum Control

The partners' trans and, concomitantly, "deviant" bodies, were viewed by many in their educational settings as bodies that ought to be controlled. Again citing Foucault, "the body becomes a useful force only if it is both a productive body and a subjected body" (1995 [1975], p. 26). Control of bodies is to exact extreme power, restriction of movement, physical restraint; deciding what is and what is not an appropriate way to behave, the creation of a system, a well oiled machine where the bodies functioning within are merely pieces, parts. Incomplete without each other, though replaceable; purposeless without the energy needed to initiate process, useless without the power to control; incapable of unique thought, utility or meaning. Such normalization of young, developing bodies exists not only in association with gender, or because of gender, but merely the result of age and how that equates to older minds and older bodies. If you are considered small, less developed, less capable, it is probable, possible, needed; no, necessary, to restrict, levy suffering, mold, create. The creation of perfect replicas, unfeasible yet always the ambition; the research partners experienced such restraint and their narratives are shared below (Sullivan, 2009, pp. 182–183).

Aidan passionately described his relationship with one of his educators:

> My first grade teacher, the first one, was a dick. And I just remember, like I would never want to sit down and do my homework. I always wanted to get up and sharpen my pencils. I didn't have any pencils that were longer than this [held thumb and forefinger 2 inches apart]. And I would wanna walk around. She would say, 'well, if you don't sit down and do your homework, you can't go out and play, or you can't do anything.' And then my next first grade teacher, wasn't a bigger bitch. But what she did was one day, I think I probably left my spelling book on top of my desk, so then she threw it away. And then sent me to the principal's office everyday during spelling for the rest of that year. I still can't spell. Yeah, that's pretty funny. And I don't know what a noun, a verb, an adjective, or an adverb is. You know, I say that to people, and they explain it to me, and I'm like yeah, that's fine. I don't have the foundation to remember what you just said. (Sullivan, 2009, p. 183)

Beth's public school experience was different than what she encountered when she was being homeschooled:

> It was like that in the classroom, it was always boring because (I already knew what they were learning). And so I would find myself moving around and seeing what the other kids were doing. Sometimes I would get cited by the teacher for not paying attention. When test time came around, I would generally get a 100 on the test. (Sullivan, 2009, pp. 183–184)

Margo felt humiliated by her teachers. She would often be found:

> Putting my hands on my hips a lot of time and rocking them. Teachers would tease me. Teachers are like prison guards; they have to keep order. And they would rather you be disruptive towards each other than be disruptive towards what they are trying to do. So teachers would pretty much look the other way when other kids would pick on me and beat me up. So I had a pretty traumatic school life. I had a hard time with other students and I also had a hard time with my teachers 'cause a lot of them are religious. (Sullivan, 2009, p. 184)

Margo described how the children were reprimanded at her school:

> In Florida they had a lot of what you consider unconstitutional punishment. You know, like, one punishment was obvious, corporal punishment. The first day of preschool, the teacher left the room and said, 'I don't want anyone to get out of their seat. I am going to go the lounge and I will be back.' She left the room and this one kid named Larry, he was sitting behind me, he springs up out of this chair and turns around. And the class just starts laughing he then runs up to the window. And this is one of those schools where they have like one of those steel mesh windows with impregnated glass. And he was too short to reach the window. And he hops up and the whole class laughs, he hops up to see out the window and falls back down again. And the class keeps laughing and he keeps hopping up and hopping up and he's trying to see where the teacher is. And then the third hop, he hops up and the teacher's face is in that window. The door flies open and she grabs this kid by the arm and starts jerking him left and right. Drags him to the desk, pulls out a drawer with blow bow paddle, you know one of those little paddle ball things, only it didn't have a ball on it. And she took that thing out and bent him over her knee and started spanking this kid with a blow bow paddle. Now my grandparents had beat me with a switch, but my parents didn't spank me,

except one time my dad spanked me with the belt. So here it is, I am in school, you know, and I am seeing this teacher paddle this kid. And that scared the shit out of everybody. And I think the teacher deliberately did it that way knowing that the kids didn't know what a big deal it was to get out of their seat. So, it is kind of like a way of imprinting that. So that was the first time I saw someone punished at school. (Sullivan, 2009, pp. 184–185)

The other time I saw someone punished at school was me. I had did something, I think I acted up while they were showing a film strip. Before they had videos and computers, they used to have these things called film strips. Yes, 35 mm film. You know, the positive transparencies that would have a caption that the teacher would have an audio visual kid that would turn the knob. And we would have those and that was kind of like our chance to cut up, 'cause the teacher would turn off the lights and you could make noise and engage in mischief and it was hard to get caught. Only I got caught, another kid told on me. So the teacher grabs me, takes me out of the class and puts me in the custodial closet. I don't know if she knew this, but I had a horrifying fear of the dark. And she put me in this custodial closet and it was the most scariest place in the world. 'Cause I remember there was like a broom in there, and one of those big industrial mops. And the only light in the room was the light coming from the crack at the bottom of the door and so my eyes would adjust over time and acclimate. And that was the scariest freaky place in the world 'cause you don't know what that stuff is when you're in the dark. And you stand real still 'cause you're just so scared that something is going to get you. And then once and awhile the maid would come and open the door and she would say, 'Why do they got you in here like this?' It was the first time I had ever saw a Black women up close, and it was scary, and I was scared of her. I never seen a Black person in real life, and this black lady at the door really scared me. And then it became a real routine to put me in there, which was okay because there was, they kept costumes in there. One of the costumes was this sequined, it was like a flapper dress, I never put it on but I remember contemplating putting it on. And I never had the guts to put it on. (Sullivan, 2009, pp. 185–186)

Lady Gazelle also experienced corporal punishment:

The days I went to school spanking was allowed. The teachers were allowed to swat the kids, discipline them, and they would just bug me and bug me until I go off and act crazy. And then they would laugh at me while the teacher would take me into the back room and swat me. So it was, school was not a good place for me at all. I got disciplined in my classes and the teachers would tell me with the same breath, 'you are so intelligent why are...' you know. And unfortunately my mother never got her GED so I never had anyone to help me with my homework when I got home.

She went on to explain that though the teachers saw her being teased by the other children, "30 years ago people choose to ignore stuff like that" (Sullivan, 2009, pp. 186–187).

The dress code for the reservation school that Lluvy Rae attended included a policy that boys must have short hair. For a transgender child who wanted more than anything to express her femininity, these haircuts were traumatic:

> I always wanted long hair when I was a kid. There were points where my hair would grow out just a little below my ear and I would get notes that I would have to get a haircut from school. I always thought that was unfair, too. (Sullivan, 2009, p. 187)

She explained in her culture, it is taboo for boys to have long hair:

> In the Navajo tradition a lot of the females aren't allowed to cut their hair until they have their puberty ceremony. For the males, it's better if you cut your hair just because, I don't know why. It's probably because it's more masculine, to define roles or whatever. But I always wanted long hair. Whenever my hair would get a little too long I would get in trouble with the teacher. And my mom would be like, 'why, why, why cut a person's hair really? Why cut his hair if he doesn't want to?' But because she didn't want conflict with the school either, she would just take me to town and I would get my hair cut. I hated it. I thought it didn't make me feel feminine anymore for the few months that it was growing back out. It made me feel like a boy when I really wasn't a boy. It was like the attention I got from the students was, 'Oh, you cut your hair. You look like a boy.' I just did not like hearing the compliments. What they were supposed to be were compliments, but I didn't like them, I didn't enjoy them, I didn't appreciate them. I hated them. That allowed me to give more of an attitude which got me into more trouble. That would just make me have a bad day. I don't know, I just thought it was funny that you would get a note from your teacher that you needed a haircut. That's really kind of weird. (Sullivan, 2009, pp. 187–188)

All of the research partners' narratives detailed above involve a plethora of modes of discipline; sometimes confinement was equal to 'prison.' Many of the accounts include physical and/or verbal/emotional abuse, usually in an attempt to remove them from the classroom (i.e. send them to the principal's office or to the closet), eclipse their sense of personhood (i.e. cut their long hair), or subject them to various other modes of degradation. As Foucault theorizes, "discipline 'makes' individuals" (1995 [1975], p. 170). It would seem that the teachers, in one way or another, were committed to 'creating' a certain type of individual, an impossible subjugated subject.

Public Humiliation

Another form of discipline at Margo's school was public embarrassment:

> The girls never got into trouble in my school. Well, the girls would tattletale most of the time and the teacher would appoint them to be monitor, like to take names. When the teacher would go out of class, usually either a goodie-two-shoes boy would get chosen or one of the girls with better academic prowess would get the privilege. They would move their desk to the front of the class they would sit next to the teacher. And so typically the girls seemed to cooperate with each other, whereas the boys taking names, there would always be a boy in class that would challenge the authority of the boy that was taking names. 'Cause I remember one time the teacher let me take names and every time a person would talk, I would put a checkmark by their name. And then they would just keep talking and I'd keep adding checks. And then I started punishing these kids that were picking on me by just writing their names on the board. I'd just write their name on the board, they didn't even do anything. I would just put their name on the board. And say, 'Anybody in here does anything, I'm going to put your name on here too.' And then those kids started throwing shit at me and calling me names. And it was real difficult period of time 'cause I was, I didn't want to be the teacher's pet. But it was a way at times, you know, if I like offered to take names, it would keep me from getting beat up 'cause the teacher would protect you. (Sullivan, 2009, pp. 188–189)
> But then the next year I had a teacher named Ms. [Name] and I offered to take names. I told her this kid was popping me in the head. And I told the teacher and she says, 'Oh you're a little tattletale, well we'll just have to make a little tail for you and pin it on you and have it say tattletale.' So I was learning that what worked with one teacher wouldn't work with another teacher. You know, it was a real weird time because we weren't regulated back then see; you actually had teachers abusing students. Even if they weren't allowed to touch you, they'd still grab your arm and shake

you in your chair or yank you out of your desk. And that wasn't considered hitting (but) teaching us students, you know? Like I remember saying, 'You're not allowed to touch the pupil.' And the teacher challenged me, her eyes bugged out, and she got in my face like, 'classroom, did you see me touch him?' And you know they wouldn't want to get in trouble so they'd go along to get along you know. So I didn't like school too much because I found that if you had friends in school, the teachers were, in order to control the class, would try to break up the cohesion of the group and kind of turn the students against each other. And then you'd have some teachers that would tolerate some students narking on each other. But then, if they didn't like you and somebody was doing something to you and you reported it, it wasn't enough to just blow you off. They would announce to the class that you fingered that person knowing full well that when you go out there in phys ed, they're gonna kick your butt. (Sullivan, 2009, pp. 189–190)

And we had teachers who would set me up for another kid to kick my butt. I had a teacher one time, she called me 'the mouth.' That was my name. She called me 'the mouth.' All I ever did was just talk too much. All the other kids would pass notes and so this teacher would punish me in very eccentric ways. Like make me stand in front of the class and she'd put a dot on the chalkboard, but put it so low that I would have to squat and put my nose on the dot. Or make me stand in front of the class and squat with my knees bent and with my arms out for several hours. That's torture under the Geneva Convention. I even brought that up and she punished me for saying that. I mean this teacher was out of control. I mean she would just dole out all kinds of bizarre punishments. It's like, she took away my art class. She took away my music class. And she took away my library class trying to punish me. The librarian spotted me one day and knew about this and called me aside and said, 'You know it's wrong to not let a student use the library. You can come by after class and I'll let you check out as many books as you want in your life.' And so that's a really good teacher. That's about the only person I cared about. And then, the principal found out what the teacher was doing and said, 'You can't do this.' And then they were just beside themselves what to do with me. They let me follow the art teacher around so I took art full time for the residual of 6th grade. Yeah, it's quite a success story you know if you think about it. Yeah, I mean it was really such a cruel punishment though, that the teacher would take away any class that you enjoyed. Nowadays people sue people, but back then teachers were a virtual tyranny. It just depends on the luck of the draw. Some teachers had a calling and some teachers hated their job, resented their job 'cause they wanted to be doing something else but they had to teach. 'Cause I think that's why I didn't care for school when I was growing up. (Sullivan, 2009, pp. 190–191)

As the above narratives illustrate, some teachers protected the research partners by allowing them to police the other children in class who were purportedly misbehaving. Such a protective tactic was not employed by other teachers, who instead felt that the research partners should be punished for their lack of conformity to gender norms. This resulted in corporal punishment and the creation of an environment that made it propitious for the research partners to be gender policed by their peers.

Racism

Some of the research partners endured intersectional discrimination as they were both trans and part of a minoritized racial group. Ironically, even within queer theory, there has been a reproduction of "the kinds of racial normalizations and exclusions demarcated by queer community" (Barnard, 2004, p. 5). Unfortunately, the terms 'lesbian,' 'gay,' and/or 'trans' often signify "white lesbians and gay men" (Barnard, 2004, p. 4). Thus, transgender children of color face multifaceted discrimination on more than one front, resulting in double jeopardy. Chris personally experienced this phenomenon:

> My third grade teacher, that was the first time that the idea of racism really became real in my life. My dad's Latino. He's Mexican and my mom is white, so I'm biracial. That really hadn't been a big factor in my life, until that point. I remember I got my first report card, basically the first of quarterly report cards. We got these handwritten, quarterly report cards and they would call in the parents to meet the teacher and look at the report card. My mom couldn't afford a babysitter, so she brought me. I remember playing around over on the side, drawing or something, and my mom talking to my teacher, Mr. [Name], he was a man. Actually, he was Mormon too, so my mom knew him outside of just school. She was going through my report card with him, there where all these great grades, like I've always gotten. Then, there was a "C." She asked, 'What is this?' And it was something really subjective; not an academic thing. I remember her asking, 'Well, why does he have a "C"?' I remember hearing him say, 'Well, people like your kid need to have, at least, some negative grades. My mom asked, 'My child? What are you talking about?' He said, 'Your child is Hispanic and it's not possible for this kid to get all As.' I remember thinking, 'What?' And my mom was totally dumbfounded at that point. She left really upset and I asked, 'What is going on?' I was in third grade and didn't really understand. I remember her explaining it to me that 'some people are really ignorant.' At the same time, she really internalized

that and, then, pushed that onto me. My skin was pretty dark and still gets really dark when I'm outside. It's lightened as I've gotten older, but my skin was darker then. I remember her wanting me to wear long sleeved shirts, that idea of being ashamed of my race, my biracial-ness, being instilled in me at that age. (Sullivan, 2009, pp. 191–192)

Lack of Support

Transgender students often feel isolated and alone, particularly if they have lack of support from peers and parents. However, this can be compounded when this absence of nurturance comes from teachers as well. Maria described such an instance that occurred in her early childhood:

> I had to go to school and I had to put up with all the gangsters and all the other guys that would call me 'sissy' and 'fag'. And I would tell them 'No, I am not. I am not a fag.' But it was obvious because of the way I acted 'cause I could not control it, as it came up naturally. But I guess people don't understand that and people are just ignorant. And there was this one teacher who told me one time, and I will never forget, 'You can never change a thousand people, but you can only change yourself. Are you going to keep fighting for the rest of your life?' She said, 'change yourself, change the way you act, change your mannerisms, try to act a little more masculine.' I said, 'I cannot change it, you know, this is what I am. And she said, 'Well, then you are going to be with problems'. (Sullivan, 2009, p. 193)

Understanding Teachers' Actions

This research partners detailed some unkind, often unethical actions of teachers. Lady Gazelle explained this in further detail:

> (When I was in) Kansas City, I remember getting home and doing (the homework). I couldn't do the homework in LA. One of the differences is I think is that I had a tutor. See, my cousin Connie, she was the same age as me and she was really smart. And so I would not have her do it for me, 'cause if she did it for me she would get into trouble. But she would help me with it. So that helped. The classes did seem easier in Kansas City then in LA. I think the teachers care less in LA, at least where I went to school they didn't (care as much). There were the Watts riots going on and President Kennedy getting assassinated and Martin Luther King. There was a lot of anger in the ghetto and the teachers never got paid enough. I didn't realize, I look at a lot of the movies now and I didn't

realize what the teachers went through on a daily basis to exist. I look at all these movies and it was like, 'Wow, yeah, and the teachers weren't there 'cause they couldn't get a job, they were there 'cause they cared.' But it was a situation where they had no control over what was going on. And it was hard for a teacher to teach without any control. Yeah, I just wow. Of all the teachers I only remember one that cared, that showed he cared. The rest of them I don't even remember them. They're just like, I don't even remember them. (Sullivan, 2009, pp. 193–194)

Although there was, at least for Lady Gazelle, an epiphany with regard to why some of the teachers may have acted the way they did, for the majority of the research partners, although in different places throughout the country, their stories all told the tale of routine harassment, mistreatment, and injustice from the teachers directed toward them.

Spaces of Resistance: Disciplinary Issues

Postmodern theorist José Esteban Muñoz (1999) asserts that identity surges forth "between a fixed identity disposition and the socially encoded roles that are available for such subjects" (p. 6). Thus, in order to survive, non-cisgender ontologies such as trans individuals will enact what Muñoz terms 'disidentification,' a term that describes the "survival strategies the minority subject practices in order to negotiate a phobic majoritarian public sphere that continuously elides or punishes the existence of subjects who do not conform to the phantasm of normative citizenship" (1999, p. 4).

Hence, some of the ways in which transgender children respond to bullying, challenges with school work, and lack of support from teachers are disobedience, rule breaking, disrespecting authority figures, and fighting. Often, these behaviors resulted in disciplinary consequences. The partners described these behaviors as retaliation for being teased and assaulted themselves or as a means to increase their personal safety at school. Some of the narratives detailed here take place in middle childhood or adolescence. However, they are relevant in that they demonstrate the outcome of bullying that began in early childhood and continued throughout elementary and middle school. This torment was able to persist as it was not eradicated by early childhood educators. Important questions must be asked while reviewing this section. What lessons did the children (acting aggressively) fail to learn in or retain from early childhood? How can we make schools safer so that transgender students do not feel compelled to fight to protect themselves or their honor? In what ways did the transgender students use violence as an act of resistance? (Sullivan, 2009, pp. 194–195).

Nonconformity to Classroom Rules

Beth and Margo were disciplined for disobeying classroom rules. Beth explained that:

> I think I did pass notes occasionally. They gave you an academic grade and a (behavior) grade. As part of the 'teacher's pet' deal, you behaved for the teacher like she wanted you to. I got attendance stars for perfect attendance. You had to be pretty bad to get a B on conduct. I can remember all the math. I did very well in math. (Sullivan, 2009, p. 195)

Margo's least favorite place in the school was:

> The principal's office, 'cause that's where I had to go when I was in trouble, and I was in trouble all the time. I was usually in trouble for talking, though I didn't fight. But I would get into trouble for clowning around, you know making noises and bringing something to school or drawing on my desk. And the teacher would punish me by bringing in a can of Ajax and having me clean it. I used to daydream and I got into trouble for daydreaming a lot. (Sullivan, 2009, p. 195)

Fighting

Gender theorist Doty argues that, when queerness becomes "uncloseted," it has been known to challenge by force ideological perceptions of what 'queer' signifies at its core (1993, p. xii). Erin holds vivid memories of acting in a violent manner and explained why she felt this was necessary:

> You do what you have to do to not get shot, killed, or beaten into the ground. And it just becomes; it gets ridiculous. You just, you get to the point where you're concentrating so much, almost like it's a game. You're trying to get a high score. How masculine can I be? And, you forget you're doing it. Like, I got violent. I remember in eighth grade this kid, he used to tease me all the time. And I had a history book, and I was reading the history book. And I was one of those kids who you had to push,

but once you pushed I snapped, and like, snapped like handcuffs. And, I remember he was sitting behind me teasing me, and I actually raised my hand and said to the teacher, who was Mrs. [Name], 'Mrs. [Name], I want you to tell this little bastard that if he says one more word to me, I'm going to turn around and break his fucking face in with the spine of this book.' And, she looks at him and says, 'Did you hear that?' He says, 'yeah,' and she says, 'I suggest you be quiet, and I suggest *you* don't do anything that's going to get you arrested.' And the kid said, I don't even know what he said. He said one more thing, and I literally turned around and swung it like a goddamn baseball bat and knocked him over the rail. Like you know those desks where they come like this, and there's the rail, and you get in this. He went over the rail. His name was Jackson. (Sullivan, 2009, p. 196)

He was the kid who tried to pay the kid to beat me up freshman year of high school. Yeah, he paid his friend to come beat me up. He tried to tackle me on a flight of stairs, and I threw him down the flight of stairs; threw him down two flights of stairs. He was really hurt. Yeah, he had a couple broken bones in his face, and I think he did something to his leg. I don't remember, but I picked him up, like, drug him, helped drag him to the nurse's office. And it was literally like it was out of a sitcom. 'Cause he's sitting there, and the nurse is trying to patch him up before they're gonna take him to the emergency room. His parents are going to come take him to the emergency room, and the principal comes in, Dr. [Name]. I wanna say his name was [Name], big black dude. Anyway, he comes in, and he's like, 'what the hell happened here.' And I looked at him, and I said, 'He fell. Didn't you?' 'Oh, yeah, I fell down some stairs, and you know, he was nice enough to help me to the nurse's office.' 'Why are you still here?' 'Just making sure he's okay. Too bad you had that bad fall.' Walked back to my class, like, you know, I was not a nice kid. 'Cause, you've got all of this stuff that you're trying to do to fit in, and it just, you just repress everything. (Sullivan, 2009, p. 197)

Maria exhibited extreme behaviors to initiate her removal from school and home:

> I was pretty much stuck- stuck, stuck, stuck. I couldn't tell my mom, 'this is what I am' cause if I did (come out), I wasn't out of the closet and I still got beat up. Imagine you know (what would happen if I told). So (that's) how that was, I was just stuck, I felt stuck, like I was tied up you know. Tied up in jeans with locks on it, miserable, angry but at the same time there is nothing you can do about it. It's just you. There, you're stuck. I guess it was so bad to be honest that when I was that age I used to do a

lot of things that... I would steal. I would do things to get into trouble 'cause it was much better to be in juvenile then to be at home, that's how sad things were. I would rather more be in juvenile than in home or school 'cause for me home and school were bad and were nothing but misery. They were unsafe, you know. So those times were very rough times, yeah. (Sullivan, 2009, pp. 197–198)

Mary had to protect herself from being bullied, but she also felt an obligation to defend Myles, her older gay brother. Other children used to call Mary:

Effeminate, they would call me a sissy. But they knew that if I heard it and it hurt me, there was going to be a rebuttal. And one day at the park, there were several boys teasing my brother. And we were walking home, and there was a field of sunflowers and it was the end of summer and the sunflowers were drying and the huge stalks of corn. These boys walked up and they were pushing my brother, and my brother was very timid and wouldn't fight. And I thought, 'These boys are bigger than me. What can I do?' And we had our swimming clothes with us, and I thought, 'What can I do to stop these boys from fighting?' Well, I remembered *Nyoka Queen of the Jungle*, and she was the woman, and she fought these natives off. And the only thing I remember is running to this field, and somehow I got the strength that I pulled these stalks up with the dirt balls on them. And I ran into the group, swinging these stalks. And children were flying, and I didn't care who I hit, but they never messed with my brother or me again. And these dried stalks was cutting these children in their face, on their arms, because it was in the summer and hot. That's the only thing I remember is, I remember Nyoka fighting these natives, and these were men, and she was a woman, and she used what was there. (Sullivan, 2009, pp. 198–199)

I'm a drama queen, I can't help it! I think about that today, and I talked about that in my book, and I thought, that's an ugly behavior. But I stopped their behavior, because from that day forward, those kids would say, 'Don't mess with [Name]. [Name] is crazy. [Name] would hurt you.' But it's true. I loved wearing that label. It made me safe. I could walk the streets, I could go to the movies, I could be out alone, and I knew that the kids, they may whisper, and run, but I knew they were never going to come up and put their hands on me again. My biological dad had guns. He was an avid hunter, and they didn't know whether or not I would have gone and got a gun. And I wouldn't have. Yet, my brother contemplated suicide. That's how depressed he was, that he even attempted suicide to kill himself. I was stronger than that. I fought back. That's the difference between he and I. And I thought, you know, those are really unresolved issues that you still feel today. Because when my brother was called a sissy, he cried. When I was called a sissy, I told them, 'Prove it.' Yes, and I didn't know, the words just came forward. And my mother would always say, 'I don't have to worry about you. You're going to survive. But Myles, he bothers and worries me in many ways.' And I never wanted to be a burden. I always wanted to be independent, to be my own thinker, and to be there if I needed that. And there were many times I did, but I enjoyed my parents coming and saying, 'Whoa, you did that by yourself. I'm so proud of you.' Yet, I never got that from my brother. My brother never heard that because he was always the docile (one). I'm sure he felt a lot like, 'Oh my goodness, I will never, ever succeed.' So, I'm sure he continues to feel that way today because of that. So, when I think about those things, it makes me very sad knowing that he never really addressed the problem. (Sullivan, 2009, pp. 199–200)

Lady Gazelle also was forced to resort to fighting as a means of safety preservation and expulsion of anger:

If they ever wanted to see a good fight and if they ever wanted to get on my last nerve, (they would mess with me) until I went for them and see if everyone else would know (not to mess with me). You know, they play and kid with me they know, 'That [Name] has had enough. Back off.' But they would put the new kids up there to mess with me. And so I can't remember losing a fight in school. I would not lose. I mean they had to pull me up off of him 'cause I would not stop until the fight was finished 'cause that was how much anger and frustration I carried around. (Sullivan, 2009, p. 200)

On one particular occasion:

A guy kept spitting spitballs at me; and at first I didn't know where they were coming from. And the whole class was in on it, but when I realized where they were coming from, well I wasn't two minutes off this guy anyway. And so, I didn't (do) anything. I said to him, 'If you spit one more spit ball at me,' the teacher sees this going on and will not say nothing, 'You spit one more spit ball at me…' I would always give them a warning, 'I am going to get you.' I would always give them warning. And he spits balls and I went over and beat the shit out of him with a chair.'

As a result of fighting, Lady Gazelle was forced to switch schools continuously.

> I went to [Name] School. I went to [Name] Junior High, and I don't remember going to any other school before that. But I can say they would suspend me for a whole semester and I would have to go to LA and to Kansas City with my father to go to school to get past that grade. And I bounded back and forth all my childhood life to Kansas City and California. (Sullivan, 2009, pp. 200–201)

Evidenced in many of the narratives detailed above, an unfortunate consequence of consistent bullying and assault was that the research partners did resort to aberrant behaviors such as violence, stealing, and fighting. For these research partners, their 'disidentification' with an intolerant, hegemonic, straight culture often resulted in marginalized behaviors as a means to survive.

Academic Performance

During the interviews, several of the partners shared experiences where they excelled at school. Academic achievement is highlighted here as education is the focus of this study. The partners expressed pride in their accomplishments and frustration when their talents were not recognized. Interestingly, the three participants who initiated dialogue about this topic had a parent who valued education, invested in their learning, and were willing to assist their children in their studies. It seems clear that they still hold sentiments constructed around values they were taught when they were small (Sullivan, 2009, p. 201).

Chris and Beth consistently achieved high marks in school. Chris explained, "I was always a very good student. It wasn't acceptable for me NOT to be a good student. My parents expected As." Beth attributes her early success to homeschooling by her mother. However, the results of her achievements posed some subsequent difficulties:

> Homeschooling had a big influence on my life. I didn't need to do first grade and so the teacher and the principal realized that a week or so into the school year. And the decision was made to promote me to the second grade with results that I was the smallest and youngest child in the second grade. And that didn't help with my feelings of- not supposed to be a boy and not supposed to be with the boys. And being the littlest boy certainly reinforced that. (Sullivan, 2009, pp. 201–202)

During her early childhood years, Lana labels herself as an, "overachiever." When she first began school:

> I was not being challenged, I would just sit there. Lots of times I would just sit there. I would do the work, and that was one of the huge problems that my teachers had with me I would do the work right there in class. They would assign me homework and I would hand it in the end of class because I did not like taking home work home. If I could do it right there then why not just do it? And then it would upset my parents because they would want me to study. Why would I study when I already knew it? I would get better grades than anyone else and I didn't even study.

She earned poor grades but,

> once they tested me they finally realized there was nothing wrong with me. I just needed to be challenged. And (then I) felt I got the proper schooling I needed. So now that was all the way 'til I was sixteen, by the time I was twelve or thirteen I was already in college courses. I was learning to program all kinds of different stuff. So, I was out of school at fifteen. (Sullivan, 2009, pp. 202–203)

Throughout her schooling, Lluvy Rae was placed in special education, standard education, and gifted education. Regardless of her placement, schoolwork was relatively easy for her:

> I have my report cards from grade school somewhere, probably on the reservation. My mom's probably stored it. Some of the comments I would get on the report cards were just, I remember one year I was looking through my stuff and I was reading them and I was, 'Oh, my God.' They were like- 'refuses to listen, acts up in class, talks all the time,' blah, blah, blah. When I think of it now I'm just like, they really made it out to be more than it was, you know what I mean? It could have been me laughing at a joke someone made in class. And them just thinking that I wasn't taking things seriously? Some of the comments, I would be afraid to take my report cards home. In grade school they had carbon copies; they had the grades and then the comments at the bottom. I was pretty much an average student after I got out of being placed in special ed. I was an average student. I went from being the highest in my special ed class to being just an average kid in the classroom, just because I was no longer in a comfortable environment. I was now back into an environment of not wanting to raise my hand, because I knew the answer. Kids at that age if you know a lot, or you remember a lot, or you just happened to do your homework that night and you come to

class the next day prepared, and you're always raising your hand, you know the answer. Kids get jealous by that. And they're like, 'You think you know it all,' blah, blah, blah, and then that translates to the teacher that I need to take a step back when the rest of the class isn't really doing their homework. So, why am I being punished for knowing something? There was a point where I would always raise my hand and they'd be like, 'anyone else?' I've seen movies that make fun of that. Like the kid that knows everything. I can relate to that. All it translates to is that the kid is doing their homework first of all, and is also just knowledgeable about a lot of things. They just want to know a lot of things. And they know a lot of things maybe because when they go home, their parents work with them on something or they go home and do, we have the internet and they research things more, or they just read more or something. (Sullivan, 2009, pp. 203–204)

For these research partners, while some expressed a verve for learning, their recollections of education were often fraught with issues; for some like Beth, being able to skip a grade resulted in further degradation and bullying due to her small size; for others like Lluvy Rae, being intelligent meant that she was frequently overlooked in class.

Parent Interactions at School

The partners came from a variety of backgrounds and family situations. Some had parents and/or guardians who were more involved than others. Most of the parents were aware that their children were being teased. Their reactions to these experiences differed. There did seem to be a common thread between partners expressing either respect and admiration for parents who were emotionally and academically supportive or a grief over those who were less willing or able to provide the educational and social guidance they yearned for as children. Although the parental responses to the educational experiences of the research partners varied, it could be argued that the multivalent power relationships enact Foucault's agonistic notion of power, that is, that power works in multiple and polymorphous ways, seen in the power dynamics not only between the research partners and their families but also between the parents and the school system (1995 [1975]) (Sullivan, 2009, p. 204).

Parental Involvement in Academics

Chris' mother was deeply invested in his life and education. When he began attending kindergarten:

She got a job as a playground aide at my school. She wanted to be with me. Yeah, she was really attached to me, so she got a job as a playground aide. Then she was offered a job at the school district as a secretary because she could type and use a computer, which was somewhat rare for the early '80s. Not a lot of people could do that very well. The school district offices were right around the corner from my school so she was still able to be close to me. I used to see her on recess when she was the playground aide, but once she went to the big office, I wouldn't see her during the day. Her work hours were longer than my school hours. I'd get out of school at three and she had to work 'til five. I would walk to her office and just hang out in her office in the little cubby. Usually, I would take a nap under the desk; maybe do homework. (Sullivan, 2009, p. 205)

When the school labeled Lana as a child with a disability, her mother visited the school to protest this decision:

She got into it with the principal one time and it got really, really heated… And she made it very clear that I was not to be treated like that. You know what I mean, that all of that was too much and that, the reason that that they wanted to put these labels on me. But they didn't want to address the fact that I was being harassed at school, you know? And she, her point was that at that age, if she is gay or if she isn't, this is her child. And she was not going to tolerate her child being called out in this way. My mother was my mother. I can honestly say, if it wasn't for the fact that my mother was so strong, strong enough to go out to the school to defend me, it would have been a lot worse. But my mother was always there and that gave me, that probably gave me a lot of strength to go to school. When I knew these people were changing that, after she made several visits, the kids finally got it and they were scared of my mom which was a good thing.

After Lana received a high score on a national exam, the entire family moved to Germany to support her education in an international private school (Sullivan, 2009, pp. 205–206).

As Lluvy Rae's mother was a single mom raising seven children and working two jobs, she had little time to assist Lluvy Rae with her school work. Several teachers seemed to pass judgement about this:

So, I (raised) my hand and then (the teacher would go) around me and say, 'Oh, well what about you?,' looking for other kids for the answer. That kind of messes my self esteem, too, as far as not being acknowledged. That kind of made me not want to be in school. And it also kind of made me think, 'maybe I don't have to do my homework if other kids don't.' I could translate that way as well. At that age a lot of kids do things to blend in with other kids. A lot of the problems that my teachers thought I had were just things that they were uncomfortable with personally. They thought and they probably felt, 'well, this is how it should be taken care of or your mom's not...' They knew my mom was a single parent, they knew she worked two jobs. They knew all this stuff because she shared it with them in the parent meetings. One of the things when I was referred to special ed was, one of the comments from the teachers was that, 'he isn't loved at home,' or something. And I'm like, 'That's not true. Even though my mom worked two jobs she knows, I mean, she made time for us. If it wasn't her, it was someone else in our family that took care of us.' What's even more funny is that a lot of my teachers were Native American, were Navajo. I didn't understand how they could say things like that when they had family members in that same situation. It didn't make sense to me. I always thought, 'why are they saying bad things about my mom?' The Navajo Reservation specifically is pretty large, however the family relations are pretty close. You might be a friend of someone who is a relative of a teacher. (Sullivan, 2009, pp. 206–207)

The above reflections by Chris, Lana, and Lluvy Rae all demonstrate a deep parental commitment to the partners' education. Chris's mother's experience was positive. However, the parental interactions of Lana and Lluvy Rae were met with resistance and contention.

Parent Responses to Bullying

Some parents were not as supportive as those of Chris, Lana, and Lluvy Rae. Beth believes that her mother was aware that she was being harassed at school. She did not interfere with the situation, however, because "I think that the attitude at that time was that I was supposed to stand up for myself. I don't recall mother or dad...ever having an audience with the teacher to that effect." Margo's parents were also aware of how she was treated at school:

> But my parents always thought I deserved it, you know. They thought I was doing something bad. In my family, if I came home and I said that the teacher was giving me a hard time or the other kids were giving me a hard time, my dad invariably would think it was my fault. So while there were some kids, if they got disciplined the parent would come down to the

school and give the principal a piece of their mind, or maybe the teacher and call them out, it was the other way around in my family. So you know, that was, that made me really introverted, definitely. You know, they led me even more into being a loner because the social rules weren't working for me. (Sullivan, 2009, pp. 207–208)

The school that Lana attended used to contact her mother when she was involved in an altercation with another student:

> As far as my education like, I moved around so much. Like kindergarten to second grade I was in Colorado. I had some really good teachers, I really must say. But yeah, I had issues with other kids 'cause I was feminine, and that was the issue. My mother was always at the school 'cause I was always fighting. Like I was being called 'fag' and I was being called other names, and I received that a lot you know? (Sullivan, 2009, p. 208)

The parental interactions when dealing with the schools varied according to the research partners' recollections. Some parents took an active part in encouraging their child's educational achievement, such as Chris's mom who volunteered at the school. Others actively defended their children (such as Lana's mother and Lluvy Rae's mother) when met with criticism from school officials regarding their children. Beth and Margo's parents adopted more of a laissez-faire attitude, as the belief was that their children should stand up for themselves. This "hands off" approach resulted in increased feelings of isolation by the research partners.

Diagnosis, Treatment, and Special Education

Theorists Phelan and Ebrary (2001) elaborate on what they define as 'sexual strangers,' those individuals who "disrupt seemingly natural boundaries and borders" (p. 29) of gender, sex, and society, who are the othered outsider, who "undermine and crack open from inside all polar categories of social order" (pp. 29–30). While it may be argued that the trans research partners are all, in some sense, 'sexual strangers,' many were othered even more so due to the fact that several of the partners were diagnosed as children with a learning disability or a mental illness. They are mostly unaware of the specifics of these diagnoses as they were not shared with them or not understood because they were given at such a young age. Aidan, for example, has virtually no memory of the intense rehabilitative physical and psychological therapies he received. It was not until he discovered paperwork later in life that he was able to piece together some of what happened to him. He is still unaware of the entirety of his "treatment." Lady Gazelle's mother took her to see several therapists at the request of her school. She explained that the school "had a really hard time with me." Lana's parents did not allow her to go to preschool. They did not feel that she was ready because she "was seeing a psychiatrist" (Sullivan, 2009, pp. 208–209).

Although she did not discuss it extensively, Lluvy Rae mentioned that she was in counseling. She seemed to appreciate the experience. She explained that other transgender children in her school were also seeing therapists. They shared this common bond.

> I was someone that just was like, all the positive influence I got in was from counselors. They would say, 'I understand you feel more like a girl,' and just talking about it. There were more of us between first and third grade. I think we all knew and that was our bond. So now when we see each other it's, 'Wow, we're all doing this,' emotional support. We'll eventually be together. It may not always be true, but that's what we thought. (Sullivan, 2009, p. 209)

Margo takes issue with bullied children being counseled on ways to deal with the abuse:

> The problem really does start at home 'cause these kids that are beating up on other kids, there is something not right somewhere. They have a sibling problem, they have a parent problem, they have an abuse issue most likely and that is transferable. I was seeing a therapist when I was in school, and there were kids far more messed up than me that should have been seeing a therapist instead of me. But those of us who see a therapist, we see a therapist because the really sick people don't see a therapist. And so we end up being the ones who go to therapy. (Sullivan, 2009, pp. 209–210)

For some of the research partners such as Lluvy Rae, their counseling experiences were deemed positive, but for others such as Aidan, these experiences, many of which he seems to have blocked out, bring a potentially painful reminder of the invasive means by which to 'treat' him.

Special Education

Some of the partners struggled in school while others earned high marks with ease. Interestingly, both Lluvy Rae and Lana were initially placed in remedial classes and subsequently placed in the gifted program. Margo, who has a genius IQ, was thought to be learning disabled at one point in her early childhood. This brings up certain important questions. Are transgender children more often labeled with learning disabilities? Some of the interviewees mentioned that they struggled to learn because they were being teased. This lowered their self esteem and increased levels of anxiety and dislike of school. Could these factors be the reason why their grades dropped to a level that they were placed in special education? (Sullivan, 2009, p. 210)

Margo recalled her experience interacting with the special education system:

> I had not been prepared for school the way some kids were, where their parents were home schooling them and you know, teaching them things so they were able to just pick right up. I had to struggle a little bit with reading. In fact, I think they thought I was learning disabled 'cause of my speech. It was how my teeth were shaped, my incisors were, you know, were coming in and the other teeth weren't. So I had kind of a lisp. And I think they thought that I couldn't hear and that was affecting my academic performance 'cause they put me into a speech class with a bunch of (special education students) and shit. And I was like, they think I am stupid, you know. But I am not stupid. I just, my teeth are making me sound funny and they figured that out eventually and they took me out of there. (Sullivan, 2009, pp. 210–211)

Lady Gazelle offered an interesting perspective regarding transgender children and special education. She believes that transgender children face difficulties when learning because they can see the world through both male and female perspectives. She asserts that each of these perspectives learns differently, and if these variations of processing exist within one child, they can become crossed and cause confusion:

> So, Kansas City school districts, I do remember doing the homework, but my father made sure I did the homework, and he didn't care how I did it, he just wanted it done. I never aced all my report cards. I got Cs and Bs. I might have gotten a B every now and then. I have a learning disability.

> I think most trans people have learning disabilities, and I just realized that at my organization just this week. I don't know why. Yeah I do. 'Cause of the way people are taught to teach, and trans (individuals) don't learn the same kind of way. Our mind is open, and I am not saying we're perfect or we're different. We're normal just like you but we have a culture as well. You know our minds are just, we got this guy and this girl in the same body. And the guy learns one way and the girl learns another way. So what happens is you have a learning disability that is just different. I don't think it is a handicap, it's just different. I definitely have a learning disability when it comes to, you know, I am dyslexic. When it comes to numbers, they start jumping around. I got some issues, learning issues. (Sullivan, 2009, p. 211)

When asked if she was ever placed in special education she replied:

> No, I was in speech classes. I've had to take some extra classes, maybe Special ED. With a report card like that, you would think so wouldn't you? But mainly because I wouldn't focus, I couldn't focus. All I could think about was, 'Why do I have to have a fight after class? I hope nobody says nothing to me. Am I going to live today or die today?' (Sullivan, 2009, p. 212)

Lluvy Rae agrees with Lady Gazelle that trans individuals are special and thus may learn differently than children who are not transgender. This can often lead to a mistaken placement within the special education system:

> Those voids are filled with what we think is love because as a child we never got the attention that we wanted. Even if we asked for attention it was like we were too needy, we were almost special, special ed. I know because there was a point where I was put in special ed, I transferred to a school and they put me into special ed because I wouldn't speak to anyone, I was really shy. I was into myself and they just thought I couldn't comprehend anything. I was looked at as dumb basically and I knew and I could understand what they were talking about and I knew I don't need to be here. I knew that, but I just never said anything. So I spent one semester in special ed. I did all the work, everything was correct; I didn't have any learning disabilities. Even at conference meetings with my mom she would come in and they were like, 'I don't know why he's in here. He's smart.' And then my mom would ask me, 'why are you in there if you can do the work?' And then I would tell her. In the teacher conferences they would share things, 'he does this a lot, he's a class clown, he keeps everyone laughing, he's the first one to participate in anything,' blah, blah, blah. And then they're like, why? I guess the question was like in other settings,

'why doesn't he participate?' It was because I was so used to the kids that we all supposedly had learning disabilities. In some way we connected because we all didn't get the attention that we wanted that we thought we deserved. We didn't get that. So we were all together and we all got along with each other because we didn't look at each other as stupid, dumb, crazy or whatever you wanted to call us, or just weird or whatever. We just all accepted each other for what we were. So after that semester I went back in January and they gave me a test. I took the test. I did really well on it and the vice-principal was upset that I had been placed in special ed for almost half the year and the principal was like, 'well I was looking at the reports and it says he never says anything in class; he doesn't participate,' blah, blah, blah. I remember the vice-principal coming and talking to me. She was female and she was so loving and caring and I was like, 'Oh, my God,' and I opened up to her. She was an authority figure, but she didn't use that like the principal did. She was like rude at the time. I didn't know it was rude, I just thought she was mean. She would yell at us and, what are principals supposed to do? I thought it was double on me because, I don't know, I was just a silly kid who made everyone laugh. So she was like, 'why don't you start participating, do your work and stuff?' And I just shared with her that I feel like no one listens to me for stuff, like we had a teacher's pet, people that wanted to answer everything, do everything first. It was never like, roles weren't spread out. Class favorites got to do what they wanted to do. When someone else wanted to do it, it was, 'oh no you can't do it because this person is doing it,' when it should have been a rotating role. Later I did go to a school where I was in a class where they did rotate the roles which was cool because I don't see anyone as the favorite. So I just basically opened up to the vice-principal and told her people make fun of me, call me names. She was like, 'well kids are going to do that to you and that's just how it's going to be'. (Sullivan, 2009, pp. 212–214)

Lana has strong feelings about her time in special education:

> As far as school, when I started out I went to a school called [Name of School] Elementary, which was a nice school or whatever. And I never really had, my problems with my first couple years of school was just like I said; they thought I was retarded. 'Cause what I would do was I would just sit there. It wasn't even, they would get their schoolwork and it would always be correct, but because I was not responsive and I would get irritated. I don't think they really understood that they would irritate me because...I would either learn things I already knew, which is very frustrating. And because I was non-responsive, they categorized me, labeled me

with all these things. Then they put me in this class with all the handicapped kids, with like Autism, Down's syndrome and all this other stuff. So I took a real liking at a young age to people with a disadvantage which is a good thing, 'cause I carried that from there, even when they moved me out of my classes to accelerated classes so, but it interesting now that I look at it. It is interesting. (Sullivan, 2009, pp. 214–215)

Many research partners discussed placement in or labeling of themselves as 'special education.' For many, this attribution was incorrect. For example, Margo was viewed as possessing a speech impediment and Lana did not participate in class. Lana's inability to participate and respond in class had more to do with her own boredom as she already understood the material. The label (and concomitant stigma) associated with 'special education' often exacerbated the isolation, anger, and aloofness already felt by the research partners.

CHAPTER SUMMARY

The partners narrated a variety of social experiences situated in an educational setting. In general, they found friendships in children possessing the same gender identity or with children who were considered outcasts. Peer relationships became increasingly difficult with age and, though not always, younger children were often more accepting of gender differences. For transgender children, there are barriers to building and maintaining friendships that for some led to voluntary or forced isolation. All of the partners were bullied, this included name calling and physical assaults. Teachers often were unaware of how to respond to transphobic jokes and comments (Sullivan, 2009, p. 215).

Most partners had both positive and negative experiences with teachers. These seemed contingent on the way the child was treated and the amount of support received. The interviewees did, however, share many more negative narratives about teachers than positive ones. These included restrictive pedagogy, physical control of their bodies, public humiliation, racism, and judgmental behaviors. Some responded to their normative school experiences by acting out, occasionally in the form of defiance of class rules and other times by fighting (Sullivan, 2009, p. 215).

Academic performance was important to many of the partners; they shared both their successes and their struggles. Parental involvement in school was also discussed. Many who earned low marks attributed this in part to lack of support from home. Several of the interviewees were involved in counseling programs at their schools, either for nonconformity to gender or social norms. A few recalled their time in the special education program (Sullivan, 2009, pp. 215–216). These social interactions occurred within the physical spaces of the school environment. How did these places influence the educational experiences of the partners? How did the partners influence the environment? The following chapter discusses the manner in which these spheres interrelated and how certain locations became associated with internalized dialogue of safety and empowerment or lack thereof (Sullivan, 2009, p. 216).

References

Barnard, I. (2004). *Queer race: Cultural interventions in the racial politics of queer theory*. New York, NY: Peter Lang.
Butler, J. (2006). *Gender trouble*. New York: Routledge.
Diaz, E. M., Kosciw, J. G., & Greytak, E. A. (2010). School connectedness for lesbian, gay, bisexual, and transgender youth: In-school victimization and institutional supports. *The Prevention Researcher, 17*(3), 15–17.
Doty, A. (1993). *Making things perfectly queer: Interpreting mass culture*. Minneapolis: University of Minnesota Press.
Fausto-Sterling, A. (2000). *Sexing the body: Gender, politics, and the construction of sexuality*. New York, NY: Basic Books.
Foucault, M. (1990 [1978]). *The history of sexuality, an introduction: Volume I* (R. Hurley, Trans.). New York: Vintage Books.
Foucault, M. (1995 [1975]). *Discipline and punish: The birth of the prison* (A. Sheridan, Trans.). New York, NY: Vintage Books.
Fuss, D. (1991). *Inside/out: Lesbian theories, gay theories*. New York, NY: Routledge.
Halberstam, J. (2005). *In a queer time and place: Transgender bodies, subcultural lives*. New York: New York University Press.
Hart, L. (1993). Introduction. In L. Hart & P. Phelan (Eds.), *Acting out: Feminist performances* (pp. 1–11). Ann Arbor, MI: The University of Michigan Press.
Miller, W. I. (1998 [1997]). *The anatomy of disgust*. Cambridge, MA: Harvard University Press.
Mikami, A. Y. (2010). The importance of friendship for youth with attention-Deficit/Hyperactivity disorder. *Clinical Child and Family Psychology Review, 13*(2), 181–198. https://doi.org/10.1007/s10567-010-0067-y.

Muñoz, J. E. (1999). *Disidentifications: Queers of color and the performance of politics*. Minneapolis, MN: University of Minnesota Press.

Parker, T., & Stone, M. (Writers & Directors). (2005). Ginger Kids [Television series episode]. In T. Parker, M. Stone, & A. Garefino (Producers), *South Park*. Los Angeles, CA: Comedy Central.

Phelan, S., & Ebrary, I. (2001). *Sexual strangers: Gays, lesbians, and dilemmas of citizenship*. Philadelphia, PA: Temple University Press.

Sullivan, A. L. (2009). *Hiding in the open: Navigating education at the gender poles: A study of transgender children in early childhood* (Order No. 3361853). Available from ProQuest Dissertations and Theses A&I (304843384). Retrieved from http://ezaccess.libraries.psu.edu/login?url=https://search-proquest-com.ezaccess.libraries.psu.edu/docview/304843384?accountid=13158.

Wittig, M. (1992). *The straight mind and other essays*. Boston: Beacon Press.

CHAPTER 6

Art Studios Versus Locker Rooms: Safe and Unsafe Places for Trans Children

The smell of a freshly open jar of paste, the sight of a new red crayon drawing a long thin mark across a piece of lined white paper, the sound of a radiator's pop and hiss, the feeling as you slide into your very own desk for the very first time, the taste of cafeteria mashed potatoes; some memories stay with us for a lifetime. Many are associated with important places. Our senses help us experience new surroundings. As we spend seemingly countless days in the same location, it becomes familiar. When we leave it, even years later, we may be able to close our eyes and recall the designs on the circle time mat, the exact locations of peeling green paint on the walls, and the dreaded fear that fills your belly at the sound of a teacher's heels on the linoleum floor. Twenty years after we have left a place, a wafting smell, unique and recognizable, can rush us back to a time when our bodies were small and our hearts were alive with possibility (Sullivan, 2009, p. 217; 2014, p. 13).

Butler expounds upon how many spaces are replete with regulatory norms, loci whose prescriptions and proscriptions become mapped on the very bodies navigating within them (2004). The educational experiences that the partners recalled for this study existed within the physical space of the school and its grounds. Certain places (whether classroom closet or tree root) represented solace or fear, entertainment or boredom, freedom or restriction, happiness or grief, or rather some variety of these multifaceted emotions. Many were tied to specific experiences with peers or adults, resulting in lifelong associations of places with feelings. As we explore these spaces, particularly in relation to safety and empowerment, we are granted increased awareness, a real and raw look into the world of our children as *they* experience it. Educators might ask themselves: How do my students exist within and interact with physical spaces? What role do I play in these relationships? How can I improve the way in which my young children encounter the school environment? How can they improve it for one another? (Sullivan, 2009, pp. 217–218; 2014, p. 14)

Research Partners' Drawings

The persons participating in the study were asked to describe and draw the first classroom or childcare center that they could remember. This question was asked as a means to help the partners recall this time in their lives, picture themselves in their old classrooms and discuss feelings and interactions that may have otherwise gone unmentioned. As they drew, they described the educational environments. What the partners remember about their early childhood classrooms is quite telling. Certain elements were particularly memorable for a variety of reasons. The narratives regarding educational environments may be of particular relevance to early childhood teachers as they design or restructure the gross layout or aesthetics of their classrooms (Sullivan, 2009, p. 313).

Aidan had few positive interactions with his first early childhood classroom. Aside from the corner and the coat closet, there were not places in the environment that he liked. Because he was often teased, "I didn't like any place where there was a lot of people" (Sullivan, 2009, p. 314; 2014, p. 16) (Fig. 6.1).

Mary felt a greater sense of security in the classroom than Aidan:

> I remember it was a very safe environment. It was very clean. There were lots of tables, lots of sunlight, lots of books; all kinds of books. There was a bookcase and I would love to go and start a quasi-high by the bookcase and if I could sit there, at the bookcase. I could be hidden and read Lorna Dune, my favorite. It was always about female heroines, poems. I was always involved in, 'I don't want people to know what I'm reading, because if they know what I'm reading, they're going to hurt my feelings.' But yet, I could make conversation with a number of people about the books: 'Well how did you know that?' And it made me feel good that I had read that, and I was a part of that conversation. And these people

Fig. 6.1 Aidan's classroom drawing

didn't know anything. They were shallow and narrow-minded. So even though we were the same age, I felt like, 'You're leaving them behind. They'll have to catch up with you.' And that was okay. (Sullivan, 2009, p. 314; 2014, p. 17) (Fig. 6.2)

Beth described the first classroom that she could remember:

> We had an old building, as I said, and the ceilings were very high. They were taller than twelve feet. As a result, we had all these old steam radiators where the heat came from hot water from the basement. The classroom, if you were standing in the door and looking at the window across from the door, you'd see a small area. Here's the front of the classroom where the blackboards were. The windows were huge. They almost went all the way up to the ceiling-not to the floor. The lower windows you could open. There were decorations up high, like fall with pumpkins. You got to show artwork on bulletin boards. Teacher's desk was to the right and the pupil's desk was to the left. Ledge for the erasers, kids wanted to clean the erasers. Rows of desks; five rows, each desk is its own unit. Here's the desk, here's the back, and underneath the chair is where you stow your books. Every

Fig. 6.2 Mary's classroom drawing

desk is a single, self-contained unit. In some years, instead of putting your books underneath, you would have a desk that opened up. The teacher could see everything that was going on. Then along the back wall there was no backboard but there was a bulletin board where you had a lot of students' artwork. (Sullivan, 2009, pp. 315–316) (Fig. 6.3)

Chris enjoyed a lot of things about his classroom:

We had desks that were for us and we put our stuff in there: things like clay and paper, all that sort of stuff. I remember, because it was the first time we got to have our own stuff, like a pencil box. It was a lot of fun, actually. I still love school supplies a lot. I was really excited about pencil boxes and things." He loved getting a new box of crayons. "You got to pick the one you wanted, with all the colors you liked. And, this was the sink; and a cabinet that had a whole bunch of other stuff in it. We had a listening station with headphones and, probably, a record player at that time, because I'm that old! What else? A door was over here. And, we had a piano, actually! I just remembered that because she used to play it! We had a piano up here. She used to be a performer, so she would play the piano. So, that gives you an idea and what it was. (Sullivan, 2009, p. 318; 2014, p. 17) (Fig. 6.4)

Erin recalls the setup of the toys in classroom:

There was a big bright colored carpet with like the big blocks of color. That's what we all sat on, and I used to always sit right here, cause there was a semicircle, and I used to sit right there. So, I don't know why I remember that, but I do. And then this was kind of a play area, and I remember that we one of the little houses you could play in and there was

Fig. 6.3 Beth's classroom drawing

the stove set, like the oven, and all the tools, and the sink, and all that stuff right over there. And then we had hula hoops, and then some kind of a box of other stuff. Her favorite place in the classroom was where she could sit with her friend. (Sullivan, 2009, p. 319) (Fig. 6.5)

Margo has a photographic memory and her drawing and description of her kindergarten classroom was more detailed than any of the other partners:

> I remember we had the ABCs running across the blackboard and then we had a number line. And then we had another blackboard and we had a solar system chart on top of the blackboard on of the right of the classroom. I remember the teacher's desk was at the very front of the class, and she even wrote cursive. And nobody had ever seen cursive before. Here is

Fig. 6.4 Chris's classroom drawing

the name of our school. And she had her name on there. And she had a wooden oak desk that had unsteady looking legs on the bottom, like that. And she sat at the very front of the room and I remember her desk was at the front of the room. And she also had a globe that was on a stand next to the desk and I actually remember this shit, I can't believe I remember it. Oh, and there was this big ass heater inside the room. And there were these ducts going through it, like that. They had, the walls were institutional green, this really disgusting green, a really pale, pale green. It was so ugly, it was aquamarine and it was green. They did beige for awhile after that too. And now they use pink for cool off premises in prisons for when prisoners go ballistic. (Sullivan, 2009, pp. 319–320)

I remember there were all these pictures. They were like a collage that were on the teacher's desk. She had just, like every year she had people like put pictures on there. And so she had pictures from all these people who had been in her class before and those were all over the front of her desk like that. And the walls were these big cinder block walls. I kind of remember those concrete block buildings, and we were in one of those mobile type buildings, except for one half of it was corrugated steel and the other half was these white concrete blocks on the outside. And the inside was

6 ART STUDIOS VERSUS LOCKER ROOMS: SAFE AND UNSAFE … 155

Fig. 6.5 Erin's classroom drawing

institutional green, we had a steel door with a mesh window, you know. And then at the end of the school day all the kids' parents would show up and so you would start to see the occasional parent poking their face up against the window, and the teacher would break away from the class and open the door and tell the parent to scram until it was quitting time. Yeah, I remember my mom would walk home with me. But the first day we had a big chalk board and the teacher had written in script, 'Welcome,' and then put the name of the school, '[Name] Elementary.' And then she wrote her name in script, and that was the first day. And everybody got a piece of play dough, you got a can of playdough, you got a ruler and some penmanship paper. They used to teach penmanship while I was in school. So you would get like this tablet that was a wide tablet with 4 lines and you would have to practice handwriting. (Sullivan, 2009, pp. 320–321) (Fig. 6.6)

As were most of Maria's responses, her answer to the question about classroom layout was brief and succinct:

Fig. 6.6 Margo's classroom drawing

> It's first grade of my elementary school. There is me right sitting down on the second table, and pretty much right here we are listening to the teachers. Then we had books set up right here, and then we had the exits set up around the classrooms. And pretty much have a pattern to every time you exited a classroom, you exit outside. (Sullivan, 2009, p. 322) (Fig. 6.7)

Lady Gazelle struggled to recall her first educational environment:

> This was preschool. My very first class I remember, okay. This was the entrance this was the, where they would take me back and swat me. This is where you would hang your coats up in the closets and these were the desks. This is the teacher's desk and this is the child's part. And this is pretty much all I could remember from the class. It was, I actually, the second class was sunny. And I remember the teacher more than I remember the class. And this other class I remember the class more than I remember the teacher that actually swatted me. I pretty much blocked all of that out. This was a horrible, horrible class for me. Only thing I remember is that, is

Fig. 6.7 Maria's classroom drawing

being teased. I don't remember what the class looked like or anything like that. A lot of stuff of my childhood I have blocked out. And for whatever reason, the real horrible stuff I can block out. 'Cause as a child, it was hard to comprehend the abuse. It was just, I was such a nice person. Come on, give me a chance, guys. (Sullivan, 2009, p. 324) (Fig. 6.8)

Like Margo, Lana's memory was also quite clear:

This is [name of school] and the school is right here and this is the square building and the square building is like this. And this area here was outside and like a brick wall. And there was like a beam that goes into the classroom. But the actual classroom, like when you went inside the classroom, we had several rows of chairs. And it was probably about three or four rows across. This was kindergarten. And kindergarten I actually remember, I sat up here probably right here. This was my seat. This was the chalkboard here. There was a cubby area here but I don't remember what it was for. I think we hung the coats over here when we came in. And there was

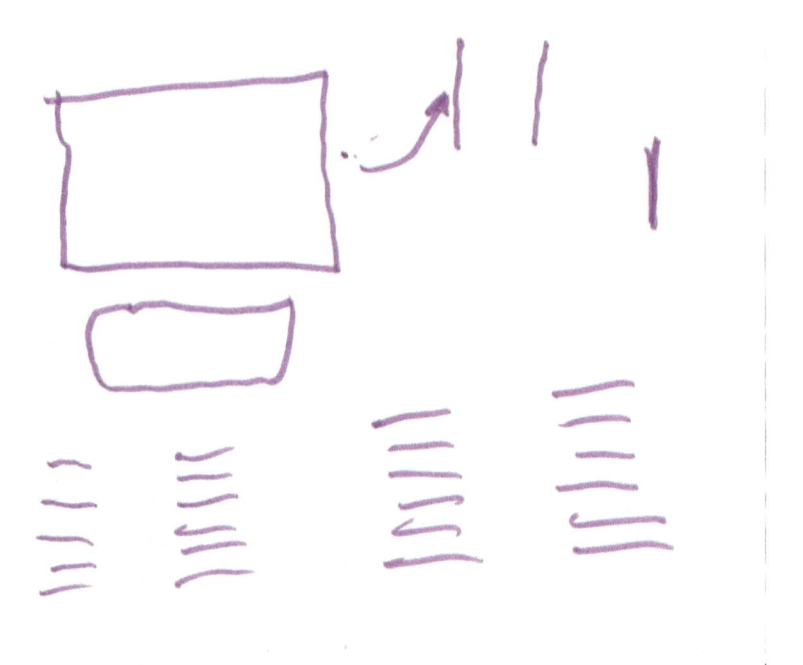

Fig. 6.8 Lady Gazelle's classroom drawing

a play area off to the left here. The way the kindergarten was set up was just outside the, like this was just like an open space and we used to play there too. All of this right here was like near a brick wall that like encased it and it had a little opening, no there wasn't an opening. You would go in inside and then you would come out and this whole thing was squared off like a jungle gym with stuff like that we used to play with or whatever; but that's pretty much how the setup was in kindergarten. (Sullivan, 2009, pp. 325–326)

Lana also described her first grade classroom and the school building in which it was located. She was the only partner who drew and described places in the larger school setting:

This was the office. The office was probably like kitty corner from the first grade. And this is where I went and did my music, the gym and all of that is right over here. And this was the stage here where we would enter into the door here, but you could go into this hallway through this set

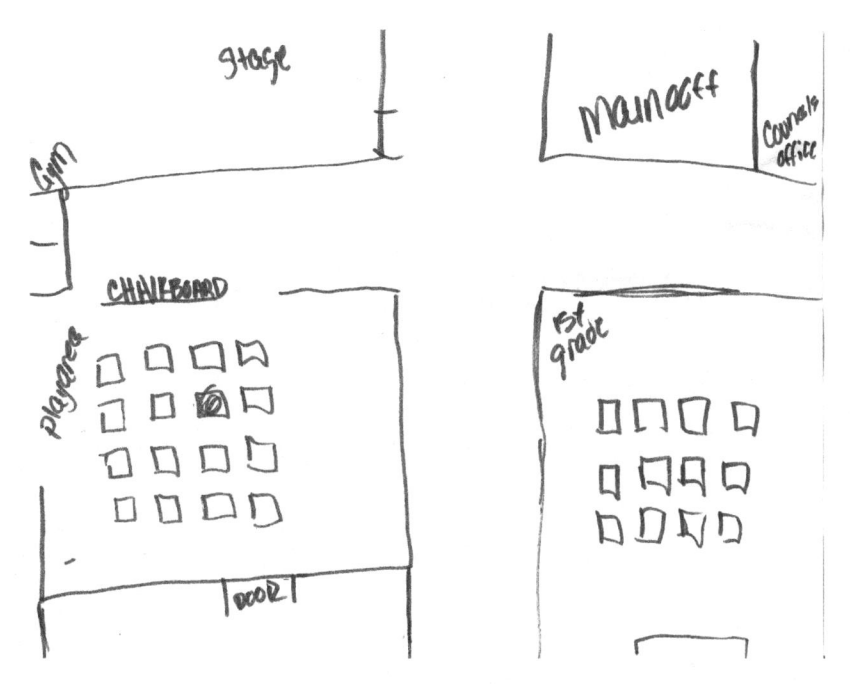

6 ART STUDIOS VERSUS LOCKER ROOMS: SAFE AND UNSAFE ... 159

Fig. 6.9 Lana's classroom drawing

of double doors. And through this double door was the gymnasium and that is where we had gym and all of that. Outside of the gymnasium was a huge gym, like the other kids other than kindergarteners on my first day of class was like here. This was the main office. Across from the main office there was like a janitor cleaning closet. But there was another classroom directly here. But my classroom was kinda off to the right there. But when you walked in there, if this was a first grade classroom, the chalkboard is up here. Again, seven rows of chairs like this and very simple, very plain. There was a table in the back and then the chairs and then the decorations. I remember decorations on the wall or whatever. And then my, where I went to second grade was the same school. You see this was the main office but I would go, 'cause they had me in counseling so much 'cause they thought something was wrong with me. My counselor's office was here in the back side of the office 'cause the main office was the principal's office. And this was the counselor's office right here and then on this side was the library and then on the other side of the library that was where I went to the second grade. (Sullivan, 2009, pp. 326–327) (Fig. 6.9)

Fig. 6.10 Lluvy Rae's classroom drawing

Lluvy Rae recalls the color-coded system that existed in her preschool. Everything was divided into, "Blue and pink and I always wanted pink. I never liked blue and there were a few times that I would switch stickers. I would switch stickers so I had a pink one. And I would get in trouble for that too" (Sullivan, 2009, p. 327; 2014, p. 17) (Fig. 6.10).

COMFORT AND SAFETY

All of the research partners existed within a construct of spatial relations, some of which enabled them to be unfettered and authentic, and others that restricted and constrained their veritable self-expressions. Gender theorist Jack Halberstam refers to the 'queer spaces' (2005) as those arenas in which queer folk engage and create spaces of comfort and/or dissent "enabled by the production of queer counterpublics" (p. 5). As we shall see, many of the partners specified places that afforded them safety and comfort, while others were forced into sites of negation and repudiation.

Finding Comfort in Teachers and Friends

Several of the partners explained that their feelings of safety were dependent on their relationship with and proximity to peers and adults. If friends and teachers were supportive, they would be more likely to protect the child from the bullying of other children. When away from these kind and helpful individuals, some of the interviewees felt vulnerable and alone. These early childhood relationships appeared to crucially impact the educational experiences of these transgender children (Sullivan, 2009, p. 218).

Erin felt safe when she was "with my one friend." Similarly, Lana recalled her relationship with a special peer:

> It's probably when I met my friend Art in second grade that probably when I would say I felt safe in school. When I got into the classroom and I got introduced to him because, I remember they brought me directly to him when I got to the class. And they said, 'I want you to meet somebody,' and we just bonded from that moment. We just started doing our class stuff together and that made it easier because they had someone they thought was like me, they said. And come to find out he was really smart too. (Sullivan, 2009, p. 218)

Similarly, Maria sought refuge in friendships:

> Here in the classroom the only time I felt safe, it was either when I was next to a person that was that was my friend or when I was with my grandparents. Those were the only times I ever felt safe, other than that I never felt safe because I was picked on. (Sullivan, 2009, pp. 218–219)

Beth felt safer:

> The closer to the teacher I was. I would not have felt safe in the back of the room at that age 'til later on. She (the teacher) would have a stack of papers and give them to me and since I had this memory of names and I knew which one matched with which face. I was called on a lot because she knew I knew the answer. She would try somebody else first and when they wouldn't have the answer, she would call on me. I wasn't one of those, 'Mr. K, Mr. K!' I wasn't one of those. (However,) I did know it and wasn't going to say I didn't. (Sullivan, 2009, p. 219)

Specific Location

For some of the research partners, it was not people but rather places that heightened their feelings of safety. It may have been a place to hide, a feeling of ownership, or a spot where they flourished educationally, a site of pride. Certain areas in the classroom increased feelings of security. Describing such places often stirred feelings of intense emotion from the partners (Sullivan, 2009, p. 219).

Aidan's story and corresponding picture are striking. He found solace in the coat closet, one of the only places in school where he could free himself from an onslaught of ridicule. This should not be the experience of our children in early childhood:

> The funny thing about kindergarten, first and second grade is I don't remember the classrooms. I remember the little locker rooms where we hung our bags. I used to always hang out in the locker room; hang out with bags in the corner 'cause there was no one else in there, and I could play with my little G.I Joe in the corner, and not be like beat up or picked on. When they used force me to go out on the playground, I would, there was this one tree root I used to just sit on the entire recess. (Sullivan, 2014, p. 17)

Erin explained that Aidan spent so much time sitting on this tree root in his youth that as an adult, "he actually took me and showed me the tree root" (Sullivan, 2009, pp. 219–220; 2014, p. 17).

Margo experienced a sense of safety when she was sitting at her desk. She dichotomized in-desk occurrences and out-of-desk occurrences:

> You know, 'cause you had activities where the teacher would sometimes put you in a circle or have you line up on the walls, and that's when kids would do things like poke you with a pencil or trip you or start teasing you or popping you when the teacher doesn't look. And sometimes you'd have a teacher, if you reported that somebody was doing something to you, they would reprimand the person doing it. Other teachers would reprimand you 'cause I remember she, she and this other teacher Ms. [name], both of them, if I would tell on someone picking on me, they would humiliate me in front of the class and say, 'Oh [name] is such a little tattletale, what do you think class?' 'Do you think we should pin a tail on him that says tattle tale?' I mean man, it was like standard issue. It seems like every teacher would say, 'I'm going to pin a tail on you for tattling,' and then other students would say, 'You get to take names,' and that person did no wrong. (Sullivan, 2009, pp. 220–221; 2014, p. 18)

Mary felt extremely safe:

> By the bookcase, by the books. I guess I've always been a drama queen. So I knew in this bookcase, there was *Jane Eyre*. I knew in this bookcase there was *Lorna Dune, Cinderella, Sleeping Beauty*, all kinds of female heroines in these books. There was also baseball books, I wasn't interested in that; *The Rookie of the Year* and all that. I wanted to see the heroines, the strong women do things. They were a part of society. It was exciting for me to read about these strong women that were making a difference and questioning, 'why?' And it made me feel important, like, 'I'm a part of this.' Because when I went home and sat, I only saw a few strong women. I saw women that were broken. (Sullivan, 2009, p. 221; 2014, pp. 17–18)

Unlike Mary, Lluvy Rae felt generally unsafe at school:

> "I didn't want to be there just because I liked staying home. But I knew it was something I had to do. I knew I just wouldn't be able to stay at home because I knew I had to go to school." (Sullivan, 2009, p. 221; 2014, p. 18)

She did, however, feel secure on the playground:

> "I think it was like that because I was able to be myself. I could play with who I wanted, getting in line (boy, girl, boy, girl). So that's the only time I felt free and not get in trouble for it." (Sullivan, 2009, p. 221; 2014, p. 19)

Unique Experiences

There were some similarities among the majority of partners, namely that there was a general feeling of being unsafe at school; however, there were certain locations where there was a sense of security. Both Chris and Lady Gazelle did not seem to fit this pattern. These outliers remind us that all children have unique educational experiences. Although transgender children appear to be bullied at a higher rate than non-transgender children and we should utilize inclusive pedagogies as a means to counteract these experiences in our schools, we must recognize that there is not one predetermined way to teach all transgender children. They are not cut from the same mold (Sullivan, 2009, p. 222).

Chris was unique among the other partners, in that when asked where he felt safe in school, he replied:

Everywhere. I remember feeling really safe in (Mrs. C.'s) class. She was, really, such an awesome teacher. She was really kind to all of the students. There was a lot of singing. And, there was a lot of singing in my house: my mom used to sing all the time, so that made me feel really comfortable, hearing someone sing all the time. I really liked my desk; I was really excited about my desk because I could put my stuff in it, had my own pens and my own pencils and markers, all my own stuff. And, they didn't change throughout the year. We got our desk and we stayed in that desk. I was really excited about that. I liked the Listening Station a lot. And the Cubby Tub had a lot of art supplies. We had some sort of table to put the art supplies on. It was just really bright, with a lot of stuff on the walls that all the Elementary School Teachers put up. There's a calendar, all sorts of fun spelling things and math things. It was just exciting! I was really excited to learn; excited to get out and start going to school. I just remember that. I really liked the classroom a lot. I think learning has always symbolized freedom because I knew that when I got to a certain point, I'd be able to be me. (Sullivan, 2009, pp. 222–223)

Lady Gazelle and Chris had distinctly opposing experiences. When Lady Gazelle was asked where she felt safe in school, she replied:

Nowhere, nowhere. Because I was the kid they picked on. You know, everybody picked on me- girls, boys, everybody. And I was always getting bullied so there was nowhere I was safe in there. I hated school. They wrote horrible stuff on my locker and teased me in the room, would play volleyball and the net was me. They were nice to me for a while, but whoever became my friend became under the gun as well. So there was no safe place for me. And the teachers in the ghetto, I was brought up in (name of town), California honey, the ghetto. The teachers were worried about their own asses. And that's what it comes down to. Instead of trying to protect other children, they were trying to protect theirselves. No, there was no place safe for me in school. It never felt safe in school. I can never remember feeling safe in school, or feeling good about being in school or about leaving the room in school. I can't ever remember that. (Sullivan, 2009, p. 223)

Understanding Lack of Safety

Margo offered a thorough explanation as to why she and other transgender children feel unsafe at school:

Yeah, I mean when you're growing up, you hang out with the kids you get along with. So this kid in your neighborhood that treats you bad, you just don't hang out with that kid. When you go to school you have to go to phys-ed with those kids whether you like it or not. And so first thing you find in school is there are groups, there is clicks and you are either in a good one or not. And that was a big part why I didn't like school, was that school took away my safety, it took away my control. Yeah, I mean, when you are at home and you are playing with your neighborhood friends, you're playing with whoever you want to play with, you know. So if someone wants to treat you badly or tease you or doesn't treat you right, that's not someone that you want to hang around with it. But when you're in school, everything is assigned to you. The teacher tells you where to sit in class, and normally if you have power, you would say, 'I'm not going to sit next to this person 'cause they're spitting on me, or they're poking me on the head,' or something. But when you're in assigned seating and stuff, it's not much fun. (Sullivan, 2009, pp. 223–224)

Methods of Safety Augmentation

Many of the participants were forced to develop ways to increase their security. Lady Gazelle developed a reputation that she was "tough" and Lana sought refuge in friendships with kind children. Margo described school as:

A real rude awaking. 'Cause I found out if I didn't clown around or pull pranks, then they would want to beat me up. So I started turning into a class clown, finding ways to keep the kids from hassling me. And I was an artist, and a lot of times I would say, 'Hey let me draw you' or 'Let me draw a car for you.' I was devolving survival mechanisms in school to stay alive. (Sullivan, 2009, pp. 224–225)

Beth was successful in school and the other children were aware of her high marks. They would request that she allow them to copy her paper during exams:

I wouldn't really turn my paper over to them, but sometimes during a test, I wouldn't put my hands over it. Listen you know, this is not my worry. And if I don't do this I'd get in trouble with the students. And if I did do this it's unlikely that I'll get in trouble with the teacher. (Sullivan, 2009, p. 225)

While for some of the research partners, they succeeded in locating 'queer spaces' in which to exist (and sometimes even thrive), these spaces varied: some were tied intimately to the presence of the teacher, while others were bound to a particular object or arena. For other partners, there was no true safe place anywhere to be found.

Empowerment

Kate Bornstein, a gender theorist who is also trans, encourages all trans individuals to become 'gender outlaws,' those who "break one or more rules of gender" (1994, p. 69). Bornstein argues that the "fluidity" of trans individuals is what can afford them power, those "principles that attend that constant state of flux that could create an innovative and inclusive transgender community" (1994, p. 69). For Rorty, even "the disempowered have their own hidden power" that involves a 'detachment' "from their experienced powerlessness by transforming their desires" (1992, p. 9).

Empowerment, thus, is the feeling of control over one's own actions, physical space, words, body; choice. The choice to befriend whom you like, move around at will, utilize your voice to express your desires and your fears; feeling supported, cared for, respected and heard. Early childhood environments can either empower or disempower our young transgender children. The continuously shifting social and physical spheres, overlapping and interacting, contour the manner in which students experience the classroom (Sullivan, 2009, p. 225).

Location

As with feelings of safety, certain specific locations represented empowerment for select partners. Erin was empowered in, "the play area 'cause no one used to screw with me. So, I kind of played by myself." Margo felt empowered:

> In my chair, again it, like any other time you can screw up, because there were times when you would come up to the front of the class, and that was the place you would feel less secure. You'd get called on to solve a problem and have to go up to the blackboard and everyone's looking at you. And the teacher would give you something to do and if you didn't do it well, that was the worst place to be, Because the class would laugh at you if you

screwed up or the teacher would reprimand you if you were not doing it right. And so you did not want to be up there, it always came down to, if you could just sit at your desk all day and be left alone, you had a good day. (Sullivan, 2009, pp. 225–226; 2014, p. 18)

Mary was empowered when she was by the bookcase because she could allow her imagination to come alive with the stories of strong women. Lluvy Rae felt empowered on the playground, "because I drew all the girls to me and I would be able to tell them all what to do and they would follow and I knew I could get away with saying, 'let's do this or that'" (Sullivan, 2009, p. 226).

Academics

For those partners who were successful in school, academics reflected empowerment. Beth relayed that:

> I felt empowered when being called on to answer something that was related to my homework because I always had my homework done. I liked going to the blackboard. It was a chance for me to show off and show what I knew and what I could do. So I felt empowered in my academic work and showing my stuff in front of the class. (Sullivan, 2009, p. 226)

Chris' recollections of educational accomplishments also brought feelings of pride:

> I think that everything in the classroom has always represented empowerment to me, actually. That's because learning was always emphasized in my family. My mom went to school, but didn't get a degree, and my dad was the same. So they both were exposed to college, but they never finished. So, for both of them, their kids going to college and finishing was really important. They really put a lot of emphasis on learning. I learned how to read when I was really young, so, I always really liked learning; just being at school really made me feel empowered. (Sullivan, 2009, pp. 226–227)

When Lana was in [name of school], she felt empowered:

> When I was doing my computer or when we were allowed to do science. It was always something I latched onto. Something I always loved.

I always loved science and I always loved math. So computers and science was a way, 'cause there were two different ways to write on the computers and stuff. You go in and learn how to write out just different stuff. So that was like, okay. And they explained to me how important it was. So, that's when I probably felt empowered. I had something that was knowledgeable, that was really good, that's something that adults were doing. (Sullivan, 2009, p. 227)

Lack of Empowerment

Unfortunately, both Maria and Aidan felt disempowered at school. When asked if there was a location in the classroom where he felt empowered, Aidan replied a simple yet powerful, "Nah." Maria's response to the same question was:

No, not really. No I pretty much felt hopeless and I felt impotent, I didn't see like an end of the tunnel. I was in the middle of the tunnel and the tunnel just kept going and going and never stopped and I was like in the universe and there was no end. (Sullivan, 2009, pp. 227–228)

Retaliation

Lady Gazelle was empowered when she was able to violently respond to the torment she incurred from the other children:

Yeah, (I felt empowered) when I had a chair in my hand and I was beating one of them over the head. Hahahaha. That's the truth because I'm not a sissy and those people underestimate us, trans people. Just because we act like girls and look like girls, that doesn't make us sissies now. And so that's what I hated, 'cause people treated me like I was a sissy. (Sullivan, 2009, p. 228)

Empowerment was experienced in different ways by the research partners. Some felt empowered for academic reasons, such as a proclivity toward a particular subject in school; for others, empowerment was tied to a particular place, such as a play area. Unfortunately, for others, they were not able to experience any modicum of empowerment at school, even leading some to retaliate with violence.

Playground

Early childhood-aged children in the United States spend important learning time on the playground. Most schools house one on the premises and the children are expected to play on it during recess. Although the playground would seem to proffer an arena of release and liberation, as Foucault would argue, power is "always already there," and that one is "never 'outside' it" (Foucault & Gordon, 1980, p. 141). Throughout the interviews, the playground was mentioned by the partners. This was either a place of entertainment or a location of contention. Aidan avoided this area as a means of protection. Maria "liked to play in it when I was in elementary, that was fun. 'Cause when I was in elementary you know, it was more innocent like." Chris was accepted by peers on the playground:

> Until we got to that puberty stage. Until we hit that stage, it didn't matter. I just related to them in ways they related to each other. I've never had much of an easy time relating to girls or women. I just see the world differently, so I don't understand. (Sullivan, 2009, pp. 228–229; 2014, pp. 18–19)

Beth described the playground as her least favorite place in school:

> I was probably the only kid in school who couldn't wait for recess to be over. The playground was very unforgiving because kids would play basketball. Of all the sports, I did enjoy basketball, (but) I didn't get the chance. They would knock you down on the court. I hated football. They would run right at you and knock you down and was just part of how they played the game, sort of like rugby. I might of enjoyed baseball and softball, but all the skilled boys would get all of the fun positions. The rest of us got stuck in the outfield and of course, we couldn't judge where the ball was and it would fall to the ground. (Sullivan, 2009, p. 229; 2014, p. 19)

She did not try to play with the other boys because:

> I didn't throw very well. I didn't try (to play with the boys). And then sometimes on the playground we couldn't go over to the girls' side. The playground was very large. We had the monkey bars, the jungle gym, and the ladder that goes above your head that you could climb, swings and slides. I remember going down the slide one time and instead of sitting up I was almost on my back. When I hit the end my back hit it and knocked the wind out of me and I was scared because I couldn't breathe. (Sullivan, 2009, p. 229; 2014, p. 19)

The research partners who did recall experiences with the playground appeared to have differing feelings; for Chris, it was not an issue until he hit puberty, and for Beth, it was consistently an issue over time.

SPECIALS CLASSROOMS: MUSIC, ART, GYM

Throughout the educational experiences of the research partners, there have been sites that enabled them to experience more freedom and liberation, and others that constrained and restricted their authentic selves. Foucault would argue that, regardless of the space, "the gaze is alert everywhere" (1995 [1975], p. 195), signifying that there is no means to exist outside of power relations. For some partners, these power relations worked in their favor in some spaces, allowing them to relish some freedom, while other spaces sought to normalize their bodies.

Music

Several of the students played musical instruments. All who participated in this activity enjoyed it immensely. The music room was Beth's favorite place in school:

> Because we, even in elementary school we had musical instruments like the drums, the woodblock. In the fifth grade we had something called the harmonica band, which was really cool. We would have these little Hohner harmonicas that were not chromatic. They were just a single scale but we could play in the key of C and of course, I had a solo. It was called *Arkansas Trapper*. Some of the other kids thought I was a smart alec because I had a solo. (Sullivan, 2009, p. 230; 2014, p. 19)

Lana has fond memories of her interactions with musical instruments:

> School was fun. Once they found out what was wrong with me in third grade I started playing music because I think they thought it would challenge me. I started out playing trombone. That didn't work. It was too loud. Saxophone chapped my lips. But I stuck with the viola for a few years which was good 'cause no one really played the viola. And my teacher Mr. [name], I will never forget him. He was a really good teacher. He had actually come from a music school to teach us. So he was really awesome. Now that was a really interesting opportunity I had there. (Sullivan, 2009, p. 230; 2014, p. 19)

She continued to explain that:

> I was in the school Orchestra. I sat in first chair as violinist and the first chair as clarinet, and played the clarinet. I really enjoyed that, but my mother could not afford to keep me in that class. You had to rent an instrument every month and she couldn't afford to do that. So that was my last passion. Everybody was nice to me. I guess musicians are like artists, very eccentric people. They are very accepting and you know, not concerned about my sexuality or anything. But that was my last passion and after that I pretty much gave it up on continuing to live a life that I was living. (Sullivan, 2009, pp. 230–231; 2014, pp. 19–20)

Gym

Unlike music class, physical education was often detested by the participants. Chris recalled that:

> It was really embarrassing in the locker room, and really painful. I would always change in the stalls. I would walk into the locker room and my face would be red, immediately. I would just shove my head in the locker, 'okay, grab your clothes and change and get out of here.' It was always really uncomfortable. I spent a lot of time in the locker room, but I certainly spent the least amount of time of anyone, probably. I just wanted to get out of here. It just, always, felt wrong. It just really felt uncomfortable and it just wasn't a good experience." (Sullivan, 2009, p. 231; 2014, p. 20)

Lady Gazelle similarly disliked changing for gym class. The locker room was her least favorite place in school "'cause I had to take my clothes off, you know. And people treated me like I had a disease. And there is no supervision in that locker room" (Sullivan, 2009, p. 231; 2014, p. 20).

Maria's negative feelings about physical education were the result of teasing that occurred while in the gymnasium:

> 'Cause the gym, oh my goodness especially in the other school, it was very rough, very rough. Gym is where I specifically would always get into fights. And the boys would pick on me and the boys would always, you know, say, 'You little girl,' or 'You fag.' And I didn't really see myself as if I was broke. But other than that I looked at myself and then said, 'Damn Mija,' I don't know but, I am a survivor 'cause all those beatings. 'Cause gym, you know, it was a perfect time and I was in the room and the teacher didn't do anything about it. And it was a perfect time for those

guys to pick on me, and get into fights. And it was pretty bad and I never had encountered any sexual abuse. But I did encounter physical abuse, and sometimes torture abuse like pinching of private parts, or punching. And so I just stayed with mostly with physical abuse and torture, lots of torture. (Sullivan, 2009, pp. 231–232; 2014, p. 20)

Mary hated gym because of:

> Dodgeball. The boys appeared to want to hurt me. And I thought, 'You wanna hurt me? I'll show you hurt.' So it made me even more aggressive, especially in dodgeball. I just chose not to wrestle. I didn't want to wrestle, so I would sit out. Swimming? Oh, I hated it. Because the boys swam nude, and I just did not want to show my genitalia. So I failed swimming, and yet I can swim. When teachers embraced my modern dance, I came alive. I taught them different steps, and I was involved. (The teacher) taught me how to tap, taught me ballet, taught me pivots. I was a quick study. I was there to be the teacher's pet, and to be a part of, 'Okay we're going to do it now. [Name], please show us how to do this. Come do this with me.' Yes, so, yes, I was very much so involved in that. (Sullivan, 2009, pp. 232–233; 2014, p. 20)

Art

Although Mary disliked "mechanical drawing," the art room was often an enjoyable place for the participants. Lana explained that in many ways:

> I think I received special treatment because I was transgender. In a good way though, believe it or not. Like I was in a lot of art classes and things like that, to develop those skills and it worked. And I won national competitions in pottery and sculpting and painting and all that type stuff and it paid off. And then I published twice for poetry and so all of that was in the special stuff they did for me and started me into around that age. (Sullivan, 2009, p. 233; 2014, p. 20)

Her most beloved location in the school was:

> Anywhere that I was doing art. Probably the art room though because I got to do pottery which I love, in the potter's room. Once I learned the pottery world I was just like, that was it, so it would probably be the art room. (Sullivan, 2009, p. 233; 2014, pp. 20–21)

It would appear that the research partners cited more enjoyment and freedom in arenas associated with fine arts, such as art and music, where they were permitted to express their artistic license on an individual level. Conversely, in the gymnasium, perhaps due to the fact that they were thrust into a foucauldian 'panoptic' arena with others, their trans bodies were on display for the consumption of all those around them, who, according to the recollections of the partners, viewed them in a highly negative and antagonistic vein.

Larger School Environment: Cafeteria, Auditorium, Library, Bathrooms, Principal's Office

The attempts by the research partners to negotiate such normalized, gendered, visual educational sites such as the cafeteria, auditorium, library, bathroom, and principal's office were usually fraught with pain and fear. In these spaces, it could be said that the hegemonic discourses around them labeled them as 'polluting persons,' defined by Douglas as those individuals who are "always in the wrong… [who have] developed some wrong condition or crossed some line which should not have been crossed and this displacement unleashes danger for someone" (2003, p. 114). Viewed as polluting persons by the hegemony, the trans partners proffered a sense of danger to those around them, for "danger lies in transitional states, simply because transition is neither one state nor the next, it is undefinable" (Douglas, 2003, p. 97).

Early childhood aged transgender students function not simply in their main classroom but in the larger school setting. During such experiences, the students had the opportunity to interact with different types of spaces as well as a variety of teachers and staff members and children of multiple age groups. Certain locations seemed to pose a higher state of discomfort than others. Although not exclusively, the interviewees tended to reflect on bathrooms and the cafeteria as being places of contention while the library and the auditorium were enjoyed (Sullivan, 2009, pp. 233–234; 2014, p. 21).

Interestingly, the locations in the school that were criticized were places of maximum control. When discussing the cafeteria, several of the partners explained that they were unable to choose where they sat or the food they consumed. These feelings of constriction and lack of control over one's own body created discouraging discourses with physical spaces defined by confinement. Mirroring Foucault's theories of panopticism, highly regimented places in the school were described on multiple occasions as being akin to prison life where one is continuously monitored and reprimanded for behavior that violates a code the "prisoners" did not themselves create (Foucault, 1995 [1975]; Sullivan, 2009, p. 234; 2014, p. 21).

Bathrooms

While discussing school bathrooms, Chris exclaimed, "Oh, God, I hated restrooms up until I started using men's rooms. It was just such a horrible experience, especially as I got older." He recalled the bathrooms he used in first and second grade. "I do remember them and trying to find bathrooms that were empty, just because I didn't like the crowds in bathrooms, ever; really uncomfortable." (Sullivan, 2009, p. 234; 2014, p. 21)

Beth has a detailed memory of the bathrooms from her early childhood:

> Elementary school, that was a three-story brick building that was built around the turn of the 20th century and therefore was 50 years old by the time we occupied it. The plumbing was in the basement and the top two floors did not have running water. If you wanted to use the bathroom, the local shorthand for that was, 'we want to go to basement.' Of course they had the girls' on the east end and the boys' on the west end. They would have the girl in the circle on the door. Boys' bathroom stank and they were always making all these toilet jokes. It was not someplace I enjoyed and of course I hated standing up to urinate anyway. The thing when you stand up would be looking around noticing you, you're tiny. And so they would make fun of me for that. Whenever I could I tried to go inside the stall and act like I was going number two. (Sullivan, 2009, pp. 234–235; 2014, p. 21)

Lluvy Rae's least favorite location in the school was the bathroom:

> I would get harassed in the boys' bathroom. They would call me names, 'sissy,' and say that I acted like a girl so I should use the girls' bathroom. Just stuff like that, probably the only place in the building that I felt uncomfortable. Didn't want to be in there, but I had to. When the teachers overheard these reactions, they would tell them to 'stop' or

they would tell them, 'it's not nice to say that.' But they continued to do it. It was addressed but it wasn't addressed as often as it should have been. (Sullivan, 2009, p. 235; 2014, p. 21)

Cafeteria

Of the participants who spoke of the cafeteria, Maria and Margo held fond memories of the experience. Maria's favorite location in the school building was, "lunch 'cause lunch was you know, I was with my friends and I was socializing and eating." Maria and Margo had drastically different cafeteria experiences. They were both social, but Maria felt included while Margo recognized that the lunchroom was yet another place where social disparities were reinforced. On Margo's:

> First day at school I had to eat school lunch, and I hated it. And I saw the other kids had brought lunch boxes and I was so confused and I thought, 'Why did they get to bring food from home and I had to eat (school lunch)?' So then the next quarter my mom lets me bring a lunch. Oh god, that was the best thing in the world 'cause I could not eat that shit. But I learned my first lesson- don't put ice in a coke-a-cola in a thermos. It is a bad idea. Then I also learned, don't let faculty know that you're bringing in a coke-a-cola to school. Bringing a coke-a-cola to school was taboo. I mean, you might as well be bringing drugs to school. So I was always trying to outsmart the system, like sneak food in. Like I would mix carnation instant breakfast into my milk 'cause I wanted chocolate milk. It was weird 'cause when you're a little kid, they give you chocolate milk in school. And then when you go to a higher grade, then they give you like prison food. It looks like prison food, plop, plop, plop. And then the kids in school would mix their food and try to gross each other out. (Sullivan, 2009, pp. 235–236; 2014, pp. 21–22)

Beth explained that, "We were very regimented in lines to go to lunch. You had certain tables you could sit in. It kept things under control. The only choice you had was either sweet milk or chocolate milk" (Sullivan, 2009, p. 236; 2014, p. 22).

She explained that sweet milk is, "just white milk. It was whole milk as opposed to buttermilk. Mississippi loved their buttermilk."

Beth continued to explain that although there were strict rules, "the lunchroom wasn't a bad place" (Sullivan, 2009, p. 237; 2014, p. 22). Chris' least favorite place in school was:

> Lunch. I didn't like lunch very much. A lot of social pressure during lunchtime, you know, in the cafeteria- where you sit, who you sit with. Especially as we got older, that felt really intense for me. So, when I was older, I would eat lunch in the library because I didn't want to deal with that, a lot of those things are tied to gender norms and being accepted by whatever group. (Sullivan, 2009, p. 237; 2014, p. 22)

Library

The interviewees tended to enjoy the library because it offered a greater amount of freedom. Margo's favorite educational spots were the:

> The cafeteria and the library. 'Cause when you go to lunch you could sit with whoever you wanted to. When you are in the classroom you had to sit in assigned seating, you had to sit where the teacher told you to sit. But when you went to the library or to the lunch room, you could pretty much sit down anywhere you wanted to sit. You had someone who was in charge of the place, it was hard for them to micromanage you on the same level the teacher micromanages you in the classroom. 'Cause when you're in a library, you're not the only class in the library, so you pretty much were getting left alone. And so I liked the library because, that was the one place I was allowed to choose what I wanted to do. And if I wanted to read a book on a certain subject then I could choose it, whereas the classroom you had to do whatever the teacher wanted you to do. (Sullivan, 2009, pp. 237–238; 2014, p. 22)

Mary's most preferred educational location was:

> The library because it was quiet. I could go to a small or intimate corner and sit. My back would be against the wall. No one could come behind me. I could sit there and concentrate. I could sit there and escape. I had all of this knowledge around me. It was a reference center for anything I wanted. And the librarian was very knowledgeable. She would direct me and show me how to use the reference books, the index cards. She was a woman. There was light, stained glass, and James and I would go there and read. (Sullivan, 2009, p. 238; 2014, p. 22)

Auditorium

Although not discussed extensively by the partners, Lady Gazelle's recollections of the auditorium are worth noting. This was her:

> Favorite place 'cause I was in the school orchestra. I was safe there. It was in an environment and in a world that amazed me and excited me. And I can't ever remember having one bad experience in the school auditorium and that why it sticks out the most to me. (Sullivan, 2009, p. 238; 2014, p. 22)

Principal's Office

As with most elementary school-aged students, trips to the principal's office are often unenjoyable. Lana spent a great deal of time in this location:

> 'Cause I always got in trouble. I had to sit in this little itty bitty room, I remember. And they had this small square window with this little fixed looking thing over the front of it. And when you got in trouble you had to sit there with it at this desk and this filing cabinet. And it had a little bed there I felt like I was in prison. So I didn't like that. I remember, so there was a bed on this side of the room and a little desk and a filing cabinet. And it was plain, there was no pictures. There was nothing, just the little squares. And I was not tall enough to see out of the squares. You could see people go past, but (you were forced to stay and) be miserable. And like, 'here I am in detention again'. (Sullivan, 2009, pp. 238–239; 2014, p. 23)

Lana was occasionally sent to the principal's office for fighting, but:

> A lot the times I used to get into trouble with the teachers because they would want me (to do it their way), especially in math. I would figure out a way to do my math work, but I would not use the formula they gave me. I would make up my own formulas. The answers were right, but they wanted me to show my work. Well if I could do it in my head, why would I do that? And that was all the way in through school. And I remember that starting, probably in first grade. And they were like, 'You have to do this,' and I was like, 'Well I don't want to do this. I just want to show my answers. So why do I need to do this.' 'Well, it's important.' 'Well, it's not important to me. So if the answers are right...' And my parents went back and forth with that for year. 'Cause the teachers, I don't know,

and they felt that was the reason. They felt that I didn't understand what they were telling me and I don't think they understood what I was telling them. It's right, so what's wrong? So what is the problem? (Sullivan, 2009, pp. 239–240; 2014, p. 23)

Chapter Summary

Although theorizing primarily about prisons, asylums, and hospitals, Foucault does mention that the ever-regulating gaze of the panoptic was also present in schools (1995 [1975]). It may be argued that the educational systems as described by the research partners are replete with modes of surveillance designed to control and correct "non-normalized" bodies.

In this chapter, the partners described their interactions with and within these normalized educational spaces. Most felt unsafe at school due to bullying and restrictions of gender expression. They found a variety of ways to cope with the lack of security, including keeping close proximity to friends and teachers. For many, particular locations in the school represented the highest levels of safety, as reflected in both their narratives and their drawings of early classroom memories (Sullivan, 2009, p. 240).

The interviewees were empowered in locations where they felt free to express themselves, where they excelled academically, or where they sought retaliation against bullies. The partners discussed special classrooms and the larger school environment. Although all had unique experiences, themes arose that categorized art class, music class, and the library as favored places while the gymnasium, cafeteria, bathrooms, and principals office were often locations of contention (Sullivan, 2009, p. 240; 2014, p. 23).

In the following chapter, the effects of navigating these physical spaces are explored. Interview-based findings are combined with theory to augment understanding of internalized societal discourses. In addition, Foucault's theories regarding the purpose and process of body normalization are examined, particularly in relationships to how this occurs in early childhood education (Sullivan, 2009, p. 240).

REFERENCES

Bornstein, K. (1994). *Gender outlaw: On men, women, and the rest of us.* New York, NY: Routledge.
Butler, J. (2004). *Undoing gender.* New York, NY: Routledge.
Douglas, M. (2003). *Purity and danger: An analysis of concepts of pollution and taboo.* New York, NY: Routledge.
Foucault, M. (1995 [1975]). *Discipline and punish: The birth of the prison* (A. Sheridan, Trans.). New York, NY: Vintage Books.
Foucault, M., & Gordon, C. (1980). *Power/knowledge: Selected interviews and other writings, 1972–1977* (1st American, ed.). New York, NY: Pantheon Books.
Halberstam, J. (2005). *In a queer time and place: Transgender bodies, subcultural lives.* New York: New York University Press.
Rorty, A. O. (1992). Power and powers: A dialogue between Buff and Rebuff. In T. E. Wartenberg (Ed.), *Rethinking power* (pp. 1–13). Albany, NY: SUNY.
Sullivan, A. L. (2009). *Hiding in the open: Navigating education at the gender poles: A study of transgender children in early childhood* (Order No. 3361853). Available from ProQuest Dissertations and Theses A&I (304843384). Retrieved from http://ezaccess.libraries.psu.edu/login?url=https://search-proquest-com.ezaccess.libraries.psu.edu/docview/304843384?accountid=13158.
Sullivan, A. (2014). Seeking solace in the music room: Normalized physical spaces in the early childhood environment and the resulting impact on transgender children. *Gender, Education, Music, and Society, 7*(2), 12–24. Retrieved from https://ojs.library.queensu.ca/index.php/gems/article/view/5168.

CHAPTER 7

Focusing the Lens: Theoretical Perspectives of Body Normalization

AN ANALYSIS OF U.S. SOCIETAL DISCOURSES: PURPOSE AND PROCESS OF BODY NORMALIZATION

The intention of research is typically to address or understand a certain problem or to situate it in a particular analytic context. Most critical social justice scholars explore an issue, usually interviewing participants or completing observations. The findings are utilized to illuminate the said issue. Some, though not all, researchers suggest ways to improve upon the topic of concern for the benefit of the population studied. Other scholars work to uncover the *cause* of the problem, prodding one to ask, as we do in this study: Why does body normalization exist? From where does it arise? How is it perpetuated? Who benefits from its existence? Why is there not a greater movement to cease its implementation in schools? (Sullivan, 2009, p. 241).

An extensive review of literature, some dating back to the nineteenth century, provided startling findings. The work of Michel Foucault and his predecessor Friedrich Nietzsche (2006 [1887]) illuminated the effect of Christianity on how bodies, particularly those considered small and weak, are regulated, imposed upon, and dominated by stronger bodies possessing social powers. Throughout this discovery process, there began to emerge a hierarchical pattern with the dominant religion and its seemingly unyielding power at the very top, and young children at the very bottom (Sullivan, 2009, pp. 241–242).

Foucault believed that Christianity interprets the Bible to suit political agendas (Lalonde, 2007). These include the procurement of funds, the expansion of power and influence, the conquest, settlement, and colonization of land and indigenous peoples, and the retainment of current followers (Pinto, 2003). The analysis of the Bible is the basis for almost all major church decisions (Nietzsche, 2006 [1895]). Some biblical passages seek to alter behavior in a way that offered power to the ruling group (Foucault, 1990 [1976]). The utilization of Bible passages to condemn homosexuality suited this goal. For Christianity to survive and flourish, it is necessary to create and maintain a following. The more children born and raised within the faith, the greater the authority gained by the religion (Nietzsche, 2006 [1895]). Sex between people of the same gender does not naturally produce offspring. Such partnerships are counterproductive to the cause (Foucault, 1990 [1985]; Sullivan, 2009, p. 243).

Homosexuality is only one form of "sodomy," which has been widely banned by several Christian religions. Sodomy is defined as a sexual act that is performed without the intention of conception. This restriction of sexuality was utilized as a means of asserting dominance over the body (Foucault, 1990 [1985]). Controlling the body is often the first step to controlling the mind (Foucault, 1995 [1975]). If Christianity asserts that one is committing a sin when partaking in sodomy, and warns of grave repercussions from such sin, then it is easier to stress the manner in which a complete and total dedication to god and the church can save one's soul. These definitions of absolute truths regarding sexuality and rule by fear (of condemnation to hell) can drive followers to live a "chaste" and "pure" life (as defined by the power structure). Resulting increased attendance at church invariably helps the collection plates to swell (Nietzsche, 2006 [1895]; Sullivan, 2009, pp. 243–244).

The construction of church doctrine is then disseminated in multiple forms (Nietzsche, 2006 [1895]). These must extend beyond the confines of the church so that believers receive constant reinforcement of church law and non-believers are bombarded by cultural cues that act as continuous reminders of who and what is in control. Presently, such doctrine can appear in blatant forms—including rituals and holidays (Christmas, Easter etc.), publications, sermons, and in more subtle capacities—the development of both written and unwritten behavioral guidelines for "moral normativity" (Nietzsche, 2006 [1887]; Sullivan, 2009, p. 244).

The proceeding model (see Fig. 7.1) displays how church doctrine constructs certain moralities. The moralities have normalized the body in

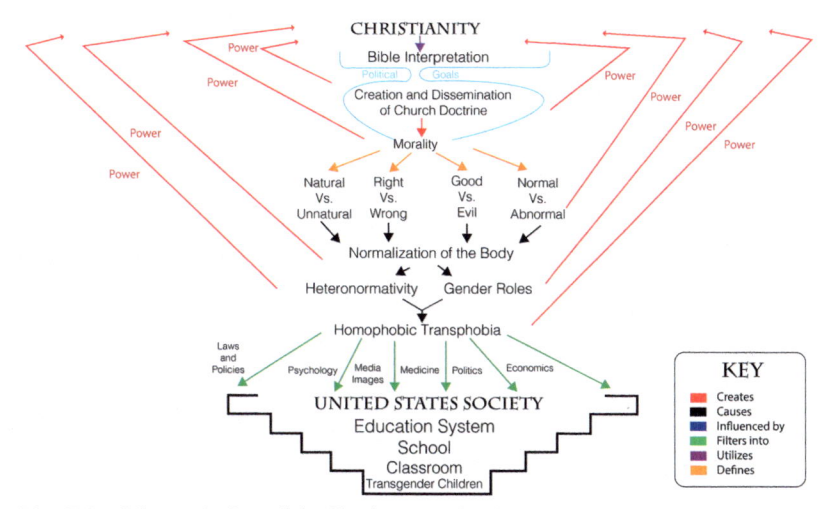

Fig. 7.1 Theoretical model of body normalization

a way that is both heteronormative and gender normative. For Foucault, "In the Christian and modern cultures these same questions- of truth, of love, and of pleasure-were to be framed, rather, in terms of the constituent elements of the man-woman relationship: the themes of virginity, of spiritual matrimony, of the soul-wife" (1990 [1985], p. 229). Christianity has culturally defined the roles of men and women, both physically and socially. Widely accepted Bible narratives continue to define customary manners of female and male behavior and dress (Kimmel, 2000). Currently, however, these "guidelines" *appear* to be cultural. However, culture originates from a source, an underlying belief system. The driving force behind the development of US culture is the Christian religion. It is important to note, that as the Bible was translated and edited, multiple books and sections that were either written by women or posited women in positions of authority, were either diluted or eliminated entirely (Bendroth, 1992; Niditch, 1979; Sullivan, 2009, pp. 244–245).

These discriminatory "moral norms" provide the kindling for a pervasive homophobic and transphobic belief system. The irrational fear and hatred of the LGBTQ community provides the religious right a common evil against which followers can unite. There must be a modern embodiment of the devil that threatens to steal the souls of the most innocent children. There must always be a scapegoat, and it is no longer socially acceptable to blatantly attack African Americans or Jewish people in such a manner. What is truly baffling is that some members of these marginalized communities (although certainly not all as many are allies and/or are part of the LGBTQ population), who just decades ago were denied basic human rights, are now spearheading the anti-LGBTQ rights campaign (Sullivan, 2009, p. 245).

The impact of these concepts is the creation of power for dominant Christian groups (represented by the red arrows) (see Fig. 7.1). As Foucault explains:

> ...Taking care of oneself in order to be able to govern, and taking care of the self inasmuch as one has not been governed sufficiently and properly. 'Governing,' 'being governed,' and 'taking care of the self' for a sequence, a series, whose long and complex history extends up to the establishment of pastoral power in the Christian Church in the third and fourth centuries. (2005 [1981-1982], pp. 44-45; Sullivan, 2009, p. 245)

The norms explored in the model filter into different aspects of U.S. society (Rowland, 2004). Our education system has been shaped by our society (Rowland, 2004). Within the system are schools, classrooms exist as part of the schools, and transgender children learn in classroom environments. The diagram (see Fig. 7.1) provides a visual adaptation of this thought process. It is a model of the link between the *cause* of body normalization and the *effect* (although not in a linear fashion) of said issue. Power dynamics are layered, complex, and evolving (Lather, 2004; Sullivan, 2009, pp. 245-246).

TRANSGENDER CHILDREN AND THE BODY NORMALIZATION PROCESS: A THEORETICAL MODEL

This model guides our understanding of body normalization. It displays this complex societal process while exploring its cyclical and ever-evolving nature. As the political and religious climate shifts, so too does the manner in which transgender children experience school. For example, so long as Christianity is granted such enormous power by its followers, and so long as it benefits from the normalized structures that it has created, our children, who are unable to conform to the dichotomous gender roles set forth for them, suffer and suffer immensely (Meyers, 2006; Sullivan, 2009, p. 247).

Lady Gazelle described how the discriminatory fundamental Christian belief system impacted her childhood. She knew that when she came out:

My mother would probably never forgive me. My father might even kill me but I felt it was something that I felt it was worth doing, that if I didn't do it I would have killed myself or someone else. And even years later after I came out and transitioned I carried that same anger and pain with me 'cause in the back of my mind I could hear my mother and father telling me that I was 'an abomination to god, I was a pervert and I am sinner.' I will go to hell and someone is going to kill me, you know. And unfortunately most trans people grow up with that. There's only a small percentage that really have family support. (Sullivan, 2009, p. 247)

The tribulations endured by transgender children have been explored explicitly in previous chapters. Their experiences are real and troubling. Thus far, this study has addressed the manner of and the purposes for enforcing normalized ideals on young bodies. It has augmented our understandings of the propagation and preservation of normalized social and physical early childhood spaces. However, the question remains: What are the internalizing effects of body normalization on the social, emotional, and educational experiences of transgender children? (Sullivan, 2009, pp. 247–248)

Implications of Body Normalization

The implications of body normalization can be both far-reaching and damaging. For oft-cited gender theorist Judith Butler, one's identity as dictated by the way society views gendered bodies often times results in an 'undoing' of the person "by withholding recognition [so that] recognition becomes a site of power. ... bound up with... the problem of who qualifies as the recognizably human and who does not" (2004, p. 2).

LET'S PLAY DRESS UP! GENDER PERFORMATIVITY

Butler theorizes gender performativity as a modality of power: "The normative force of performativity-its power to establish what qualifies as 'being'-works ... through reiteration" (1993, p. 188), signifying that the notion of having to 'perform' a particular gender is the driving force that enacts that gender into being, reinforced through repetition time after time. The normalization of the body also occurs over time, and begins the moment parents learn the sex of their child. As Donna Rose explains in *Wrapped in Blue*, the "seemingly obvious proclamation, based solely on a visual inspection of a newborn baby's genitals, is the single most defining moment of any child's life" (2005, p. 22). Everything shifts into high gear from the moment "it's a girl" is declared. No longer does the child live in a world of green and yellow, the colors our society has labeled as gender neutral. It is time to bring on the pink! But that pink color is merely a representation of expectations for the child's life (Rose, 2005). What kind of person will she become? What kind of job will she have? Whom will she marry? What should I teach her? What will she wear? All of the preceding questions are answered at the precise moment a doctor declares the baby's sex (Sullivan, 2009, p. 248).

Children with XX chromosomes (and sometimes XXY chromosomes) learn what it means to be a girl (Bornstein, 1994). This occurs through the constant reinforcement of what one is, or what one is not, the redirection when a child behaves in a way incongruent with gender norms, and the replication of behavior of adults of the same gender (assuming of course, that only two genders exist) (Butler, 2006). Judith Butler calls this process gender performativity. For Butler, "Performativity is not a singular act, but a repetition and a ritual, which achieves its effect through its naturalization in the context of a body, understood, in part, as a culturally sustained temporal duration" (2006, p. xv). Aidan agrees with Butler, that "Kids will figure it out, because guess what? They pay attention. And when it makes sense to them, and they start understanding it, and they can understand why adult people act this way, then they'll start conforming." Mary was trained that boys bow and girls curtsy. She detested being asked to bow as this performance reinforced masculinity (Sullivan, 2009, pp. 248–249).

Erin explained that it was the other boys in school who taught her how to be a boy:

> Do this or we'll kick your ass. Don't swing your hips when you walk or we'll kick your ass. Don't cross your legs when you sit or we'll kick your ass. Don't discuss your feelings. Boy, what else? There's so many. (Sullivan, 2009, p. 249)

It took Erin years to perform to a level where she passed as male. She needed to learn how to do so, because she was at risk of physical assault:

> I used to be really good at acting like a guy. I used to carry a gun and drive race cars. You know what, that guy is not a queer. Yeah, the guy with the pistol in his waistband, driving the fast car so the cops don't catch him, that guy's not a queer. (Sullivan, 2009, p. 249)

Gender is not static; rather, it evolves as it is produced and reproduced (Butler, 2006). The manner in which gender is performed is based upon societal norms; and borders defining appropriateness are quite rigid (Thurer, 2005). It is possible to misplace who you are in this process. Aidan's mission for his battle to conform was survival:

> You just kind of shut down, and you pay very close attention to what people, the teachers, they cut you up into groups. They say, 'Okay, you go over here because you're similar; because you're all girls, or you're all boys, or you're all four foot eleven,' or whatever. 'And you go over here.' You know, they break everything up. 'You go by arts and crafts, and you guys go by G.I. Joe.' You pay very close attention to this predetermined group of people that you're forced to sit with. How do they act? How do they sit on chairs? Okay, I'm going to mimic that so I don't get my butt kicked by the people over here. It's all just about trying to not go insane and survive at the same time. (Sullivan, 2009, pp. 249–250)

Butler (2006) elucidates that mimicry of masculine behavior does not make you a man if you do not feel like a man. It is merely an illusion. For her, "Such acts, gestures, enactments, generally constructed, are performative in the sense that the essence or identity that they otherwise purport to express are fabrications manufactured and sustained through corporeal signs and other discursive means" (Butler, 2006, p. 185). Chris's experiences illuminate Butler's argument:

> I just remember not being very good at being a girl. It's the way that people see the world. The people I was supposed to relate to and have something in common with, I didn't. It didn't make a lot of sense to me to put a lot of effort into relating, 'I just don't understand why that's important to you.' I would just get frustrated and want to go play basketball, or I'd want to go read. (Sullivan, 2009, p. 250)

Tea Parties and Trucks: Gender Segregation

Cromwell argues not only that "the terms 'sex,' 'sexuality,' 'gender,' and even 'bodies' are social constructions, none of which can any longer be taken as natural categories" (1999, p. 31) but also that a governing set of socially accepted and reinforced rules, the 'body politic,' "dictates what constitutes legitimate sex and gender, normal sexuality, and even what identities are considered appropriate" (p. 32). One way in which this body politic functions is to reinforce and teach gender norms, that is, to separate boys from girls during various activities. This demonstrates to children where they belong and also where they do not belong. If they are different from the group in some way, it is quickly apparent. If the majority of the boys want to play with trucks, and one boy wishes to play with dolls, the child with the unique preference will seem odd (MacNaughton, 2005). He will likely face ridicule. Segregating children in this manner can utilize group-think as a means to self-regulate (MacNaughton, 2005). Even efforts of teachers to gender integrate early childhood classrooms are often resisted by children who have already internalized gender segregation in play (Paley, 1986; Sullivan, 2009, p. 251).

Erin's kindergarten classroom had segregated tables. She can also recall the location of the "boys' toys." Margo's classroom was similar:

> For me, I would say before school I hung out primarily with girls. But then when I went into school, it was taboo and they really discouraged it 'cause I remember boys on one side of the class and girls on one side of the class. Boys' restroom, girls' restroom, girls' table, boys' table; everything starts getting segregated. You play kick ball, you have the girls playing the girls and the boys playing the boys. So school was making me acutely aware of social strata, pecking order. (Sullivan, 2009, p. 251)

For Beth, the division extended to the playground: "At the time we had segregated play areas on the schoolyard. I couldn't really go over to the girls' merry-go-round or girls' swings. That made it even worse because I was stuck over there with all the boys" (Sullivan, 2009, p. 251).

Segregating by gender can be frustrating and upsetting for transgender children (Bornstein, 1994). The presence or absence of a penis (and not the presence or absence of a vagina) determines the parts she will be offered in the school play, the color goodie bag she will receive at a classroom birthday party, and the sports she will participate in on the playground (Bornstein, 1994; Sullivan, 2009, pp. 251–252).

The gender divide in Aidan's classroom forced him into isolation. He would rather play alone than play with the girls:

> That's why I would hide in the corner and play with G.I. Joe. Heaven forbid I get caught with a G.I. Joe. Oh yeah, even to the activities. Like girls over here made arts and crafts, and the boys would go over here and touch each other's penises. I don't know. Like, you know what I'm saying. They separated everything. (Sullivan, 2009, p. 252)

Lluvy Rae described gender segregation as "painful":

> Like how I wasn't able to participate or I didn't want to participate because there was always the divide- boys against girls or, I didn't like that. I never enjoyed boys against girls. Or when it was like trying to do a class play or something and we had to, if we wanted to be in it, we had to be a role. Like the male or female role. We couldn't try out for something that we wanted to be. Which is kind of like what theater is anyway, you know what I mean? It's like if you go back way like the history of theater it was really just men, it was men in makeup. You know? And so, I think it's kind of ridiculous to say, 'Oh, you can't try out for that part because you're not a girl,' or for a girl to be told, 'you're not a boy.' And that just leads onto like the suffering inside. (Sullivan, 2009, p. 252)

Lluvy Rae feels that the deliberate separation of children based on assigned birth gender has had lifelong implications for her:

> I think my earliest revelation of being trans was probably around three years old. But I think it's earlier. Because when I went to preschool, even in preschool they had the whole color coded system. Blue and pink and I always wanted pink. I never liked blue and there were a few times that I would switch stickers. I would switch stickers so I had a pink one. And I would get in trouble for that too. At the end of the day they'd be like, 'the girls line up over here and the boys line up over here.' I hated that. Like snack time; boys line up over here, girls line up over here. We're going outside to play, line up boys or only girls. I think that's what affected me early on. In preschool, knowing that the rest of my life I'm going to be separated boy or girl and not really grouped (all together). I think that's really what messed my self esteem and making me became the shy person. And this person that doesn't really want to do anything or be involved with anything they know is going to be gender role specific. I remember at my preschool graduation, or ceremony, I think it was called a ceremony, they wanted all of us to dress traditional and that meant I had to wear slacks and a shirt. But I remember my mom going to buy the fabric to make my shirt. I remember shopping for that event and I remember participating in it. I hated it. I didn't want to wear, I didn't want to dress like the traditional. I like traditional clothing, but I did not want to wear what a man wears. And I knew I was never going to wear a dress, that was never going to happen. But I was just unhappy. I remember people being happy, but I was not happy because I was wearing something else. Until we got the gowns. We had little gowns that we put on and I was like, 'yeah!' It's like a dress. Until after the ceremony when we had to take it

off and give it back. Now I have to be seen in this and pictures were taken. And those pictures are still there to this day. I go to my grandma's house I see those pictures and I'm like, 'Oh, my God.' It's funny, I laugh because I knew at that age I did not want to wear male clothing; I knew it. (Sullivan, 2009, pp. 253–254)

During early childhood, Lana's teacher formed the class into segregated lines to walk to and from activities:

And I would get mad, 'cause I remember at first I was okay because I got to hold the boys' hands, 'cause we used to have to line up on both sides of the wall. But then it wasn't okay 'cause I wanted to be with the girls. There were a couple of times when I would get into the girls' line and the teacher would tell me I was not supposed to be over there. And I would just look at her crazy and then I would just go stand in the other line. And then just stand there and be mad. I think that's when I started to develop my attitude 'cause I didn't know how to express that. You know what I mean? I remember even at the youngest age, especially at kindergarten, that I would get so upset with not being able to get in line with the girls. So I made it a point every time we would go out to recess, all the girls would play wall ball and I would go and play with the girls. I made it a point to always play with the girls not the boys, despite my teachers. But that's where I felt that I belonged, I really did. I remember I got into trouble a few times for using the girls' bathroom. But sometimes at naptime, I would go sleep with the girls because I felt more comfortable with them. I don't know why I never really was as comfortable with boys. Other than that I would say (we were segregated) when it came to doing or playing certain games or sports. When there was events, 'cause it was always boys versus girls, I always wanted to be with the girls and I always had to be with the boys and I didn't like that. (Sullivan, 2009, pp. 254–255)

Lana's countering of authority was a way to subvert the dominant power structure (Foucault, 1995 [1975]). The resulting penalty (redirection to an alternate physical space) disciplined the child to reinforce adherence to pre-established codes of behavior. The child is functioning within a panopticon where maximum control correlates the body with the gesture (Foucault, 1995 [1975]). For Foucault, "The regulation imposed by power is at the same time the law of construction of the operation" (1995 [1975], p. 153; Sullivan, 2009, p. 255).

Like Lana, Margo attempted to:

Join the girls. I remember jump rope. How good I was, how easily it came to me. Well, Double Dutch is a rite of passage for little African American girls. And I teach Double Dutch today to the boys *and* the girls. And I remember sixth grade. The little girls were out there doing Double Dutch, and there was a fence where you could go through the slats. And I was playing volleyball, because there were portions where we played, and I saw them playing Double Dutch. Well, I Double Dutched with these kids at home. And I slid through the slats, and I was over on the girls' side, maybe about ten minutes before the bell rang. And I was turning the ropes, and they would go, 'Oh [name], you really turn Double Dutch well! I can really, really jump well.' The recess teacher went, 'What are you doing over there on the girls' side?' 'Well, you saw me turning Double Dutch.' And just really blew it out of proportion. (Sullivan, 2009, pp. 255–256)

Margo's act of resistance pushed back against rigid, gendered boundaries. Her act of defiance reflected her authenticity in the queering of hegemonic, cisgender spaces. As Halberstam explains, "'Queer space' refers to the place-making practices within postmodernism in which queer people engage and it also describes the new understandings of space enabled by the production of queer counterpublics" (Halberstam, 2005, p. 5).

'NO PLACE FOR ME AS I AM': GENDER ROLE CONFORMITY AND INTERNALIZED SELF-REGULATION

Our society has constructed clear and strict boundaries of masculinity and femininity. These extend beyond apparel and appearance to behavior and mannerisms (Rupp & Taylor, 2003). All are subject to such guidelines, including children in early childhood education (Butler, 2006). Those "gender outlaws" whose existence challenges what is considered appropriate are quickly reprimanded (Bornstein, 1994). Discipline is utilized in the form of isolation, ostracization, ridicule, public humiliation, physical restraint, and violence (Deacon, 2003). The most powerful tactic of all, however, may be the result these methods have on the psyche. Individuals are "othered" in an attempt at forced self-governance (Cook, 1993). This Orwellian practice singles out and makes abnormal all that is non-cisgender. As a result, such individuals question their actions in comparison to societal discourse and make attempts to conform (Foucault, 1995 [1975]).

This internal regulation, as described by several of the partners, is often a matter of survival (Sullivan, 2009, p. 256).

Margo exemplified this process as she described when she began to realize that she was unlike her peers:

> I didn't know there was anything wrong with me and there were kids whose parents were saying, 'I am not allowed to hang out with you 'cause my dad says you're a queer.' And I don't know what that is 'cause I was like a kid in grammar school in second grade and stuff. And you've got parents who won't let their kid play with you 'cause they think you're a queer and I'm like, 'I don't even know what that means.' (Sullivan, 2009, pp. 256–257)

Mary also received external input that her behavior was "unnatural." She says:

> I was at [name of school] as a kid, maybe first, second grade. I was sitting at the table with other students and there were paper dolls. And I chose to grab the Katie Keene, I'll never forget, the Katie Keene paper dolls. Katie Keene was a movie star that was very glamorous, and she wore beautiful gowns and she drove beautiful cars and she dated three men…the fantasy. And one of the girls at the table looked at me and said, 'Boys don't play with paper dolls,' and then pushed me because she knew that I wanted to play with them, and yet I wasn't really a boy. And I thought, 'I'm better at this than you,' because I put Katie Keene in this white and blue dress, but here you have the same Katie Keene paper doll, and you're putting the wrong dress because they were posed. And I thought, 'Her arms doesn't match this dress. How dare you tell me that I don't know how to play paper dolls when you're putting the wrong dress on the wrong girl? This dress belongs to [name], not Katie.' I said that, and I was right, but somehow I felt bad because I thought that I shouldn't have said that to her. (Sullivan, 2009, p. 257)

Lluvy Rae explained that she was often identified as a girl by people who did not know her well.

> Because I was always with the girls and I had a high pitched voice and I don't know, I guess I just blended in with the girls really well. It wasn't really the kids, it was more the adults. Like other teachers that came into the classroom. They would make loud comments. Like my teacher would call my name out and then I'd come up. And when I'd turn around and be walking away I would hear comments like, 'Oh, that's a boy, Oh that

looks like a girl,' or you know what I mean, comments like that. It was almost a failing in a way but at the same time it was like, 'God, that's kind of neat.' The way it was mean was they were talking about me, that's what I thought was mean. If you have a comment you should probably say it in another room or when I'm not there, you know? It's so funny how some people think that kids that young don't really, they're not aware of things like that, but I was aware of a lot of things. (Sullivan, 2009, p. 258)

Erin was often scolded by her teacher for utilizing gender nonconforming behavior during play. She enjoyed spending time playing in the toy house:

And I always thought it was really funny when they would kick the boys out of a house. Because you'd have all these girls in there playing house, and then it's just like a lesbian orgy household. I mean, I'm not saying there's anything wrong with that, but I mean, if you're going to do the you know, American flag, baseball, and apple pie version of Andy Griffith America, you want to have at least one male in the house. It just would seem to me, right?! I mean, fuck. You know, it's a lesbian orgy house, and that would be an awesome reality show. But I don't know that it would be at a kindergarten. (Sullivan, 2009, pp. 258–259)

Aidan also spoke of the issues that can arise in the "housekeeping" play area:

Good god, I mean what do you think the whole point of playing house is? To teach a young girl what her gender role is. And that's fine and dandy. I mean, I'm not saying take the house out of the kindergarten you know. Just don't demand that they play with it, or don't correct them if they don't, or don't correct little boys if they do. (Sullivan, 2009, p. 259)

Like Erin and Aidan, Lluvy Rae also recalled the "housekeeping" area of her classroom. Her teachers did not feel that it was appropriate for her to play with the toys in this location:

They had a little plastic kitchen. And there was a ball that they let the boys play with and the girls could play in the kitchen. I was automatically drawn to the kitchen area and I think a few of the guys saw me playing in the kitchen, and you can be a boy or girl in there. There were a few teachers that thought they could fix it by making me play football and really aggressive sports. It just wasn't my nature to be aggressive like that. I just wouldn't participate. They would throw the ball at me and I wouldn't catch it on purpose or I would run the other direction. I would always do something that would make them say, 'Just don't play.' (Sullivan, 2009, p. 259)

It is fascinating and disturbing that five-year-old children can become the gender police (Paley, 1986). Even those who easily conform occasionally act in a manner incongruent with gender codes. A boy who cries because he falls off his bike and scrapes his knee may be told by his father to "stop crying and take it like a man." A little girl who has a tendency to shout loudly at her friends may be reminded by an adult that "it is not ladylike to yell." If children internalize these direct and indirect messages, they reenact what has been taught by adults (Paley, 1986). This seemingly external peer regulation occurs in part as a means to internally regulate the conforming child: "See how masculine I am? I fit in because I determine that you do not. Thus, you are unable to tease me" (Sullivan, 2009, pp. 259–260).

As Foucault explains, the process of using peers to regulate the group, is similar to military training (1995 [1975]). Aidan, who served in the military, described how this theory operated within his own childhood classrooms:

It's the pressure, the societal pressure. And you know, the military does the same thing, and it's a perfect example. Okay, you're in boot camp, and you have a little recruit that's not behaving properly, so what do they do, they punish everybody else. So if your drill instructor, or your teacher, okay, Erin here is just not exceeding at math. Well, guess what, it's your fault 'cause you're not helping her out. You're the student sitting next to her. It's your fault. Why aren't you helping out Erin? This is your problem. You have to do three hours extra homework, because you didn't help Erin to solve her math. So now who are you mad at? Erin, cause now you have to do three extra hours of homework, cause she's a dumbass, right?! It's an example. But at the same time, you know, you should have helped her. She should have asked for help. You should have been like, 'hey you're struggling,' but you don't know that. You don't make those connections, so it's a group mentality kind of thing. So, we are not conforming to the gender play that we're supposed to be having in kindergarten and first grade. So, what is everybody else going to do? (Sullivan, 2009, pp. 260–261)

Margo's play was also regulated by her peers:

It seems that girls can be taught, 'eww that's gross, don't play with that.' Whereas I had female friends who were tomboys and we'd go to the creek and look for salamanders or catch butterflies and play with barberries or creepy crawlers. Like they used to have this Mattel thing called 'The Thing Maker,' and you could get this plastic goop and make plastic bugs with molds and put them in the oven and bake then. They didn't have the cyber toys back then, and it was a different time, you know. I don't know if I would have grown up the same, if I had grown up now. But the era I was in, I think I was fairly normal, 'cause a lot of the kids played army and I wanted to be a nurse. And I remember the kids saying 'he wants to be a nurse, he wants to be a nurse.' And they were all teasing me 'cause I remember I had my mom's cape and hat that I had borrowed when we played army, and I wanted to be the nurse. I got teased for that. It was all about finding out what the normal things were and what the barriers are. (Sullivan, 2009, p. 261)

As a young child, Margo struggled to survive in a hostile and unforgiving environment:

You know it was my world and everything was okay until I started making adverse contact with the system, you know. And so there was this progressive disclosure where I started realizing that you know that, that I am living my life in my head as a child, but as I am getting older I am being subjected to other people's rules, social annoyance and stuff. Each time I entered a different rite of passage, whether it was grade school or high school, it was kind of like knocking down the social norms and finding out that I didn't fit in even more. (Sullivan, 2009, pp. 261–262)

Preschool Outlaws, Rebels with a Cause: Gender Rebellion

Kate Bornstein explains that, 'gender outlaws' are those individuals who ascribe to a gender fluidity, those "principles that attend that constant state of flux that could create an innovative and inclusive transgender community" (1994, p. 69). Whether it was Lana's insistence on standing in the girls' line, Margo sneaking through a fence to play jump rope with the girls, or Chris cutting his hair short without his mother's permission, many of the partners tested gender boundaries. They blatantly violated rules to make themselves more comfortable. One partner told the story of a child who, unbeknownst to his parents, lived in his true gender for an entire summer while at camp. At home he was a girl, at camp he was a boy. The only person who was aware this was occurring was his brother, who was sworn to secrecy. Neither the camp staff nor his parents ever learned of his courageous act which, if revealed, could have posed devastating consequences (Sullivan, 2009, p. 262).

Margo disclosed an account of a time in her life when she too defied authority to live comfortably in public, if only briefly:

> I met another kid who cross-dressed. He had a mentally (disabled) sister and he would dress in her clothes. She wasn't capable of telling anyone 'cause she didn't talk. And so me and him started putting on her clothes after school. And then one day he saw another kid get in trouble for talking, and the teacher humiliated this kid by putting a dress on this other kid. She literally put a dress over this kid's clothes and it was a very ill fitted dress. It was a dress with cap sleeves, and it was too tight on him. And this kid was crying and struggling, she forced him to put this dress over his clothes and then marched him into the lunchroom. So me and my friend [name] were like, 'Why don't we pick out our own clothes and bring them to school act up and then we can dress up?' We did that. Yeah I thought I was funny as shit, because I was like, you know, rather than me get in trouble 'cause the teacher made me do it. And that's the way I saw it, and the teacher wouldn't let the other kids mess with you. In fact, if you mess with someone that was getting that punishment, they would take that dress off that person and then put it on the person that was making fun of them. So that detoured most of the kids from teasing you for it. (Sullivan, 2009, pp. 262–263)
>
> The teacher did do that to me twice because me and [name] actually brought some of his sister's clothes and the teacher actually did it. But I think she was the one who told my parents, 'cause I remember when I got home that night, I was in deep trouble. And my dad got so mad that he managed to get me transferred out of that class. And I was forbidden for playing with that kid again... I remember he was a diabetic too, and it was really bad- we ended up moving. I almost wondered if that had something to do with my family moving from Florida to Atlanta. Because it was right after that my dad started interviewing, he had interview for a job in New York and my mom and dad went to New York. And then they did it in Atlanta, and then he took a job in Atlanta and we moved that year. So there's a part of me that wonders if my dad put in for a transfer or something because of that incident. Because he found out that I was in one class that that kid was in and he hit the roof because he had gone to all this trouble to have me transferred out of the same class as that kid. But I

was in a speech class that that kid was in and he found out and just hit the ceiling and then a few months later we moved to Atlanta. (Sullivan, 2009, pp. 263–264)

CHAPTER SUMMARY

This chapter discussed the purpose, process, and implications of body normalization in the United States. Foucault's theories were analyzed and a theoretical model was created to demonstrate the links between his research and the population studied for this project. The research partners recalled narratives about gender performativity, segregation, normalization, and role conformity. The following chapter will conclude the study. It will include a summary of overall findings of the study, research partner suggestions for students and educators, and implications for future research (Sullivan, 2009, p. 264).

REFERENCES

Bendroth, M. (1992). Fundamentalism and femininity: Points of encounter between religious conservatives and women, 1919–1935. *Church History, 61*(2), 221–233.
Bornstein, K. (1994). *Gender outlaw: On men, women, and the rest of us.* New York, NY: Routledge.
Butler, J. (1993). *Bodies that matter: On the discursive limits of 'sex'.* New York, NY: Routledge.
Butler, J. (2004). *Undoing gender.* New York, NY: Routledge.
Butler, J. (2006). *Gender trouble.* New York, NY: Routledge.
Cook, D. (1993). *The subject finds a voice: Foucault's turn toward subjectivity.* New York, NY: Peter Lang.
Cromwell, J. (1999). *Transmen and FTMs: Identities, bodies, genders, and sexualities.* Urbana: University of Illinois Press.
Deacon, R. (2003). *Fabricating Foucault: Rationalizing the management of individuals.* Milwaukee: Marquette University Press.
Foucault, M. (1990 [1976]). *The Care of the Self: The History of Sexuality: Volume III* (R. Hurley, Trans.). New York, NY: Pantheon.
Foucault, M. (1990 [1985]). *The use of pleasure: the history of sexuality: Volume II* (R. Hurley, Trans.). New York, NY: Vintage Books.
Foucault, M. (1995 [1975]). *Discipline and punish: The birth of the prison* (A. Sheridan, Trans.). New York, NY: Vintage Books.
Foucault, M. (2005 [1981–1982]). *The hermeneutics of the subject* (G. Burchell, Trans.). New York, NY: Palgrave Macmillan.

Halberstam, J. (2005). *In a queer time and place: Transgender bodies, subcultural lives.* New York: New York University Press.
Kimmel, M. (2000). *The gendered society.* New York, NY: Oxford University Press.
Lalonde, M. (2007). *From critical theology to a critical theory of religious insight.* New York, NY: Peter Lang.
Lather, P. (2004). Critical pedagogy and its complicities: A praxis of stuck places. *Educational Theory, 48*(4), 487–498.
MacNaughton, G. (2005). *Doing Foucault in early childhood studies.* New York, NY: Routledge.
Meyers, R. (2006). *Why the Christian right is wrong.* San Francisco, CA: Jossey-Bass.
Niditch, S. (1979). The wronged woman righted: An analysis of genesis 38. *The Harvard Theological Review, 72*(1/2), 143–149.
Nietzsche, F. (2006 [1887]). *On the genealogy of morals.* New York, NY: Barnes & Noble.
Nietzsche, F. (2006 [1895]). *The antichrist, a criticism of Christianity* (A. M. Ludovici, Trans.). New York, NY: Barnes & Noble.
Paley, V. (1986). *Boys and girls: Superheroes in the doll corner.* Chicago IL: The University of Chicago Press.
Pinto, H. (2003). *Foucault, Christianity, and interfaith dialogue.* London: Routledge.
Rose, D. (2005). *Wrapped in blue.* Scottsdale, AZ: Living Legacy Press.
Rowland, D. (2004). *The boundaries of her body.* Naperville, IL: Sphinx Publishing.
Rupp, L., & Taylor, V. (2003). *Drag queens at the 801 cabaret.* Chicago, IL: The University of Chicago Press.
Sullivan, A. L. (2009). *Hiding in the open: Navigating education at the gender poles: A study of transgender children in early childhood* (Order No. 3361853). Available from ProQuest Dissertations and Theses A&I (304843384). Retrieved from http://ezaccess.libraries.psu.edu/login?url=https://search-proquest-com.ezaccess.libraries.psu.edu/docview/304843384?accountid=13158.
Thurer, S. (2005). *The end of gender: A psychological autopsy.* New York, NY: Routledge.

CHAPTER 8

Where Do We Go from Here? Dos and Don'ts When Working with Trans Children

Gender theorist Marjorie Garber (1993) describes society's propensity toward defining and categorizing individuals as an action that is steeped in fear and misunderstanding: "The boundary lines of gender and of subjectivity, never clear or precise, their very uncertainty the motivation behind the anxious desire to define, to delimit, to know, are... constantly redrawn" (p. 333). As has been consistently demonstrated throughout this project, the research partners' reflections on their early childhood educational experiences showed how they fought to survive in chiefly hegemonic, cisgender spaces. Although their recollections were at times painful and raw, the articulations of these memories can be utilized in order to shift the pedagogical paradigm of how to educate trans children, chiefly via the means of educational supports, resources, and tools for educational institutions and the community at large.

This concluding chapter thus offers suggestions for how to improve the educational experiences of transgender children. They are offered by the partners themselves and supported by relevant research studies. The partners also speak directly to transgender students, currently in early childhood. They provide suggestions for successfully completing school in the safest manner possible. In addition, the research partners share advice with administrators regarding the creation of more-inclusive settings for transgender children to learn and grow. The project concludes with implications for future study (Sullivan, 2009, p. 265).

Advice for Teachers

"You can't play in the house because you're a boy. Boys don't play with dolls." Many preschool teachers have witnessed such interactions occur between children in their classrooms. Is it enough to say, "Boys can play with dolls if they'd like to, let Hayden play with you?" The response is often a protest, or a strange look aimed in the teacher's direction. When supervising a student teacher during circle time, we witnessed the student teacher asking a student to sort small plastic toys. Half of the toys were orange and the other half were yellow. He began to divide them and place them into separate piles. When the student teacher asked the child why he had chosen to sort them in this manner, he replied, "Orange is a boy color and yellow is a girl color." The student teacher then picked up an orange toy and asked, "What if this is my favorite color? Can it be a girl color then?" "No," he replied as he looked at her, half puzzled and half annoyed, "Orange is for boys" (Sullivan, 2009, p. 265).

At four years old, this child's ideas about gender were already so ingrained that he was unwilling to accept new ideas. What are his parents teaching him? What are his peers teaching him? What is he learning from his teacher and the physical classroom environment, perhaps even unbeknownst to his educators? How would this little boy respond if his male-assigned peer came to school in a dress because that is what felt most comfortable to his peer (Sullivan, 2009, p. 266)?

Though the research partners experienced early childhood education, several decades prior to the completion of this study, the work of Judith Butler, Mindy Blaise and others demonstrated to us that, in many ways, things have not changed very much (Blaise, 2005; Butler, 2006). It is vital that we train teachers so that they can support the Lanas, Margos and Aidans of our world. There are transgender children in our early childhood classrooms. Fifteen years from now, will they offer narratives similar to Chris's or Maria's? There is much work to be done to adequately support our current generation of three to eight-year-old transgender students (Sullivan, 2009, p. 266).

The partners expressed strong opinions when asked, "Where do we go from here?" They offered advice for teachers working with transgender children or students perceived to be transgender. Themes arose from their suggestions, and they clearly relate to the narratives offered in previous chapters. Those partners who felt a lack of protection from their teachers tended to suggest that teachers increase safeguards for transgender children. Similarly, interviewees who felt stifled mentioned that adults should provide children with increased freedom. The primary themes include:

- Allow children to be themselves
- Abandon assumptions
- Eliminate gender segregation
- Involve parents
- Create a safe environment
- Support and protect transgender children (Sullivan, 2009, pp. 266–267).

Allow Children to Be Themselves

Maria felt as though children should have the right to freedom of gender expression:

> The advice for the teachers that I would give them (is)- do not dodge. I am not saying you have to accept it, no you don't, but what I am saying is just give them that space. They need it and deserve it. Give them that space and give them the respect and love that they deserve 'cause they are also human beings. And I guess my advice that I would give them, 'cause regardless whether it is you are accepted or not, they're going to still do it. I mean it's like me saying, 'Oh well now I am here in the United States, I am not going to speak Spanish. I'm going to stay this way because it is what I am, it is how I was born and it is how I am going to stay,' the same thing. With people when it comes to the transgender community, I was the way I was born. That's the way I am and I am not going to change. The best advice would be, is not to judge them. And you don't have to accept it but give them space and protect them against bullies. 'Cause there is a saying that goes, 'what goes around comes around.' And for all those teachers that think that my sons and daughters are not like that, think twice 'cause maybe your son or daughter is just like that and you just don't know it. (Sullivan, 2009, pp. 267–268)

Aidan feels that adults perpetuate the problem of discrimination in schools:

> You know, children wouldn't give a shit if the adults didn't correct them. None of the kindergarten kids would've cared if the parents wouldn't have

made such a big deal about what was going on. Cause kids don't know that. (Sullivan, 2009, p. 268)

Chris agrees with Aidan. He discussed a circumstance where a parent might mention that she did not want her son in the classroom with a transgender child:

> Well, if I were the teacher, I would say, 'Well, then, you can ask that your student be taken out of my class, because this little girl is very happy, very kind kid. She's a happy little girl and we are going to make sure this is a safe place for her. Your child doesn't have any problems with her, so don't create them. Just let them exist as children and get to know each other; maybe they'll be best friends.' (Sullivan, 2009, p. 268)

One of the most vital supports for transgender children is to address them by the pronouns and adjectives that they use (Hansbury, 2005). While some transgender persons use the pronouns "she" or "he" others use "they" "ze" or "hir." Utilizing the appropriate pronoun and adjective demonstrates support of and consideration for the transgender individual (Pronouns, A Resource for Educators, n.d.). The Gay, Lesbian, Straight Education Network (GLSEN) offers the following advice to educators regarding pronouns:

- If you feel comfortable, introduce yourself with your pronouns as a model. For example: "Hi, I'm Anjelique. I use she/her and they/them pronouns" or "I'm Milo, and I use they/them pronouns."
- Practice, practice, practice! Use gender-neutral pronouns such as "they" and "ze" while visualizing the person who uses them.
- Whenever possible, take the lead from the transgender and gender non-conforming (GNC) students and educators in your school, especially during the planning stages.
- Welcome feedback and be ready to make adjustments as you continue to make your spaces more inclusive: "If you have any feedback for us on how to make this gay-straight alliance (GSA) a more welcoming space for transgender, gender nonconforming and gender non-binary people, please let us know!"
- When addressing groups of people or people whose pronouns you haven't been told, use gender-neutral language such as, "friends," "folks," "all," or "y'all," rather than "guys," "ladies," "ma'am," or "sir" (Pronouns, A Resource for Educators, n.d.).

Abandon Assumptions

Many young children who are assumed by adults to be transgender, are actually gay or lesbian. This is because gay children are functioning within a heteronormative environment where it is presupposed that only boys like girls, and vice versa. As Rust explains, "as individuals' locations shift, so do their relationships to landmarks in the sexual landscape" (1996, p. 67). A young girl might *assume* for a short while that she is really a boy because she feels herself drawn to girls, and in society it is only acceptable for boys to like girls. However, that child might actually be a transgender boy. It is best to resist assuming a child's gender identity. The partners mentioned that it is important to abandon assumptions, listen to children without judgment; while doing so, utilize understanding of how norms of gender and sexuality can impact homophobia and transphobia (Sullivan, 2009, p. 268).

As Beth is a physician, her opinions are both medical and personal in nature:

> I'd say be sure that, if the fact is known, because it's not always known. Parents will transfer their child to another school and let them start over in another gender. And if that's the case, then my advice is to treat that child as a girl or boy who's in a transition state. And don't make any distinction because they're going to be going by a new name and you don't want to single them out for any sort of special attention. If it is a child who is struggling with gender confusion and has remained at their old school, then it's much more. I would counsel the teacher to have compassion for the child without making a huge scene over them and without making them a teacher's pet. I think that most teachers who go into early childhood education would be understanding, unless they have a major religious issue. If they don't have the issue, I think they would be supportive of that child. (Sullivan, 2009, pp. 268–269)

Aidan feels that placing assumptions on young children can be detrimental:

> I think that they should stop their perception. Stop their perception, and stop their ideology in that terms. The fact of the matter is if teaching itself caught up on that, they're going end up influencing. And the poor one kid every three years who actually has an issue is just going to get harmed. I think if teachers just laid off the segregation; they laid off the, ya know, you can do this cause you're a boy, and you can't do this cause you're a boy. If they just kind of let them do whatever the hell they want to do.

And then there's some schools where they don't even have, you know, up until third grade, the bathrooms aren't segregated, and they just kind of let the kids go wherever they want, set up their own standards and develop in that area. What happened to us when we were children, you know that was adults forcing adult socialization, and adult gender norms, and adult patterns of behavior on five year olds. Five year old kids can't conceive that. Like, they don't understand why the adults are saying well, 'you're a girl,' and 'you're a boy.' But, they just know that the adults are saying that. Like, okay I can't go here. I don't understand why I can't go here, but I can't go here. So, then they start to make up their own reasons and their own patterns. And, as those twenty or thirty kids are doing this collectively, it spins their own social development. And I think if you just let the kid go; like, stop to the extent of yes, you have a vagina, and you have a penis, and that's what makes you different. Leave it at that. If a boy wants to go play house, no teacher should ever discourage it. If a girl wants to go play G.I. Joes and cowboys and Indians, no one should ever discourage it. Just take it as it is, and the kid will eventually grow up, and figure out what they need to do anyways. (Sullivan, 2009, pp. 269–270)

Eliminate Gender Segregation

Butler explains that, "as bodies, we are always something more than, and other than, ourselves" (2004, p. 25). This can be interpreted to signify the multiple discourses acting on and through bodies constantly. The ramifications of such forces greatly impact LGBTQ individuals. In previous chapters, the research partners discussed the ways in which their educational experiences were segregated by gender. They also revealed some of the internalized implications of such policies. Below, the interviewees further express their concerns about this ongoing practice. To some, this visual representation of gender binaries perpetuated in-group/out-group dynamics (Sullivan, 2009, p. 270).

Chris believes that:

There are certain structures that could help to alleviate some of (the problems). I remember having a boys' and a girls' line for everything. When you'd walk around the school, going to music class or going to gym, it's always boys and girls. Maybe something that makes it easier for students who aren't comfortable with a binary gender or who are trans or that are genderqueer or anything. 'Well, we need two lines. You get to pick the line you go to, but you stay in it all week.' But just creating an environment that's less segregated by gender, I think, would be a positive step. Well, I think it would be cool if everyone worked a little harder to encourage everyone to play with tools, because I think it's important for boys to learn how to nurture and to learn how to play with dolls and be comfortable with it. There are a lot of boys who want to play with dolls, but then feel bad about it. So, I think that creating a safe place for little boys to play with dolls. (Sullivan, 2009, pp. 270–271)

Erin expressed her concern for lifelong implications of gender segregation:

I think part of the reason that we have so many people with transvestite fetishes, and things like that, is because it's so taboo. You know, like all these kids who shoot themselves with handguns. You never hear about a kid in a house where the dad shows him what the handgun is, and teaches him how to use it, takes him to the range, shooting himself with a handgun. It's always the parent who has it locked up in a drawer, or out on a high shelf, where they don't think the kid can reach it, and the kid is not allowed to touch it, and not allowed to see it. And it's taboo, so now he's going to go looking for it. It's a little red button sitting there. But, yeah, I think segregation, segregating the sexes like that does nothing but hurt. You know, I mean, everyone says that chauvinism is bad. But you know, you're already teaching that girls should do, should stay in the kitchen, and guys should be out doing the physical stuff. You know, you just forgot to add 'barefoot and pregnant.' (Sullivan, 2009, pp. 271–272)

Lluvy Rae commented on the perpetuation of gender segregation. Although she is no longer in school, she is aware that it continues:

When my niece started late she was a really big part of her classroom and was always volunteering. And there was a few times they would have a class party and they would come in, and I remember there was this one party that the parents had the party for the class. She had a princess theme for her daughter but she still brought in pink and blue plates. Like looking in at the party, I was nineteen and I thought oh wow, why can't they have the same colored plates for everyone. I think also just letting the kids as a whole decide if it's going to be an animal theme or whatever, but just let them choose. Allow them to pick and have their say without having boundaries, but the boundaries not being so strict. Allowing a little leeway in some aspect of it so it's fun. (Sullivan, 2009, p. 272)

Involve Parents

It is impossible to discuss children in schools without also elaborating on the child/parent/school relationships. Many of the partners expressed grief over lack of parental involvement and understanding. Firstly, the interviewees want schools to encourage parent participation. They want adults who care for children at home to be aware of what is going on at school so they can assist with homework. Secondly, the partners believe that because the school environment is an educational setting, it is a springboard for educating parents about transgender children. They believe that the school should have a fundamental knowledge base that they are able to share with parents and community members. The interviewees do recognize, however, the conservative nature of the field and social/legal ramifications of discussing certain topics with parents. They did not always have the answers to these ethical quandaries. However, they often suggested approaching parents in a reserved manner, particularly those who are resistant to allowing children freedom of gender expression (Sullivan, 2009, pp. 272–273).

Beth recommends that if a teacher suspects she has a transgender child in her class, she should:

> Involve the school counselor. Hopefully…the school counselor would have a bit of knowledge about the subject, would be motivated; if they don't have much knowledge that they would seek more information about the topic. And then have an audience with the parents and say, 'I'm not sure you're aware but I want you to be aware that certain things occur.' Should they talk to the child first or the parents? That's a hard question. There are legal issues at play there too. So I think that you have to talk to the parents first. (Sullivan, 2009, p. 273)

Beth explained that, often, parents of transgender children will force their child to live as their assigned gender. Despite disagreements between parent and teacher:

> I think that legally speaking there is very little that a teacher can do. However, I think there's one of the things a teacher can do is make information available to the parents. So they know it is your right to pursue this type of counseling but know that there are alternatives. And please if you have the opportunity, at least go to this website- mom I want to be a girl. And this is one of the biggest reasons that kids leave home as soon as

they can because their parents will not accept any evidence of transgender. (Sullivan, 2009, pp. 273–274)

Margo emphasized, that despite a parent's opinion about the way their children should behave, students are independent people who should be granted certain levels of autonomy:

> Parents, well the problems are that kids aren't property. And I believe in child rights. I don't want to see a day that the kids are having the parents busted because they are not getting what they want for Christmas, but I do think that we are at a point now where you can have stubborn parents who make their kids objects in schools, 'cause the parents dress their kids a certain way, that kid is going to get picked on. (Sullivan, 2009, pp. 274)

Margo's thoughts about personal autonomy led to a discussion about the balance of rights:

> I think they (transgender children) need to be supported to a greater extent. But then, you have to also balance parental rights with that. If I was a parent, I wouldn't want anyone telling me how to raise my kid. And depending on which side of the law you're on, because there are some people that are progressive and some people that are regressive. And I feel sorry for any kid who has regressive parents, because they are like birds. They can take flight if you let them. If you put them under a ceiling, then they can't go anywhere. They need to allow their kid to really be who they really are. These kids are really not their possession, they are small adults. (Sullivan, 2009, pp. 274–275)

Margo also believes that the way parents raise their children at home can contribute to, or help alleviate, the problem of bullying in school:

> So I think a large part of it is at home, it's not just at school. I think it's part of the problem. Parents are lazy as shit, they want the school to do everything. And I know why. It's 'cause you work all the time, you don't have time to do stuff and you want your kids to be easy to deal with. And so they think that whatever discipline these schools level is good. And it's not, because it's usually done by disturbed people for the wrong reasons. And I think that a big part of it comes from the home environment as opposed to the school. And parents should get involved too. I mean everyone has a right to an education. And it's not fair that some people go to school to be left alone and be able to concentrate on school and study,

while other kids spit in their food or kick them in the butt while they are walking down the hall. (Sullivan, 2009, p. 275)

Lady Gazelle recognizes the fallibility of all people, including parents. Her advice for parents about recognizing the beauty in their transgender children teaches all of us who interact with these students an important lesson:

> It is so crucial what you say to a child. When I see parents with children, everybody makes mistakes. There is no easy remedy for a trans child 'cause the child is mad 'cause he can't be like other boys or other girls and they are cursed. He cannot be like gay men, 'cause we are cursed. But you can take a negative and make it a positive, I think being a trans is a positive thing, you know. Our spiritual level is so elevated. (Sullivan, 2009, pp. 275–276)

Create a Safe Environment

For Chris, a child's ability to be himself is tied to feelings of safety at school:

> I really think that the best advice to anyone working with children is to allow kids the flexibility to just be who they are, and not force our ideas on them as to who they should be. I think that goes for everybody- aunts, uncles, parents, teachers; because kids are going to self-determine, at some point, and it's just a matter of whether that's easier or harder for them to think. Growing up Mormon in a family that wasn't okay with my gender performance, unless it was what they wanted, there's a lot of shame and a lot of fear that I internalized, definitely, about who I am and who I was. That made my process harder; so, anything to avoid those things, like, creating a safe environment for kids to really feel out who they are. (Sullivan, 2009, p. 276)

Maria believes that schools would be safer for transgender children if teachers worked to reduce bullying:

> For all those teachers that think by letting all those students pick on them or beat the up, just think for a second, and look for a second, and look at the person straight into the eyes and ask yourself, 'Now gee, what if this was my son or daughter? What if this was me?' You never know. If

you could one day be like that, what would I do then? Just ask yourself, for all of the teachers and that are willing to judge others, just ask yourself, 'Would I like for someone to throw rocks at me?' 'Would I like for someone to treat me that way?' And ask yourself you know that, think for a moment, you know. We are not just toys, we are human beings. We came from placenta world and we have flesh and bones. (Sullivan, 2009, pp. 276–277)

Margo extended Maria's discussion by stating that schools must be safe for *all children*, including those who are transgender:

And so I can't help but think that you know, we gotta have safe schools but we gotta make them safe for everybody. 'Cause that's why people don't cooperate, 'cause when it's okay to make fun of one kid, but not okay to make fun of another kid, then that makes no sense. And kids you can probably see a mile away. 'Cause I remember there were special needs students who were mentally (handicapped), and they could do anything they wanted. The teacher would let them just sit in the class and not give them anything to do, and the teachers protected those kids. And so kids could do no wrong even when they did do wrong, and they created a lot of disruption. And they made it damn hard to teach class. And so the teacher would protect them, the most important thing in the world. And so these other students would count the minutes until that the teacher would let their guard down and they would always do something egregious to them. So knowing that has happened before makes me think that is not as simple as we think. It is 'cause kids want to rebel. (Sullivan, 2009, p. 277)

Support and Protect Transgender Children

The partners explained a need to feel validated. In general, they expressed a need for nurturing teachers who were willing to protect them from abuses. The educators that they recalled with the greatest fondness and respect were those who took extra time for them, supported their interests, and encouraged their successes. In addition, the teachers who simply listened to them were held in high regard. They wish for the current generation of transgender children to exist in classes with such teachers (Sullivan, 2009, pp. 277–278).

Mary, who is herself a teacher of young children, asserts that educators should:

Encourage the child, without questioning them or ridiculing or putting them down or making them feel less than; because words will hurt you and come back, and it's so hard to dismiss that pain. You may have made an impact, but you could've done horrible damage. And that child will relive…I am *still* reliving things that happened to me as a child, thinking, 'Oh, I'm past that.' But the curtsy and bowing brought back old issues. That's why it was very important for me not to punish the child, but to let them know this is not the right behavior. I need to take this, and you too need to come out. That way, the child did not say, 'Oh Ms. B. come and told me that blah… .' No. I do not want that kid on a couch twenty years later saying that I scarred him in any way. No. I do *not* want that. If anything, I want that that baby to look up and say, 'Had it not been for Ms. B. to allow me to *be*.' Yes, I want the flowers, the incorruptible seed to grow, and say, 'Woah, Ms. B. was interested in me and helped me to realize, even though I didn't know who I was.' Those are the words that I wanna hear. (Sullivan, 2009, p. 278)

Lana advised that teachers demonstrate:

Patience. And also if they are in a classroom and having problems with kids calling them out with names, address it. But do it to where they both are there, like you and I are sitting down. And say there is a teacher and they are both addressed, you know what I mean, where they both know, 'No, it's not right for him to call you this. Let him know that you know it's not right.' You know what I mean, where they're both there. Because that's something that never happened to me, so that's why I cannot really say whether or not the consequence or disciplines (the bullies that teased me) received was good. 'Cause I never really knew what consequence or disciplines they ever received. I just knew that it was at a point and time that I was just being left alone. (Sullivan, 2009, pp. 278–279)

Similarly to Lana, Lady Gazelle reflected on her own experiences when offering advice to teachers:

I think that teachers, it's their personal responsibility as a mentor to take time to hear what that child has to say. Always take more time out for that trans child, 'cause that trans child, because that trans child is on a different level spiritually then most of those children in the class. And you know that as a trans child, you should really hear what that child has to say. And the reason is because they're usually more confused than anybody else in the class. They're smarter, but on certain things it's almost like dealing with someone who has, what is that that (disorder)...autistic? It's almost like dealing with someone who is autistic. It is almost like dealing with an autistic child, you have to explain things to that child clearly, don't make nothing up. Don't say that the tooth fairy is going to come and get the tooth from under your pillow or anything like that 'cause they know that you're lying. But, if they come to you and say, Mrs. (Name), 'Why do I have to play with the boys and not the girls,' well you can't say to a trans child, 'That's just the way it is honey.' They don't understand that. You have to break it down and explain to them, 'Well boys play with this and girls play with that. What are you more comfortable playing with?' It is, 'cause you don't treat them like a (person with special needs) like everybody else does, because they don't understand it. You know, just take that time like Mr. (Name) did with me. And I remember him better than any teacher I had in class. And I went through a lot of teachers by the time I was twelve years old. They had 86ed me out of all the elementary schools districts in Los Angeles because no one of those teachers would take the time. They might take the time to have one conversation with me and realize oh, 'W. is really a smart child,' and that is really as far as it went. (Sullivan, 2009, pp. 279–280)

Lluvy Rae believes that teachers should:

Have a lot more patience, [be] more understanding, [be] more sensitive, and not make inappropriate gestures. Kids pay close attention to these and they would not want to made fun of because that would make me look like a bad kid. I think just trying to be more understanding and just lightening up in a way that makes everything positive. Make things more neutral so it's not always girls and boys. There's always some of that that makes you uncomfortable. (Sullivan, 2009, p. 280)

Margo had a distinct opinion about protecting transgender children that was not shared by any of the other partners:

Be careful how you protect the child because some teachers mean well, and if you try to buffer the child too much, it makes them pay after hours. 'Cause there were a few teachers that would protect a few students, and I think they meant well, but I don't think that they realized that made them desirable targets. And so after school, whether it was phys-ed or the cafeteria, that's when these people get their crack onto these people. And so a lot of times, like the kids with special needs teachers would put them at the front of the class, you know, and it brought a lot of resentment.

So I think you have strike a balance between buffering kids, but don't set them up for being victims at the same time, or even violating their civil rights. You cannot tolerate any disparity, once you have done that you have set the thermostat because that's the watermark. And if a kid knows they can get away with something, they are going to do it. And so kids are typically probing teachers' responses trying to benchmark what they can and cannot get away with. So with one, had you want to protect them, but I think you go too far. It backfires on you 'cause I've seen kids that have been protected before, and they get a reputation for being the teacher's pet. And it seems to build a lot of resentment where it makes them a lot high profile target. 'Cause I can think back to every student that would like go get coffee for the teacher, or get to take names. It was like being in prison where the snitch gets beaten up, it is very similar to that. (Sullivan, 2009, pp. 280–281)

Advice for Students

The research partners offered a great deal of advice to early childhood teachers with transgender children. They had fewer suggestions for the children themselves. In some ways, this may be because speaking to the children is in a way like speaking to themselves, all those years ago. What do they wish they had known? What would they have changed? For many, the feelings that the interviews stirred are still painful, for several, unresolved. This discussion around this topic was illuminating (Sullivan, 2009, pp. 281–282).

Erin and Aidan are married, and were interviewed together. The dialogue that ensued between the two when discussing advisement of transgender children is quoted below. It is interesting to note their strikingly different opinions:

Ashley: "What advice would you give transgender kids about school?"
Aidan: "Nothing. Absolutely nothing and I'll tell you why. They don't know what the hell they're going through. It's going to take them years to figure out, and then they'll be like, 'Oh, no shit.' There's nothing you can tell a kid. 'Cause again it goes back to that whole, you tell them something and they don't understand. They hear what you're saying, and it makes sense, but they don't understand why they're saying it and what it means."
Erin: "Keep your head down."
Aidan: "I wouldn't even tell them that."
Erin: "I would."

Aidan: "Kids need to get picked on. I know that sounds a little harsh, but everybody gets picked on. Maybe some get picked on to a greater extent. The reason kids like us are picked on more so is because of teachers. It's because of the society that forces them to try to be gendered, like I was explaining to you. So, I think if that decreased, then kids like us wouldn't get picked on so much. We'd just get picked on normally like everybody else."
Erin: "Yeah. We could go back to picking on people 'cause they look funny. Like the kid with the harelip, or the redhead." [This was a playful jab at Aidan's red hair.]
Aidan: "If you allow that to happen, then they're not going to have to keep their head down. Cause it's just going to be normal."
Erin: "I think 'keep your head down' is good advice for anybody entering school."
Aidan: "Now, see, you never learn. If you keep your head down, you won't learn. How much crap did I miss out on sitting in the corner of the room?"
Erin: "Well, I don't know. Keep your head down" (Sullivan, 2009, pp. 282–283).

Beth discussed generational differences between herself and transgender children currently within the early childhood education system:

I think that the world has changed a lot since I was in elementary school. In some ways there is a lot more knowledge out there and you wouldn't have the situation where I had where I really didn't know what was going on with me. It's possible for children and parents to know what's going on. (Sullivan, 2009, p. 283)

As Margo indicated:

There are some children who may demonstrate to some degree cross-gendered behavior and not turn out to be transgender. But at least the parents can know to keep this in mind and some children are so intensely transgender that it's obvious even as an elementary school child. But in some ways it's a more dangerous world because children are expected to conform, and when they don't, they can be subject to bullying and true physical abuse. And so I think that discretion is important and children need to be aware, yes you know that there are things that happen in your life that are really wonderful, but you have to be safe first or you won't make it there. (Sullivan, 2009, pp. 283–284)

Beth helps to facilitate an annual transgender community event. It was held one week after this occasion that Ashley interviewed her:

> I would advise a child to avoid dangerous situations. I would let them know that a lot of people have gone through this and they can survive it. But there are persons to avoid and places to avoid. And I look at Lawrence King that was shot and killed this year, and I think that the person should have avoided some of the situations that got themselves into. A fourteen-year old wants to be loved and accepted and wants to be loved as a gay or possibly a transgender individual, but was a little too aggressive. Kids are not aware of everything. And that would be my concern is that you are a person at risk and you would very likely not be able to transition, maybe not as a child as soon as you are on your own. But you must know the extra precautions you'll have to take to avoid violence and other life threatening situations because they're out there. There is support and you need to realize that transition involves a long time and it's not going to happen overnight. You're a special child and you have a wonderful life ahead of you. But you don't want to do anything that would be dangerous for you. I think the main thing for transgendered children is their safety. (Sullivan, 2009, p. 284)

Similarly to Beth, Margo was also extremely concerned about the safety of transgender children. She suggested that they should:

> Know your allies, be guarded about sharing because some people want to gossip. And I think a lot of times people want so badly to be accepted that they make a bad choice that they trust someone that is not really trustworthy. So I think that you have to err on the side of caution and not give too much of yourself because you don't know nothing about the other kids. And if you don't know nothing about the other kids, then it's probably not a good idea to have them know a lot about you. You want to know more about them then they know about you. (Sullivan, 2009, pp. 284–285)

For many of the partners, the advice given seemed to arise from a mixture of experiences in childhood and current employment/community involvement. As Mary is a teacher, the advice she was offering was not just for some notion of hypothetical students existing somewhere in the world, she was speaking for unknown children as well as *her own* students:

Just stay in school no matter how many people tell them, 'You're not good enough.' Find out what you do, what comes easy for you, and stay in school. Get an education. Education is the key, because once you get that degree, no one can hold you back. And it's really about dreaming, whether or not they can get it. They don't believe it, a number of them. If you're AEP (Advanced Education Plan), yes, but not the IEP (Individualized Education Plan). They come in with that baggage already, and those are the ones that I breathe hope into. The AEPs, you don't have any problem. They *know* academics is key. They *know* that's where they're going to stay, especially their parents. But the ones with the IEPs say, 'Well I'm not gonna do this anyway. Miss Thing said I wasn't gonna...' And they start believing it. I was one of those babies. I know. And they didn't have IEPs during my day. I had to make sure that I stayed, and it was a constant challenge and a constant battle because all of the outside is brought into, because of all the stimuli, positive and negative, and I had to make sure that I did it the right way. And I'm so glad that God allowed my family to stay together, and my mom, and my stepmother, and stepfather, and biological father, to give me that, 'Atta boy. You can do it.' And then finally, 'Woah, I did it. I didn't think I could do this.' And then, all of the sudden, you look up and go, 'Look what else I've done. Woah, if I can do that, then I can do *this*.' And if you have God on your side, you can do it. You have to believe that you can do it. I feel so good that I had the courage to take that risk and make it happen. (Sullivan, 2009, pp. 285–286)

Lana and Mary have similar views about schooling. Lana's advice to transgender children was:

No matter how you are treated or what goes on, get that education. It is the most powerful thing you will ever have in this world, but the most lacking in the trans community I think. A lot of, the average person does not live above a certain economic level, but the majority of the trans do not have an education. And I feel if the trans community can get empowered through education, then they could have a more powerful movement, because knowledge is power. (Sullivan, 2009, p. 286)

Lady Gazelle runs a community program for transgender people in the Southwestern United States. She is extremely visible and involved in the community. When speaking to transgender children, she would advise that:

Definitely education is important. But what's even more important is for you to educate yourself about your own culture, that's so important. When you go to a Black school they want you to learn all about your

Black culture. You go a Jewish school; they want you to learn about your culture. Transgenders, we have a culture, we have a history, you know. And we should study that and get your education. But more than anything, educate yourself as much as you possibly can on who and what you are so you're able to explain to other people who and what you are. It's very important. Yeah, be yourself. But more than anything, if they educate themselves, today a nine year-old child can go into a school and find something on [being transgender] in the library. (Sullivan, 2009, pp. 286–287)

> I think a transgender child should always find one adult that can be a mentor to him. And I think what is not done enough is that most people have ulterior motives, but I think a transgender child should familiarize themselves with transgender mentors or with mentors that actually, that definitely understand and know how to nurture a transgender person. That's so important because you don't find a transgender in every class you go to. You know, there are questions that you can't go to your mother and she have the answer. That's when it is so important. And when a teacher teaches a class, they are actually teaching that class to become teachers. And so that's what's so important. And if you don't have a proper role model, someone you can come to and ask questions, your education is then lost or is put off for a longer period of time. And so I think mentors are important. And there are mentors in schools today that are safe people to be around. More than anything, I do not suggest that children be promiscuous these days because it comes back to bite you in the butt. And the bottom line is, the only thing a whole lot of sex will get you into to is whole lot of problems. So you need a mentor that you're able to talk to about your sexuality, because if you're not able to talk about it, you're not able to grow. (Sullivan, 2009, pp. 287–288)

Lady Gazelle also added:

> Find that positive energy and use it, that positive energy and use in a good way. We have a gift 'cause we have to give, and if we are greedy then we will be miserable. We have to give, but we have to give on our terms. (Sullivan, 2009, p. 288)

When asked what advice she would offer to transgender students, Lluvy Rae replied:

> I think just letting them know, reassuring them that it's okay. It's really hard to say. Nobody came to me at that age and talked to me about the

way I act. I guess I would tell them to be confident. And express how they really feel and not hold it in. They don't feel like they're not being paid attention to. You may always hear some really hard things, but there is another day. That person might have a different experience that night that might bring it to a stop. I know that like even through grade school I had friends whose parents were alcoholics. It kind of why they were lashing out and see why they're saying the things they say. In the end, they're not getting the relationship they wanted. I guess a lot of them have feelings of jealousy or feeling that they have to say those things because they wanted to be the cool kid. I guess I'd say to them to try and hang in there the best they can. It seems like a really long time, but it goes really fast. That's a really hard question to answer. I would say to be yourself, don't pay attention to what people say. There's still the bullies and the name calling, people, the teachers that don't support because they think you're different. (Sullivan, 2009, pp. 288–289)

ADVICE FOR ADMINISTRATORS

Although we never specifically asked the partners to speak of the principals or superintendents of schools, several of the partners brought up issues related to the larger school system. After reviewing this data, it was clear that academic administration, policy-makers, and curriculum developers were emergent themes:

> Well, that's like, take Europe for example, you know what I mean, you don't have as many, all these hate based things. Unless it's based on religion, which is the good old fashioned way to kill people! And it's because for the first three years of education, it's immersion. Like in the United States, it's you will do this, and you will sit and learn this, and be graded on this. And there, they just expose them to all this stuff. And then they start advanced education. And people in America are like, oh, that will make us fall behind. But we have the worst education in the industrialized world, so apparently they're doing something right. You know, I mean I think this 1950s bullshit that we do is just holding us back. (Sullivan, 2009, pp. 289–290)

Margo explored Foucault's notion of the panopticon (Foucault, 1995 [1975]):

> Kids now are like in a prison, I mean metal detectors. One day we drove by a school and (I said) that the school looks so strange, it looks like a

prison. They build them that way with narrow windows and stuff they are building them that way. And do you know what they are planning now? They are talking about having a GI start teaching. They want to start having ex-military people into the classroom. I don't think that is a good idea at all. I mean, 'cause they are going to just lose it on one of these kids. I know why they want to do it, they just want to boost discipline and they have too much discipline as it is in school now. They are teaching you to be a robot. (Sullivan, 2009, pp. 289–290)

Lana discussed the value of acceptance in elementary school:

> For instance, when I found out that there was a trans, there was a gay school, I actually found out about it when I was ten years old in California. Well, I don't know if you would call it a gay school, but they were really open to the gays. I packed my bags and I saved $113.00 and I tried to run away, and that's where I was going. I was going to California. And that was where I was going to live my life in California, until I got arrested. And the police said, 'Why are you on the street at ten years old and walking around at midnight all by yourself?' I would say, 'To be around people like myself.' If you feel out of place you're probably not going to do as well. You're not going to be concerned with what's wrong with me, why don't I fit. You're never going to focus on the real reason you're there and that is education. (Sullivan, 2009, p. 290)

Lluvy Rae warned that, without support, transgender children:

> Just kind of shut off school. I think anyone will do that, even if they are gay, if they're another minority, going to a school that's predominantly, for example, if someone's African American, if an African American went to a school that's predominately white and if someone who's white went to a school that's predominately African American or Latino or what have you, I'm sure they'd have issues too whether they feel like their issues aren't being addressed. (Sullivan, 2009, pp. 290–291)
>
> Just give support. If they could have a gifted program in school; I think many trans kids' minds work in so many different ways. So I think a talented gifted program. I was in the gifted program in school. I think if they just allow us to do painting or dance. If they had a group that was transgender, I think it would make the bond stronger with the other kids. Eventually, I think it would roll over into being more accepted in schools and with the staff. My mom did support me because I told her how I was getting support or this is what works for me. She would understand

that. I think parents need to open up. There is really nothing they can do to change their child's life. It would be good to have training for parents and the staff. If you don't support your child at home and don't let them express themselves, it's going to leave them lying which will lead to drugs, or other chemical dependence, some survival drugs or unprotected sex, survival sex. I think it would be helpful to have panels of people at school who have experience in some of these programs would be helpful. Or stories of people who are incarcerated where they made a bad decision because they would hurt or kill someone because they were hurt, or they were being abused or expressing who they really are, which ultimately led to jail. It's the reality of it. This is what it leads up to if you don't give enough support to your child. Emotionally, I think we're all affected emotionally and some of us are able to overcome it and go on in life. It all comes down to support throughout school, the parents, the community. Just letting them be aware of that because we can't be hiding anymore. The bad treatment needs to stop and it won't, but people need to be aware of it. (Sullivan, 2009, pp. 291–292)

Lana explained that there are ways to make schools more inclusive for transgender children:

One way I would say is youth group, like (the group we have locally). Youth groups are an awesome way to do it. It empowers children first of all to know what they are. But they get their strength from power in numbers. It provides an opportunity for a safety net or safety blanket. The bad part about it is that other students put them out. But if the school is embracing them as a whole, then that shouldn't really be a problem. Or even do it in community youth groups, like I mean, boys and girls club things of that nature. And you also have to start with the parents. Like I stated, my mother always knew. If the parent thinks that their child is transgender or if they are gay or something, then they need to reach out to the resources that are available in the transgender, gay, lesbian and bisexual community to help that child. I think that is very, very important that way the parents can know how to empower their children to know how to deal with difficulties in life. (Sullivan, 2009, p. 292)

There are a plethora of guidelines and suggestions that research has shown will better the educational experiences of LGBTQ individuals. The recommendations below closely follow what many of the research partners discussed above. This is not designed to be an exhaustive list but rather a compilation of several ideas that research has shown to be valid, and that yield positive results for both LGBTQ and non-LGBTQ students alike.

- GSAs and other related clubs have been shown to decrease hostility directed at LGBTQ individuals, reducing instances of victimization and increasing safety (Diaz, Kosciw, & Greytak, 2010).
- Clearly defined and enforced anti-bullying/harassment policies that list specific protections for students based on sexual orientation and gender identity improve the school climate for LGBTQ and non-LGBTQ students alike (Diaz et al., 2010).
- Accessibility to support staff (counselors, social workers, psychologists, behavior specialists etc.) can reduce feelings of isolation and victimization among LGBTQ students and can augment a sense of belonging (Diaz et al., 2010).
- Proper training for school counselors (to effectuate best practices regarding the advisement and protection of LGBTQ students) is crucial in the development of a tolerant and inclusive school climate (Gonzalez & McNulty, 2010; Smith & Payne, 2016).
- Development and maintenance of a positive relationship between LGBTQ students and their families engender favorable results for both children and their parents (Burt, Gelnaw, & Lesser, 2010).
- Being mindful of the language that teachers, administrators, counselors, and support staff utilize when working with LGBTQ individuals, taking particular care to use proper terminology such as pronouns (he/she/they) and adjectives (his/her/their) assists in bolstering the LGBTQ individual's confidence and comfort (Gonzalez & McNulty, 2010).
- Incorporating the lived experiences of LGBTQ individuals who are racially and linguistically diverse as part of the curricula and praxis of educational institutions makes the school environment more inclusive of all types of individuals (Gutierrez, 2004).
- Creation and/or support of fine arts programs that encourage creativity of all students provides a safe space for LGBTQ youth seeking to self-identify through such practices (Meyer, Tilland-Stafford, & Airton, 2016).
- The presence of experts at the district or board level who can provide training and support to administrators and teachers can buoy anti-discrimination educational practices and schemas (Meyer et al., 2016; Singh & Burnes, 2009).
- The integration of discussions of gender diversity throughout the curricula and inclusion of social justice issues by educators will lead to a school climate that is more affirming of gender diversity (Meyer et al., 2016; Vecellio, 2012).
- Allowing transgender and other gender creative, gender expansive, non-binary, etc. students access to sex-separated facilities, programs, and activities based on those students' gender identities (including restrooms, locker rooms, physical education classes, etc.) reduces the

stigma associated with being LGBTQ and consequently helps foment a tolerant and inclusive school culture (Orr et al., 2015).
- Support for and celebration of LGBTQ culture and politics—including involvement of students in activist practices within schools, permission for LGBTQ students to dress according to their gender identity and expression, access to literature that promotes and explains LGBTQ issues and culture, and support at the school level for students to contact local government officials to consider passing LGBTQ-inclusive legislation, would provide a means for LGBTQ and non-LGBTQ students to promote understanding of and appreciation for related issues (Vecellio, 2012).
- Infusion of LGBTQ issues, such as National Coming Out Day bulletin boards, activities related to Pride (Pride Day/Week/Month/Celebration, etc.), and queer-related media and books on visual display in schools serve to initiate the discussion of LGBTQ-related events and encourage non-LGBTQ students to become allies for their LGBTQ peers (Singh & Burnes, 2009). Such practices will help educators "envision and implement pedagogical practices that challenged, resisted, or disrupted heteronormative, gendered assumptions about student identities" (Smith & Payne, 2016, p. 44).
- The creation of a Gender Support Plan/Gender Transition Plan can provide a template for any educator to use in developing a strategy to protect transgender students in schools (Orr et al., 2015). An example of this plan is provided in the text *Schools in Transition: A Guide for Supporting Transgender Students in K-12 Schools* (Orr et al., 2015, pp. 52–59). The entire text may be accessed via the following webpage: https://www.genderspectrum.org/studenttransitions/.

CONCLUSIONS

This study explored the early childhood education experiences of ten transgender adults. Through portraits, the research partners offered a glimpse into their youth, their interests, and personalities. Post-portraits, they shared their social interactions with friends, peers and teachers. The implications of bullying and violence were discussed, sometimes resulting in retaliation and other times isolation. The interviewees critiqued pedagogy, racism, parent interactions, and gender norms. They shared stories about their academic performance, special education, and diagnoses. The partners opened up regarding interactions with physical spaces- the playground, specials classes, and the larger school environment. They talked about where they felt safe and where they felt empowered. The data analysis concluded with the purpose, process, and implications of body normalization (Sullivan, 2009, pp. 292–293; 2014, p. 23).

The interviewees illuminated the manner in which transgender children navigate social and physical educational spaces. There were similarities: all were bullied, most befriended children with the same gender identities, and each found her/his/their own way to cope with being teased. One of the most important things they taught us, however, is that transgender children experience early childhood education differently depending on their race, gender, socioeconomic status, location, sexual orientation, religion, and family status. Mary, Lana, and Lady Gazelle are all Black and also transgender. They lack white privilege and thus faced racial discrimination unknown to Aidan, Beth, Erin, and Margo. Nonetheless, Margo was ostracized due to her socioeconomic background in a manner that Erin did not experience. It is impossible to discuss gender identity without also addressing other diversities as well. The issues are layered and complex (Sullivan, 2014, p. 293).

As Chris, Lana, and Beth demonstrated, being transgender does not equate with academic failure, although it may increase the possibility of misdiagnosis. Mary and Lana assert that being transgender provides a level of spirituality that opens up opportunities unknown to non-transgender children. Lana was, in fact, singled out for positive treatment by her teachers as a result of her gender identity. Certain Native American cultures revere two-spirit people, and assert that they have a higher level of spirituality than those who are not two-spirit (Bornstein, 1994; Sullivan, 2014, pp. 293–294).

Conservative Christian religions continue to be a major threat to transgender children. They spearhead hatred and discrimination that incites violence in the same manner as the Ku Klux Klan (a hate organization founded on Christian principles), only on a much larger scale. Several of these religious groups have organizations, including Focus on the Family, which advocate for the forced adherence to assigned gender and reparative "therapy" (Stanton, 2009). This "treatment" includes restricting all things of the "opposite" gender (including toys and clothing) from transgender children. For example, a MTF child would be unable to play with dolls, draw girls, or even color with a pink crayon. Such restrictions can lead to suicidal ideations (Bornstein, 1994). We, as educators, possess an enormous responsibility to protect the most vulnerable citizens-our children, and it is with a greater understanding of differences among these children that we as instructors must operate.

In summation, all embodied individuals are bound up in a multiplicity of gendered discourses that are polyvalent, sometimes constraining and restrictive, but often encouraging and liberating (Sunderland, 2004). The gender ontologies examined and voiced in this project instantiate the importance of inveighing against the stereotypical and traditionally accepted, dichotomized poles of sexuality and gender and advocating instead for the often blurred, complex, and layered middle with regard to differenced gender constitutions. The research partners, in one way or another, all demonstrated the desperate need for spaces of affirmation and safety where they were unfettered in their gendered articulations. In essence, they enact what gender theorist Julia Rodríguez describes as a "rhizomatic" concept of identity formation, defined as a process in which identity is construed as an 'and' instead of an 'is,' focusing on processes, dimensions, and sites of rupture where new identity formations are engendered (2003, p. 22). Thus, they accomplish "the breakdown of categories, questioning definitions and giving them new meaning, moving through spaces of understanding and dissension, working through the critical practice of 'refusing explication'" (Rodríguez, 2003, p. 24), and, hence, highlight the multivocality of the many differenced sexual constitutions they identify with and express.

The findings of this study are not intended to be generalizable, to answer the question, "How do all transgender children experience school?" They are meant rather, to ask questions, questions of ourselves as educators and members of the US society. And so we pose this to you the reader: Where do we go from here? There is clearly still much to be done. What can you do in your own classroom to make transgender children feel safe and supported? How can you create an environment ideal for all to learn? What can you do in your family, school, and community to educate others about what transgender children need and have to offer? There is no one right answer to any of these inquiries. Every child and every school are situated among social and political contexts that must be given thorough consideration (Sullivan, 2014, p. 23). And so we conclude with a quote from Maria, which, though directed at transgender children, can truly teach us all:

> Hey, you have to be strong. You have to just be strong and have your claws out and be like a cat and hold them tight, and get ahold of anything that you can grip on. And if there is not enough space, make up space, grab some extra dirt wherever you can. But grab some where it will keep you

there, hang you there. Be strong and be yourself, and don't let anybody change you. 'Cause no matter how they try, it is no good. And that's another thing I have to say to the students or any other kid or young guy who will listen to this is. If you think that you are fooling everybody else by trying to act straight, you are just fooling yourself. You're fooling yourself 'cause no matter how much you try to satisfy society, it's not going to work. One day the truth will come out. If you're the type of person that says, 'Oh out of convenience, 'cause they have money or to make more money, or so my parents will help me with my school and they can help me get a house and I can just act straight and just live life normally so I can have everything in life financially,' well guess what, one of these days the truth will come out. So you're better off just telling the truth from the beginning and just accept who you are, step out of the closet. We are in different times. Just get out of the closet, damn, make life simpler. If your parents are supportive, then talk to your parents about it. But if you find yourself in a dangerous situation like I once did, get some help either with the police or with one of your family members that support you, or other organizations. We don't have to put up with that stuff anymore. We have lots to protect us. And all I can say is, if your parents work with you, I know that it sounds hard to do it, but put your pants on very tight and tighten up your belt and have enough balls and get help and get out, get out of the situations. And anyone, no matter if he is a president or the Queen of England or whoever it is, don't let anybody step on you. Accept yourself and be happy with who you are and don't try to change for anybody else. 'Cause life is short and we only live once. And if you don't take advantage of this love we have, and if you waste it all in life, then guess what? You die and guess what? You look back and say, 'Why didn't I just decide to do it when I had the time to do it, like I wanted to?' Love yourself, be happy, love yourself, love others. And that's it, end it. Let freedom reign, let the gay part live, hell yeah. (Sullivan, 2014, pp. 294–296)

References

Blaise, M. (2005). *Playing it straight*. New York, NY: Routledge.
Bornstein, K. (1994). *Gender outlaw: On men, women, and the rest of us*. New York, NY: Routledge.
Burt, T., Gelnaw, A., & Lesser, L. K. (2010). Creating welcoming and inclusive environments for lesbian, gay, bisexual, and transgender families in early childhood settings. *Young Children, 65*(1), 97.
Butler, J. (2004). *Undoing gender*. New York, NY: Routledge.
Butler, J. (2006). *Gender trouble*. New York, NY: Routledge.

Diaz, E. M., Kosciw, J. G., & Greytak, E. A. (2010). School connectedness for lesbian, gay, bisexual, and transgender youth: In-school victimization and institutional supports. *The Prevention Researcher, 17*(3), 15–17.

Foucault, M. (1995 [1975]). *Discipline and punish: The birth of the prison* (A. Sheridan, Trans.). New York, NY: Vintage Books.

Garber, M. (1993). Spare parts: The surgical construction of gender. In H. Abelove, M. A. Barale, & D. M. Halperin (Eds.), *The gay and lesbian studies reader* (pp. 321–336). New York, NY: Routledge.

Gonzalez, M., & McNulty, J. (2010). Achieving competency with transgender youth: School counselors as collaborative advocates. *Journal of LGBTQ Issues in Counseling, 4*(3–4), 176–186.

Gutierrez, N. (2004). Resisting fragmentation, living whole. *Journal of Gay and Lesbian Social Services, 16*(3–4), 69–79.

Hansbury, G. (2005). Mourning the loss of the idealized self: A transsexual passage. *Psychoanalytic Social Work, 12*(1), 19–35.

Meyer, E. J., Tilland-Stafford, A., & Airton, L. (2016). Transgender and gender-creative students in PK-12 schools: What we can learn from their teachers. *Teachers College Record, 118*(8), 1.

Orr, A., Baum, J., Brown, J., Gill, E., Kahn, E., & Salem, A. (2015). *Schools in transition: A guide for supporting transgender students in K-12 schools.* New York, NY: American Civil Liberties Union. Retrieved from https://assets2.hrc.org/files/assets/resources/Schools-In-Transition.pdf?_ga=2.256010443.1989119643.1557079732-1114610386.1554941422.

Pronouns, A Resource for Educators. (n.d.). *GLSEN.* Retrieved March 19, 2017, from https://www.glsen.org/article/pronouns-resource-educators.

Rodríguez, J. M. (2003). *Queer latinidad: Identity practices, discursive spaces* (1st ed.). New York: New York University Press.

Rust, P. C. (1996). Sexual identity and bisexual identities: The struggle for self-description in a changing sexual landscape. In B. Beemyn & M. Eliason (Eds.), *Queer studies: A lesbian, gay, bisexual and transgender anthology* (pp. 64–86). New York: New York University Press.

Singh, A. A., & Burnes, T. R. (2009). Creating developmentally-appropriate, safe-counseling environments for transgender youth: The critical role of school counselors. *Journal of LGBT Issues in Counseling, 3*(3/4), 215–234.

Smith, M. J., & Payne, E. (2016). Binaries and biology: Conversations with elementary education professionals after professional development on supporting transgender students. *The educational forum, 80*(1), 34–47.

Stanton, G. (2009). Answering parents' questions on gender confusion in children. *Focus on the family.* Retrieved from http://www.focusonthefamily.com/parenting/parenting-challenges/gender-confusion-in-children.

Sullivan, A. L. (2009). *Hiding in the open: Navigating education at the gender poles: A study of transgender children in early childhood* (Order No. 3361853).

Available from ProQuest Dissertations and Theses A&I (304843384). Retrieved from http://ezaccess.libraries.psu.edu/login?url=https://search-proquest-com. ezaccess.libraries.psu.edu/docview/304843384?accountid=13158.

Sullivan, A. (2014). Seeking solace in the music room: Normalized physical spaces in the early childhood environment and the resulting impact on transgender children. *Gender, Education, Music, and Society, 7*(2), 12–24. Retrieved from https://ojs.library.queensu.ca/index.php/gems/article/view/5168.

Sunderland, J. (2004). *Gendered discourses.* New York, NY: Palgrave Macmillan.

Vecellio, S. (2012). Enacting FAIR education: Approaches to integrating LGBT content in the K-12 curriculum. *Multicultural perspectives, 14*(3), 169–174.

Epilogue

By Tyler Titus, Board Member for Erie, Pennsylvania, School District

After being asked to pen an epilogue for this book which captures the early childhood educational experiences of transgender individuals, I reflected on my own struggles as a transgender child growing up in a small, rural town in America. It was long after my elementary years that I became equipped with the words I needed to express to someone what was happening inside of me. I needed those words when I was a child, but they simply weren't available as the people in my environment were not using them, or if they were, it was to make a flippant and derogatory statement.

It wasn't until my teacher asked us to line up to use the bathroom, boys in one line and girls in the other, that I started to feel uncomfortable. The heaviness landed in my stomach and pushed on my chest. For a moment I imagined breaking the rules. I imagined what it would be like to go in the other line. But I didn't move to the other line. I walked up behind my female peers and stood. I followed the directions because that was what good kids did—they listened to the teacher. My eyes fell to the ground and I stared at my feet. That was the beginning of the solidification that I was different. It was also when I started looking down as I walked.

School became the second space I felt out of place, the first was my father and stepmother's house. Whenever I was there, I was forced to feminize myself. They wanted me to be what they envisioned. They did not like the version of myself that I presented. They were not quiet about their disgust with my dirty, torn jeans and my unkempt hair. Those two planted my first seeds of shame. School watered them and kept them alive throughout my primary and secondary education.

In fact, school is where most transgender students have their negative self-beliefs affirmed. Most trans students go into school every day with a sense of displacement. We seek to find refuge from the commotion spinning around inside of us through our connections with friends, to know that we aren't broken, and that someone, somewhere sees and thinks we are amazing.

We look for ourselves. We look in the stories we read. We look in the examples given out in classes. We look at the posters on the walls. We listen to the words those around us are using.

We find ourselves, but often it's in the punchline to a joke. It's a debate in the lunchroom. It's a conflict over the bathroom. We are the undertone to every intentional misgender or refusal to use our chosen name. These interactions become our inner language. Our inner language are the whispers, the condescending terms, the hurtful remarks, and the dismissive pronouns.

Many of us fight the urge to disappear while desperately wanting to be seen for who we are, and simultaneously being terrified about what will happen when our inner world is exposed. I have read this book several times and it is because I find myself in the pages. I find myself in the experiences that are shared throughout the pages. This book connected our stories—our struggles and triumphs—and created an understanding of how transgender children have to precariously navigate the physical structure of the school. The stories of the other individuals in this book shed light on how transgender children are forced to navigate through often tumultuous relationships with school personnel. I knew I was different. I knew I wasn't like the other kids in my class. I wanted to be, and I tried to be, but when I kept failing, I gave up trying to fit in and embraced standing out. I took the power back from those who tried to shove me into a mold I wasn't ever supposed to fit in.

Most of us are always assessing our surroundings. Do they see us? Do they know our truth? And what do they think about us? Do they see us as broken?

I knew I wasn't seen as a person who made sense to others. I knew I confused them and I always carried the burden of their judgments. The looks, the laughs, the stares, the shoulder checks, the "Girls don't wear that," every "Ew, what are you?!" All of it remained present within me and came barreling out whenever I saw my reflection. I would stand in the mirror and assess myself with such disappointment and disgust. I would whisper, "They are right. You are a freak."

As I sit here now, thinking back to my time spent in school, my whole body tightens. Dozens of emotions race through me and collide into each other—the anger, the fear, the sadness, the desperation, the hope, the disgust, and the helplessness. However, the one always pushes its way to the forefront is frustration. I am frustrated that I was led to believe that my worth was dependent on external perceptions of who I was as a person. I am frustrated that the suicide contemplation and attempt rate continues to hover between 40 and 60%. I am frustrated that my school story continues to be the same story of so many trans youth today, that so many youths still struggle to find themselves represented, acknowledged, or affirmed within their communities, their homes, and their schools. I am frustrated that so many in the world of education still are disconnected from the power to make a difference that lies within their hands.

This frustration propels me forward as I believe it can be different. I believe that transgender students can be more than just affirmed, that they can be supported in their scholastic institutions. As a transgender male, this book resonated with me for so many reasons. The stories that outlined the experiences, the interventions and suggested approaches for teachers, are the very thing I was hoping to find when I was in school. This book provides an insight to a trans youth's world and gives those in that child's life tools to connect, protect, and support them.

The things that I experienced while in school caused an enormous amount of harm, but this doesn't have to be the truth for students today. This book will help us create a space where trans students don't just survive, but where they may thrive.

As an advocate for transgender and gender non-binary youth, I work to create the understanding and changes outlined in these chapters. I travel across the country and share the research around transgender suicidality rates. As a therapist, I work with transgender youth and their families to help them navigate the world around them in safe and supported way. Just like the individuals outlined in this book, my clients have been faced with exclusion, rejection, isolation, and discrimination. I work to help them heal from being in spaces where they were not acknowledged, affirmed, or supported. As an elected school board member, I challenge the staff within our district to meet each child with unconditional positive regard, especially those who are navigating through internal revelations such as gender identity. As a father, I hope that my children will continue to encounter teachers who accept their family and understand that we are composed of love for all beings regardless of our perceived differences. As an individual who continues to face discrimination, oppression, and rejection, I encourage anyone who plans to enter the world of education to spend time with the stories and information inside these pages so they can learn ways to make this world a safer place for all children. It is my hope that this book will find its way onto the shelves of libraries around the country and be utilized in curricula of teacher training programs so that transgender students are no longer held responsible for creating their own safe space. This book works to eliminate the stigma that surrounds transgender individuals. I believe this book will change hearts, open minds, and save lives.

Appendix A

Interview Questions for Research Partners

This research project seeks to understand the lived experiences of transgender children in early childhood education. I will ask you to think back to the time of your life between preschool and third grade. Any time the word early childhood is mentioned, it refers to this educational period.

1. If your childhood was a book, what would your chapters be?
2. Describe the first classroom or child care setting you can remember. Can you please draw it for me?
   a. Please describe what you have drawn.
   b. Where did you feel:
      i. safe?
      ii. empowered?
   c. What were your favorite/least favorite places in the classroom and the school?
3. What advice would you give early childhood teachers who are working with transgender children or children who are perceived to be transgender?

4. What advice would you give transgender children about school?
5. Is there anything else you'd like to add?

(Sullivan, 2009, p. 335)

Appendix B

Demographics Questionnaire filled out by Research Partners

TRANSGENDER CHILDREN AND INTERNALIZED BODY NORMALIZATION IN EARLY CHILDHOOD EDUCATION SETTINGS: A NARRATIVE REFLECTION OF TRANSGENDER ADULTS

Pseudonym_____
Age_____
GenderIdentity_____
Race/Ethnicity_____
Area Where You Grew Up_____

Types of schools and child care settings you attended from pre-school-3rd grade (public, private, charter, home etc.)
_____
_____
_____

(Sullivan, 2009, p. 333)

Index

A
Academic empowerment, 167
Academic performance, 103, 109, 136, 143, 146, 221
Acting out, 94, 146
Advice for administrators, 217
Advice for students, 212
Advice for teachers, 200
Age affecting peer relationships, 100
Agency, 23
Agender, 3
Aidan, 9, 60–62, 70, 101, 106, 113, 116, 123, 142, 150, 162, 168, 169, 186–188, 193, 194, 200–203, 212, 213, 222
Art classroom, 98, 128, 172, 178
Auditorium, 115, 173, 177

B
Barriers to friendship, 100, 101
Bathroom bill, 1, 2, 6
Bathrooms, 2, 6, 120, 122, 173, 174, 178, 190, 204, 227, 228
Beth, 9, 10, 63–66, 86, 96, 104, 105, 108, 113, 115, 118, 124, 132, 136, 138, 140, 141, 151, 161, 165, 167, 169, 170, 174–176, 188, 203, 206, 213, 214, 222
Bigender, 3, 7
Body normalization, 6, 7, 123, 178, 181, 183–185, 197, 222
Bornstein, Kate, 33, 41, 45, 46, 166, 186, 188, 191, 195, 222
Bullying and violence, 11, 19, 20, 22, 26, 28, 29, 36, 103–105, 108, 111, 112, 131, 136, 138, 161, 178, 191, 207, 208, 213, 214, 221, 222
Butler, J., 17, 20, 33–35, 41, 43, 45, 53, 98, 149, 185–187, 191, 200, 204

C
Cafeteria, 149, 173, 175, 176, 178, 211
Causes of bullying, 108

Childhood crushes, 97–99
Chris, 9, 66–70, 95, 100, 113, 114, 129, 136, 138, 140, 141, 152, 163, 164, 167, 169–171, 174, 176, 187, 195, 200, 202, 204, 208, 222
Christianity, 12, 181–184
Cisgender, 7, 10, 18, 22, 23, 25, 27, 29, 35, 43, 49, 54, 191, 199
Cisnormative, 18, 51, 53
Classroom drawings, 151–160
Comfort and safety, 10, 23, 49, 68, 94–96, 98, 100, 103, 111, 113, 117, 131, 135, 137, 147, 150, 160–162, 164–166, 178, 190, 195, 200, 202, 204, 208, 211, 214, 219, 220, 223
Comfort in teachers and friends, 161
Compromise bill, 2
Coping with bullying, 109, 111
Curriculum methods, 119

D
Demigender, 3
Diagnosis, treatment, and special education, 141, 143–147, 221
Disgust, 47, 103, 228, 229

E
Economic disparities, 102
Educational curricula, 24
Empowered locations, 178
Empowerment, 150, 166–168
Erin, 9, 62, 70–73, 96, 119, 132, 152, 155, 161, 162, 166, 186, 188, 193, 194, 205, 212, 213, 222

F
Female to male (FTM), 11, 35, 54, 94, 108
Fighting, 109, 111, 130–132, 134–136, 141, 146, 177
First-Third grade, 114, 142
Formal curriculum, 25
Foucault, M., 6, 11, 19, 34, 42, 100, 112, 122, 123, 127, 138, 169, 170, 174, 178, 181–184, 190, 191, 194, 197, 217
Friendships, 9, 94, 95, 97, 99, 100, 110, 146, 161, 165
Friends with outcasts, 96, 97, 146

G
Gay Lesbian Straight Education Network (GLSEN), 19, 20, 28–32, 52, 202
Gender, 3, 4, 6, 17–19, 22, 24, 25, 27–29, 32–36, 41–45, 47–51, 53, 54, 59, 66, 68, 93, 97, 100, 112, 123, 131, 141, 183, 185–189, 191, 193–195, 199, 201–205, 208, 221–223
Gender Confirmation Surgery (GCS), 45, 48, 50, 60, 66, 73, 89
Gender creative, 3, 34, 220
Gender Dysphoria (GD), 46, 49, 50
Gender expansive, 3, 23, 24, 35, 220
Gender expression, 1, 19, 20, 22, 27–29, 31, 34, 43, 99, 101, 178, 201, 206
Genderfluid, 4
Gender identity, 1–5, 7, 18, 20, 22, 25, 26, 28, 30, 32–35, 43, 45, 48–50, 52, 53, 59, 62, 84, 94, 95, 97, 102, 146, 203, 220–222, 230

Genderless, 3
Gender non-binary, 4, 202, 229
Gender non-conforming (GNC)/variant, 4, 53, 202
Gender outlaws, 33, 166, 191, 195
Gender performativity, 35, 185, 186, 197
Gender questioning, 4
Gender rebellion, 195
Gender role conformity, 70, 129, 191, 197
Gender segregation, 51, 187–189, 201, 204, 205
Gender spectrum, 26
Grounded theory, 7, 8
Gym classroom, 170, 171, 204

H
Hegemony, 27, 33, 173
Heteronormative, 27, 33, 54, 183, 203, 221
Heterosexism, 19, 20, 100
Heterosexual matrix, 17, 20, 33, 98
Hidden curriculum, 25, 43
Historical treatment of trans children/youth, 46
Homophobia, 10, 19, 20, 32, 203

I
Inside, 81, 93, 141, 154, 155, 157, 158, 174, 189, 227, 228, 230
Internalized self-regulation, 191
Intersex, 4, 7, 45, 53
Isolation, 25, 34, 101, 109, 141, 146, 188, 191, 220, 221, 229

L
Lack of empowerment, 168
Lack of support, 130, 131, 147
Lady Gazelle, 9, 10, 73–76, 80, 95, 99–101, 104, 118, 125, 130, 131, 135, 136, 142–144, 156, 163, 164, 168, 171, 177, 184, 208, 210, 215, 216, 222
Lana, 10, 76–79, 95, 98, 99, 108, 110, 111, 113, 116, 117, 137, 139–143, 145, 146, 157, 158, 161, 165, 167, 170, 172, 177, 190, 195, 210, 215, 218, 219, 222
Lesbian, gay, bisexual or transgender (LGBTQ), 2, 3, 9, 20–36, 50, 66, 80, 93, 98, 109, 184, 204, 219–221
Library, 31, 128, 159, 173, 176, 178, 216

M
Male to female (MTF), 35, 52, 53, 80, 94, 99, 108, 222
Margo, 9, 10, 86–89, 95, 96, 102, 103, 105, 109, 111, 120, 121, 124, 127, 132, 140–143, 146, 153, 156, 157, 162, 164–166, 175, 176, 188, 190–192, 194–196, 200, 207, 209, 211, 213, 214, 217, 222
Maria, 10, 83–86, 95, 101, 105, 112, 114, 130, 133, 155, 157, 161, 168, 169, 171, 175, 200, 201, 208, 209, 223
Mary, 9, 12, 89–91, 109–111, 117–119, 134, 150, 152, 163, 167, 172, 176, 186, 192, 209, 214, 215, 222
Mass media, 52
Methods of safety augmentation, 165

Music classroom, 128, 170, 171, 178, 204

N
Name calling, 103, 105, 107, 127, 146, 210, 217
Nietzsche, F., 181, 182
Nonconformity to classroom rules, 132

O
Outed, 28
Outside, 71, 89, 93, 111, 129, 130, 155–159, 169, 170, 189, 215

P
Pangender, 4
Parent interactions at school, 138, 141, 221
Parent involvement in academics, 138, 146, 206
Parent responses to bullying, 140
Playground, 104, 106, 116, 118, 139, 162, 163, 167, 169, 170, 188, 221
Postmodernism, 42, 191
Postmodern theory, 41
Post-structuralism, 42
Post-structuralist theory, 27
Preschool and kindergarten, 21, 25, 28, 51, 60, 62–64, 66, 71, 77, 78, 80, 99, 111, 113–115, 119, 124, 138, 142, 156–158, 160, 162, 189, 193, 194, 200
Principal's office, 123, 127, 132, 159, 173, 177
Public humiliation, 127, 146, 191

Q
Queer theory, 8, 27, 41, 54, 129

R
Racism, 119, 129, 146, 221
Rae, Lluvy, 9, 80, 81, 83, 94, 95, 97, 99, 101, 105, 106, 114, 120, 126, 137–144, 160, 163, 167, 174, 189, 192, 193, 205, 211, 216, 218
Research partners, 6, 8, 9, 11, 12, 41, 59, 94, 97, 99–101, 105, 108, 109, 111–113, 117, 119, 122, 123, 129–131, 136, 138, 141, 142, 146, 150, 160, 162, 166, 168, 170, 173, 178, 197, 199, 200, 204, 219, 221, 223
Results of bullying, 112
Retaliation, 109, 131, 168, 178, 221

S
Safe environment, 150, 201, 208
Same-gender friendships, 94
Sex, 1–4, 7, 18, 22, 24, 33, 34, 43–52, 54, 94, 118, 141, 182, 185–187, 216, 219, 220
Sexual orientation, 20–22, 26, 28, 30, 32, 43–45, 222
Social interactions for trans youth, 28, 221
Spaces of resistance- disciplinary issues, 131
Special bond, 117
Specific locations, 162, 166
Struggles for trans individuals, 11, 21, 22, 27, 29, 41, 49, 50, 53, 54, 227
Support of transgender children, 12, 30, 202, 209, 218

T

Teacher education training, 21, 23
Teacher relationships negative, 20, 28, 119, 146
Teacher relationships positive, 112, 113, 119, 125, 146, 222
Transgender, 1–7, 9–11, 17–26, 28–30, 32, 34, 35, 42, 43, 46–54, 59, 62, 73, 75, 76, 80, 82–86, 89, 91, 93, 94, 96, 97, 100–102, 112, 113, 116, 126, 129, 131, 132, 142, 143, 146, 161, 163, 164, 166, 172, 184, 185, 188, 195, 199–203, 206–209, 211–216, 218, 219, 221–223, 228–230

Transgender tales, 52
Transphobia, 6, 19, 20, 203
Two spirit, 4, 7

U

U.S. societal discourse, 178, 181, 191
Understanding lack of safety, 164
Understanding teachers' actions, 130

V

Victim discourse, 24
Violence, 2, 8, 28, 50, 54, 103, 105, 108, 136, 168

Printed by Printforce, the Netherlands